☆ BUILDS BODIES 10 WAYS

Al Jaffee's
NEXT BOOK

Al Jaffee's
NEXT BOOK

Written, Drawn, and Quartered
by Al Jaffee

Assembled by
Harry Jaffee

with special thanks
to Jim Ruth

A SIGNET BOOK
NEW AMERICAN LIBRARY
TIMES MIRROR

NAL BOOKS ARE ALSO AVAILABLE AT DISCOUNTS IN BULK QUANTITY
FOR INDUSTRIAL OR SALES-PROMOTIONAL USE. FOR DETAILS, WRITE
TO PREMIUM MARKETING DIVISION, NEW AMERICAN LIBRARY, INC.,
1301 AVENUE OF THE AMERICAS, NEW YORK, NEW YORK 10019.

SIGNET TRADEMARK REG. U.S. PAT. OFF. AND FOREIGN COUNTRIES
REGISTERED TRADEMARK—MARCA REGISTRADA
HECHO EN CHICAGO, U.S.A.

SIGNET, SIGNET CLASSICS, MENTOR, PLUME and MERIDIAN BOOKS
are published by The New American Library, Inc.,
1301 Avenue of the Americas, New York, New York 10019

First Signet Printing, August, 1977

1 2 3 4 5 6 7 8 9
Printed in the United States of America

Foreword

Years ago when Al Jaffee started writing books I desperately wanted to write a foreword for one of them. But each time I asked Jaffee to let me do it he would say, "Wait till my next book." Well, this is *"Al Jaffee's next book"* and, by golly, I'm holding him to his promise.

Now at the outset, let me say that I never cared for the author or his work. That may seem like an unusual way to begin a foreword, and perhaps that is why Jaffee kept stalling me off about writing one. In any case, when I presented this foreword to the author I distinctly said to him, in front of witnesses, "You're probably too narrow-minded and chicken-hearted to print this," to which he replied in a holier-than-thou manner, "I don't like censorship in any form and anyway I'm not afraid of anything you have to say."

Jaffee and I met under rather depressing circumstances. It was at the annual Christmas party of the accounting firm of Blick, Hargrove and Estrus. Jaffee and I were personal clients of F. Michael Estrus, CPA, and he introduced us as two people who ought to know each other because we "have so much in common." It was not the first time that I was impressed by the astute insight of members of the accounting fraternity. When Jaffee and I compared notes we found that what we had in common was that I was a leading shrink and Jaffee was a leading nut. Since I do not care to bring my work into social situations, I realized I must somehow get away from this perfect example of abnormal development. I exhausted every escape ruse——sudden illness, the call of nature, etc.——to no avail. Jaffee had his grubby hands firmly locked on my arm and insisted on showing me his first book. I succumbed to his blandishments and agreed to read it. Now suddenly I was *really* ill and felt the urgent need of a bathroom. But Jaffee would not release me from his steely grip until I had looked at a draft of his second book, which he quickly produced from one of his pockets. Survival suddenly became a question. Then, out of the blue, the answer came. Revenge. With a determined glint in my eye I offered to write the foreword. But something was wrong. He was suspicious. Was it the determined glint in my eye that tipped him off? Or was it the fact that not only did I *not* laugh at his cartoons, but also derisively sneered at everything else in his book, including the table of contents? As the years went by I kept after him. Finally I shamed him, before witnesses, into the situation I explained before regarding this book.

So now you know all about how I got to write this foreword.

By the way, if you really want to have fun and enjoy rich, truly infectious humor——something that books of this sort couldn't hope to achieve in a million years——then get yourself invited to the annual Christmas party of the accounting firm of Blick, Hargrove and Estrus. Those guys are a riot.

—*S. Adler Jungfreud, M.D., Ph.D.*

A Marvelously Maladroit Movie-making Maneuver

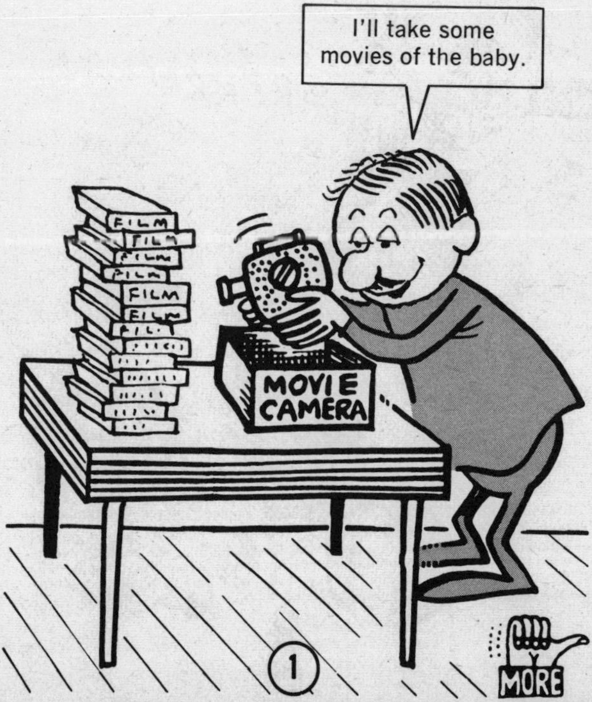
I'll take some movies of the baby.
FILM
FILM
FILM
MOVIE CAMERA
MORE

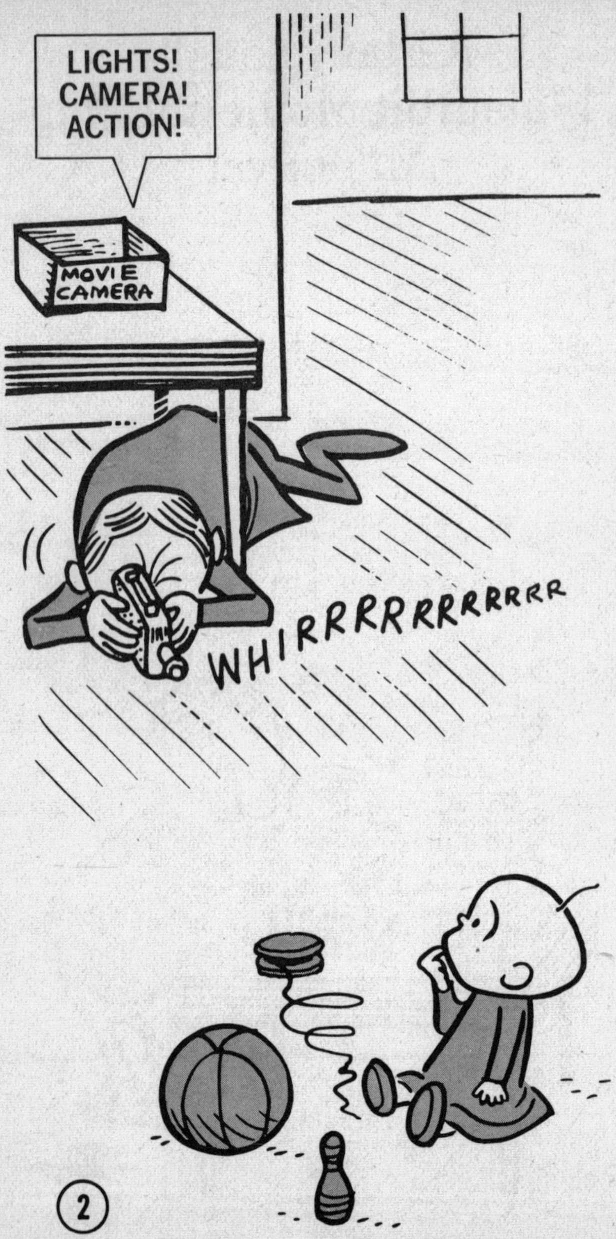
LIGHTS! CAMERA! ACTION!
MOVIE CAMERA
WHIRRRRRRRRRRRR
2

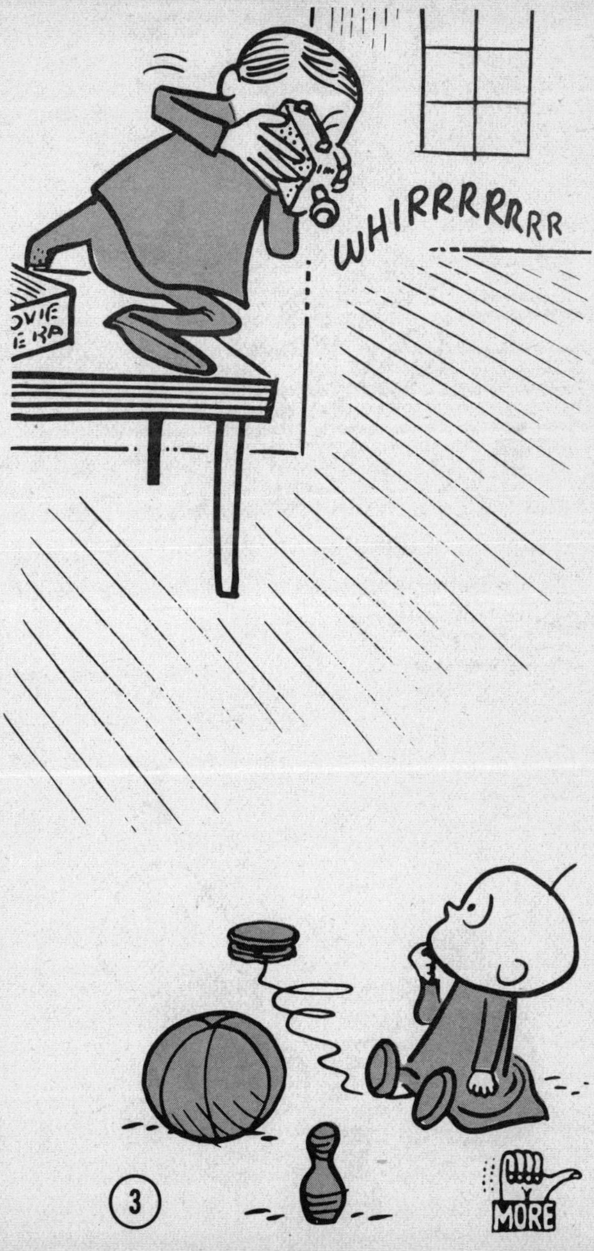
WHIRRRRRRRR
MOVIE
EKA
MORE

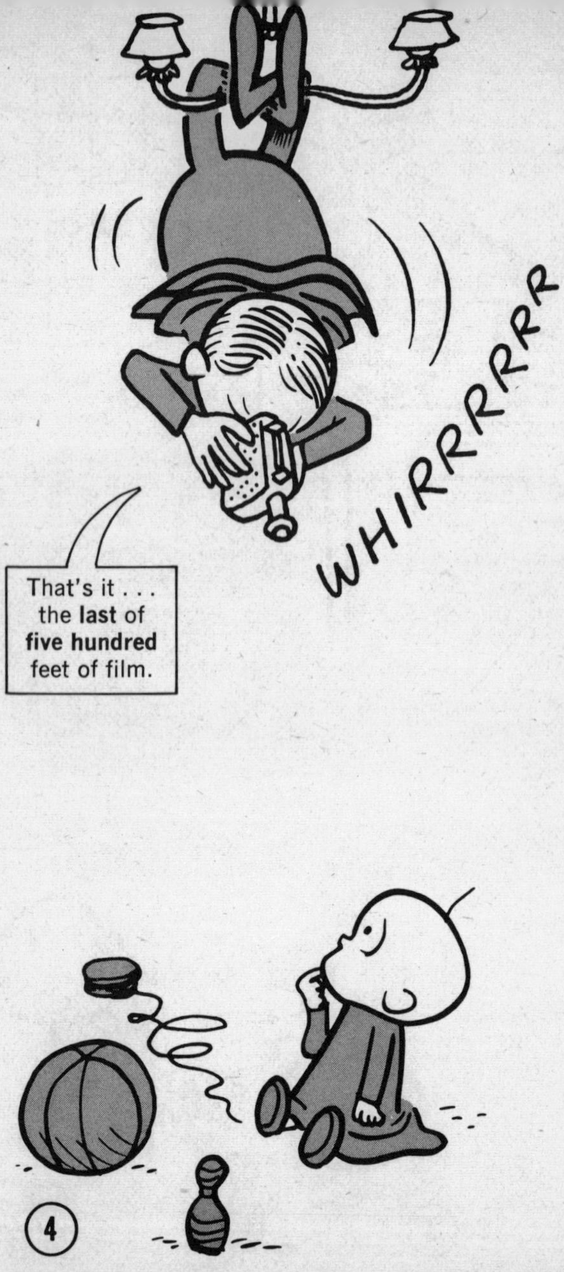

That's it . . . the **last** of **five hundred** feet of film.
WHIRRRRRR

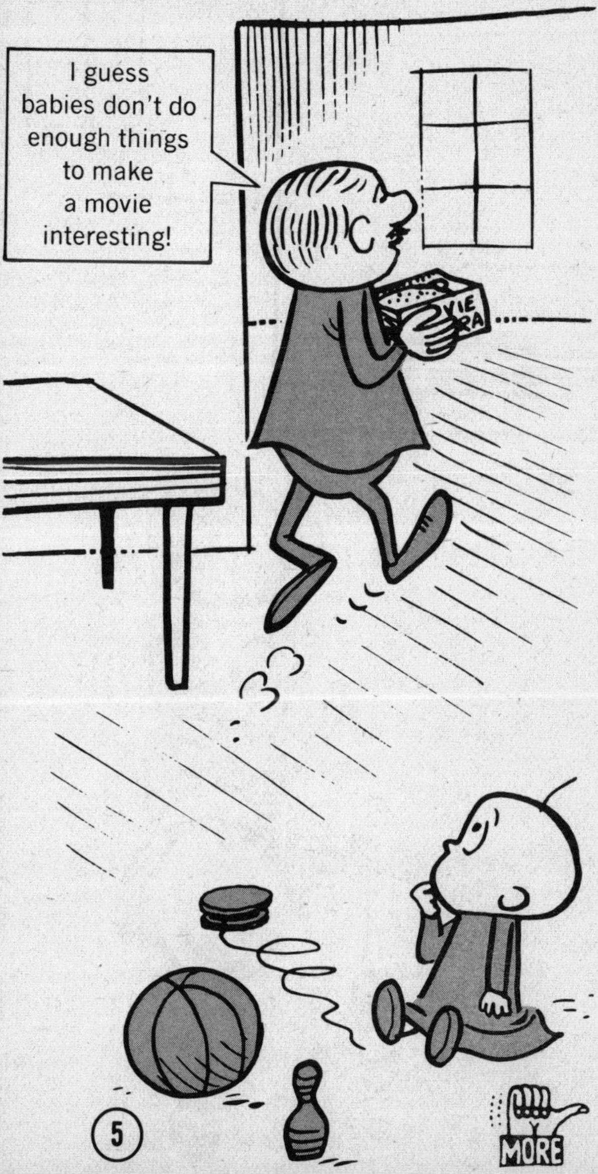
I guess babies don't do enough things to make a movie interesting!
MORE

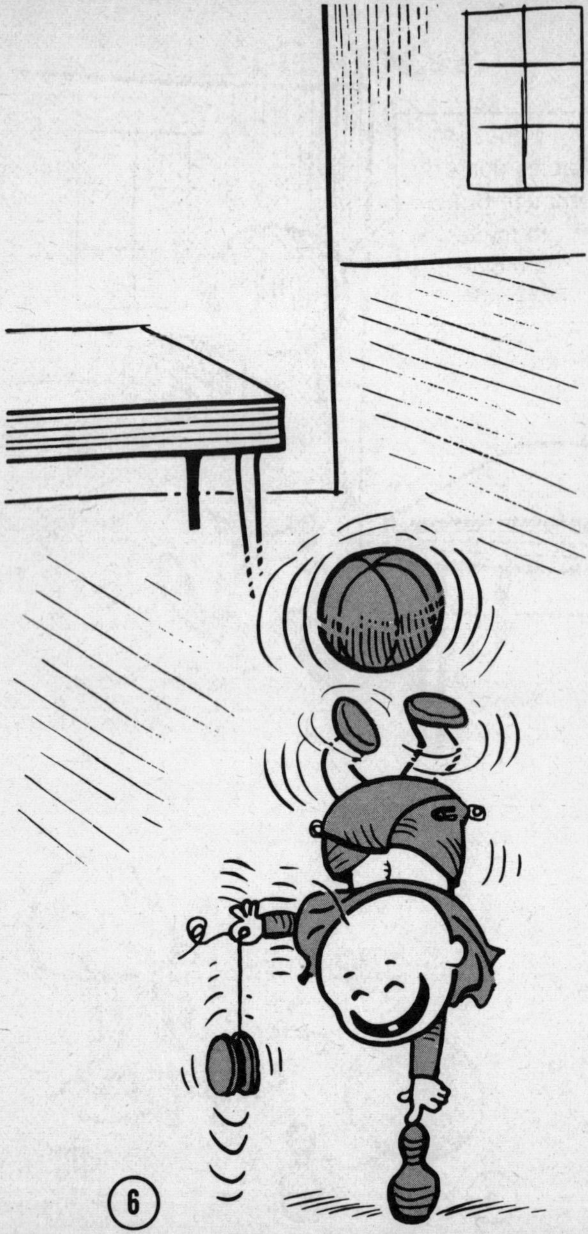

6

A Superlative Ingathering of Astounding Absurdities

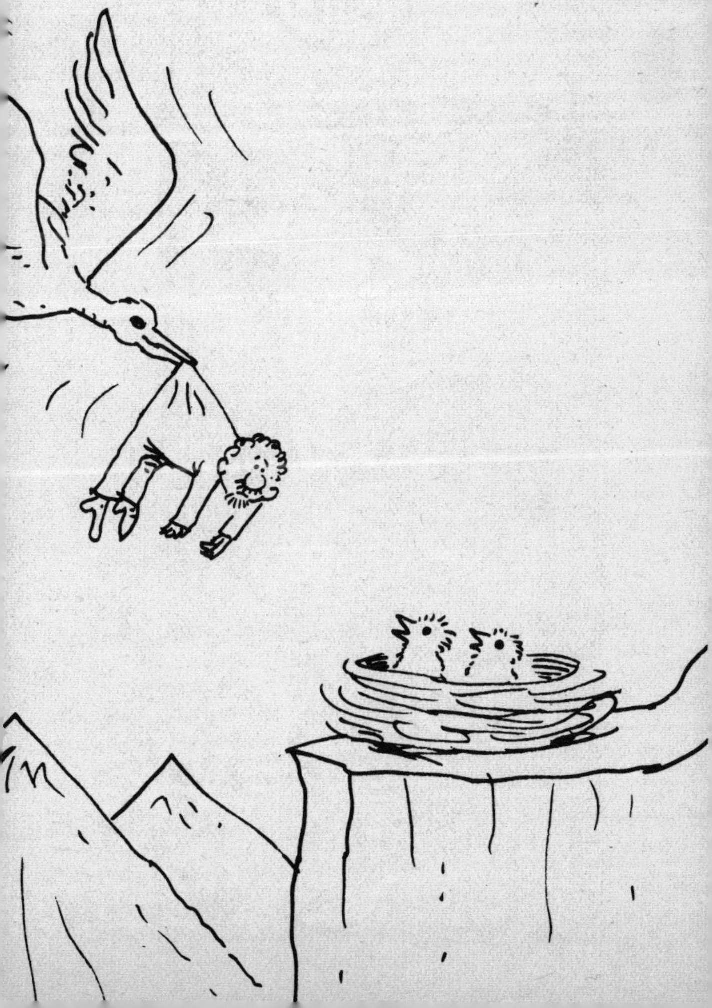

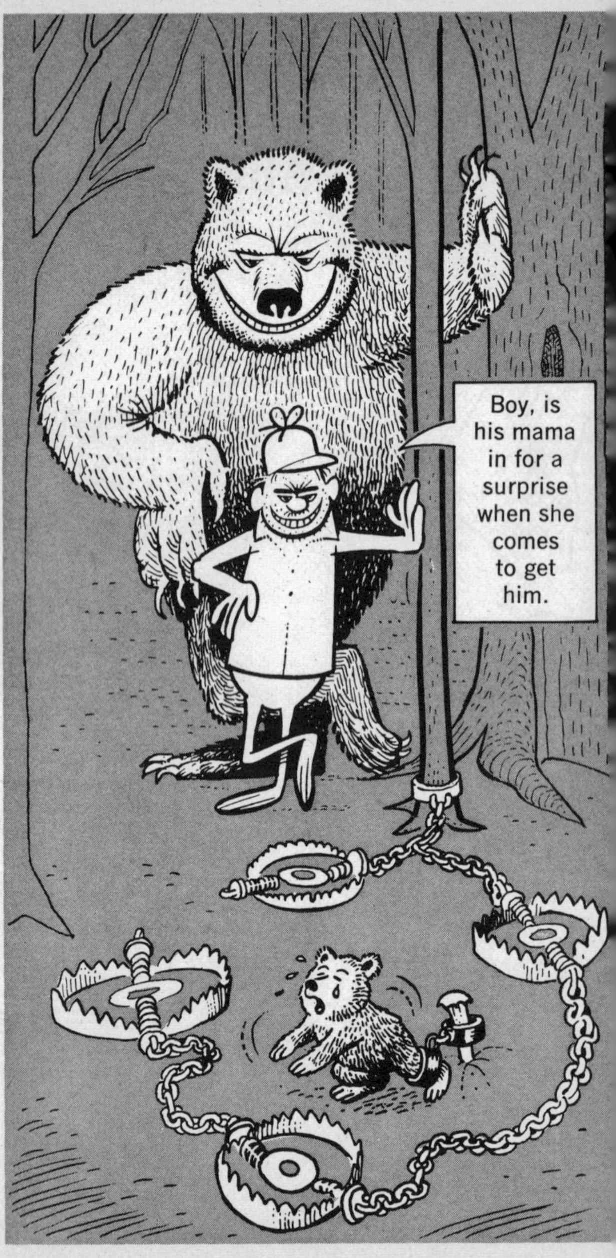
Boy, is his mama in for a surprise when she comes to get him.

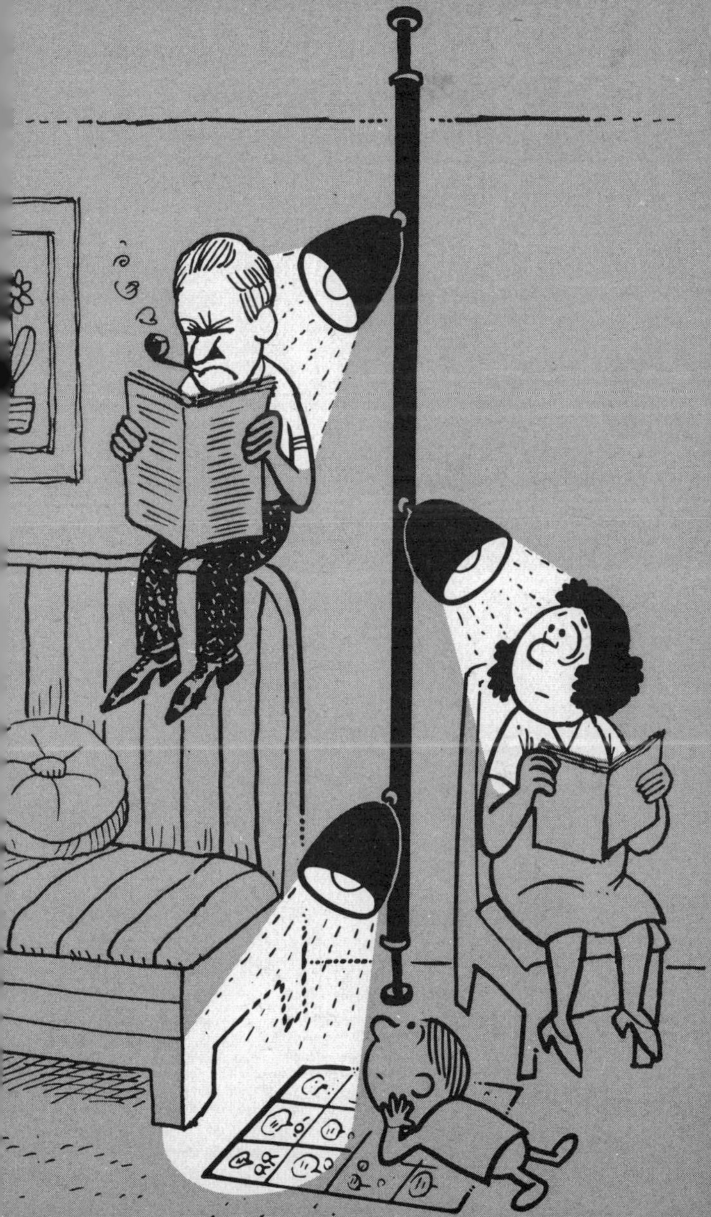

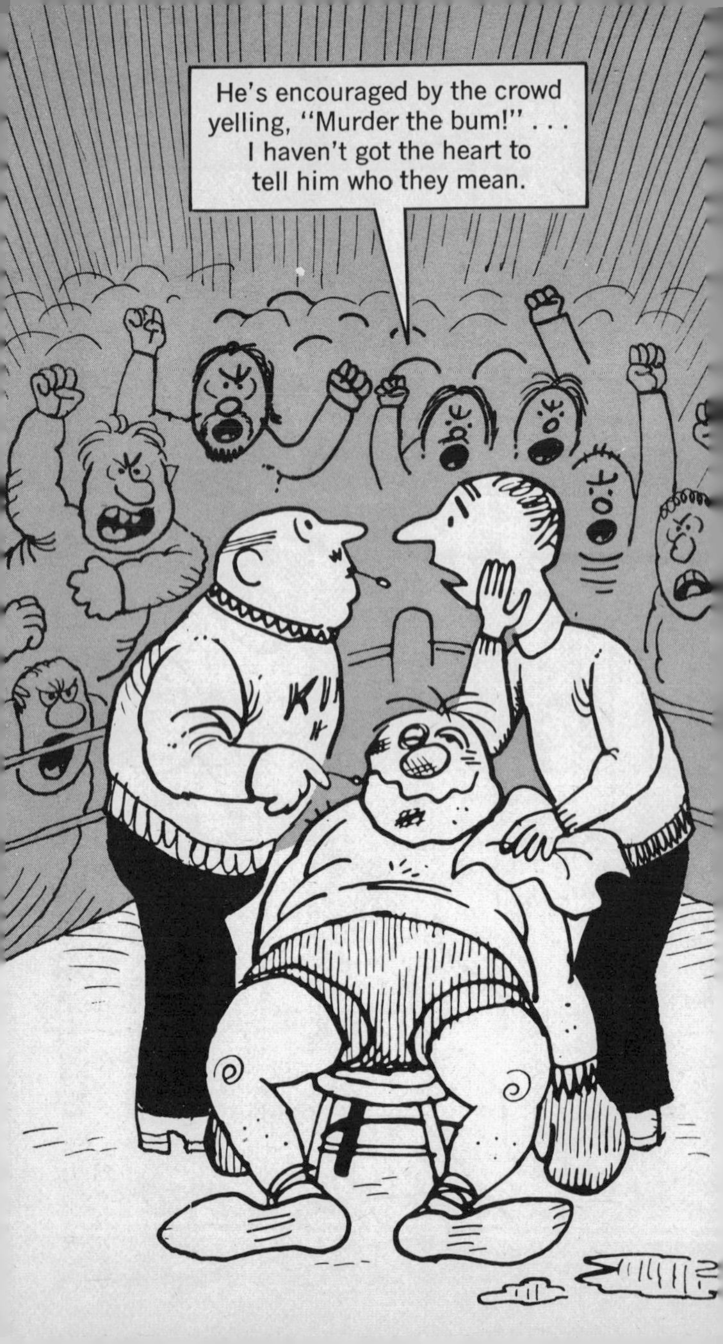
He's encouraged by the crowd yelling, "Murder the bum!" . . . I haven't got the heart to tell him who they mean.

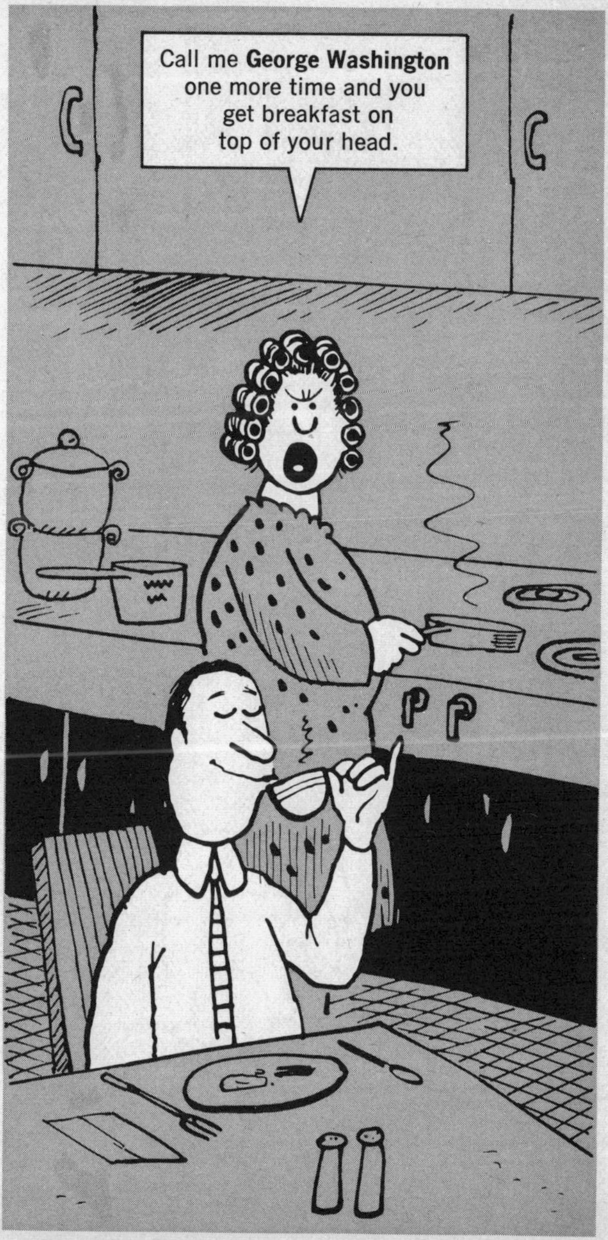
Call me **George Washington** one more time and you get breakfast on top of your head.

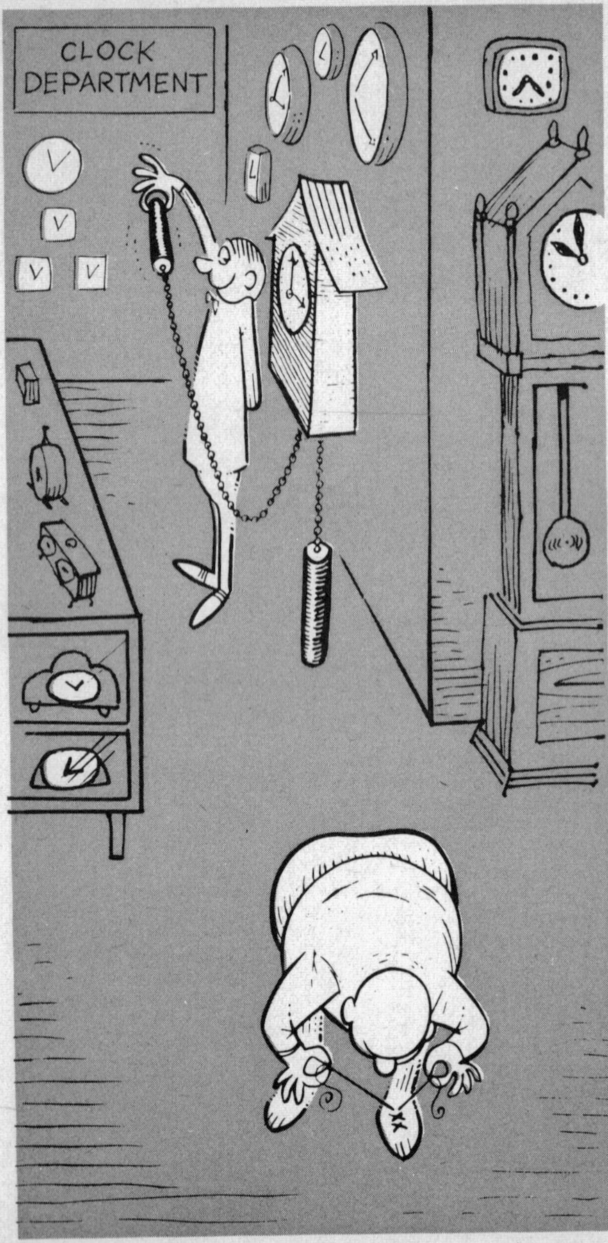
CLOCK
DEPARTMENT

A Captivatingly Contrived Cat Caper

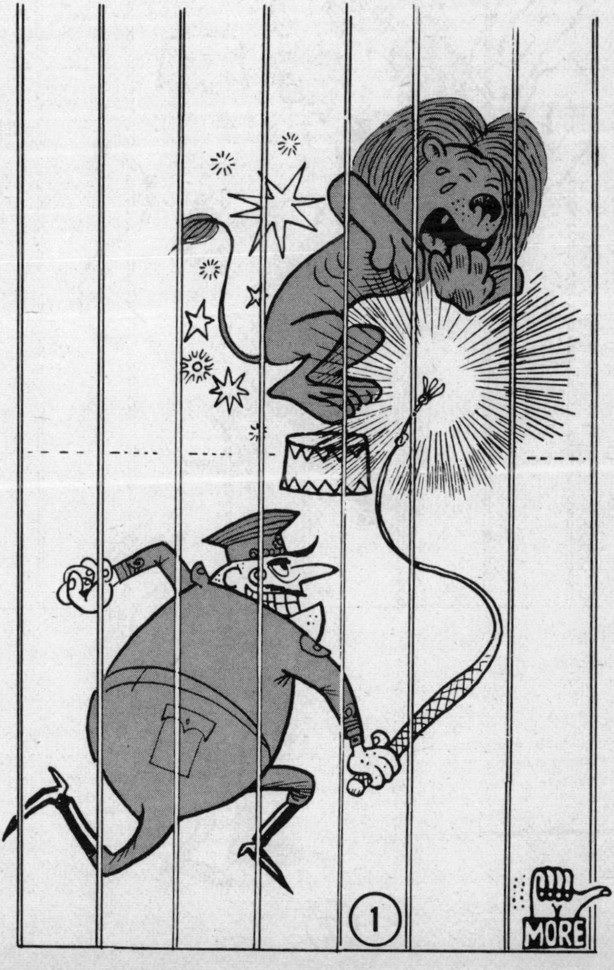
MORE

ROWR

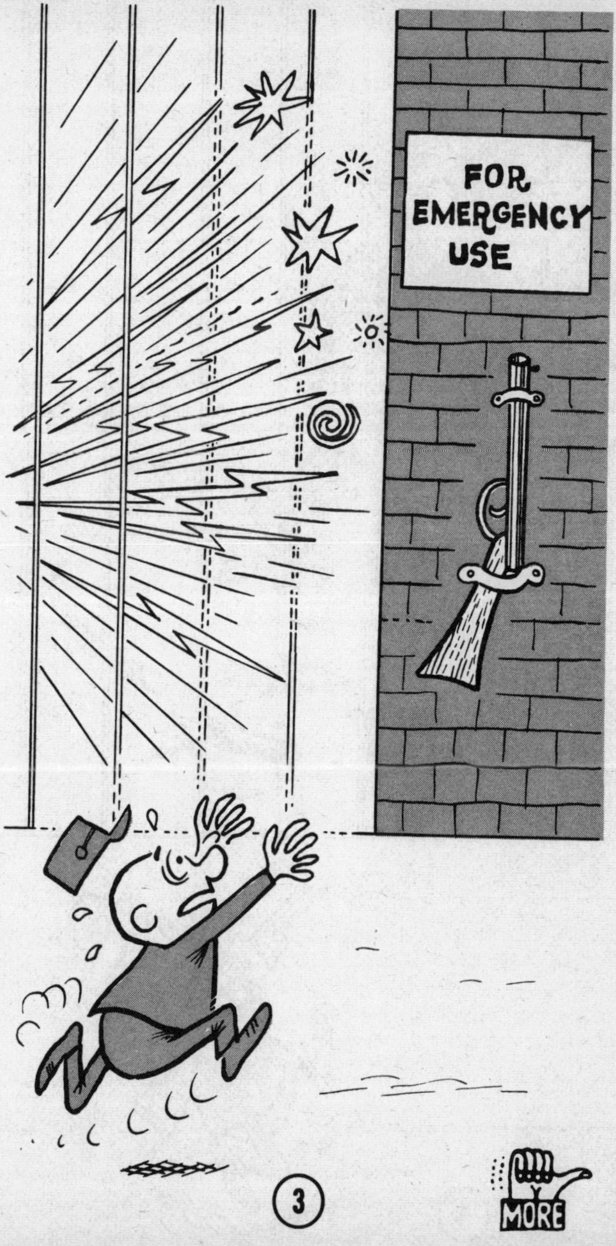
FOR EMERGENCY USE
MORE

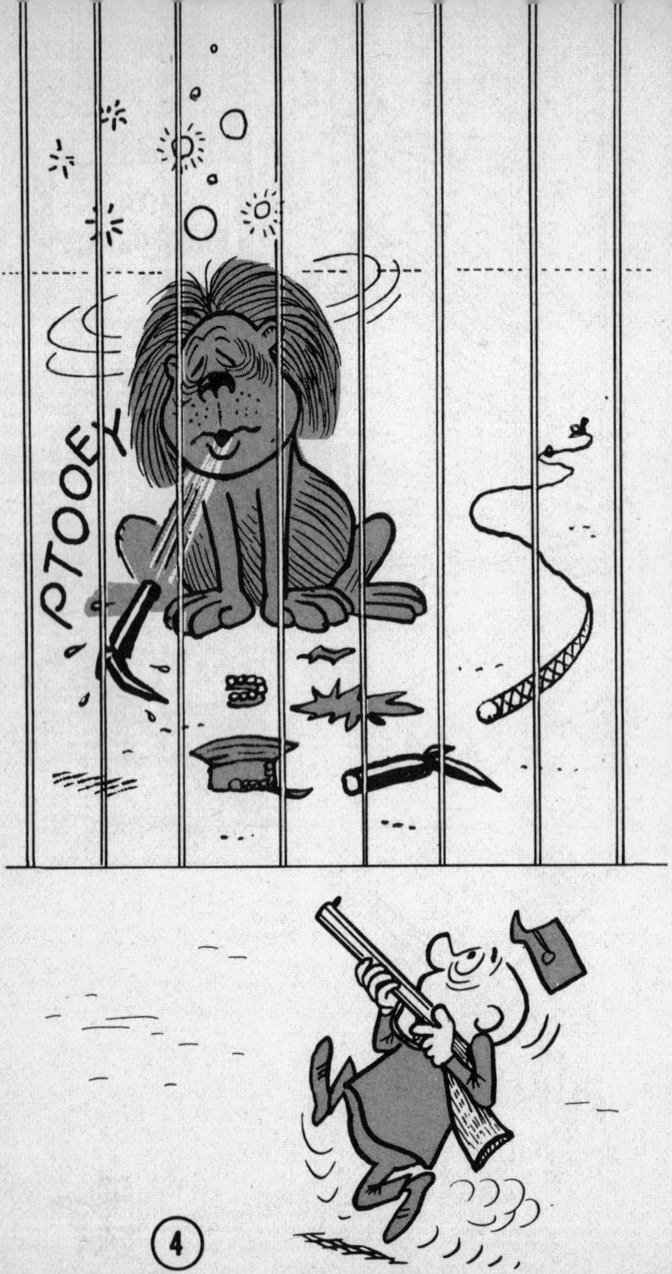
PTOOEY

4

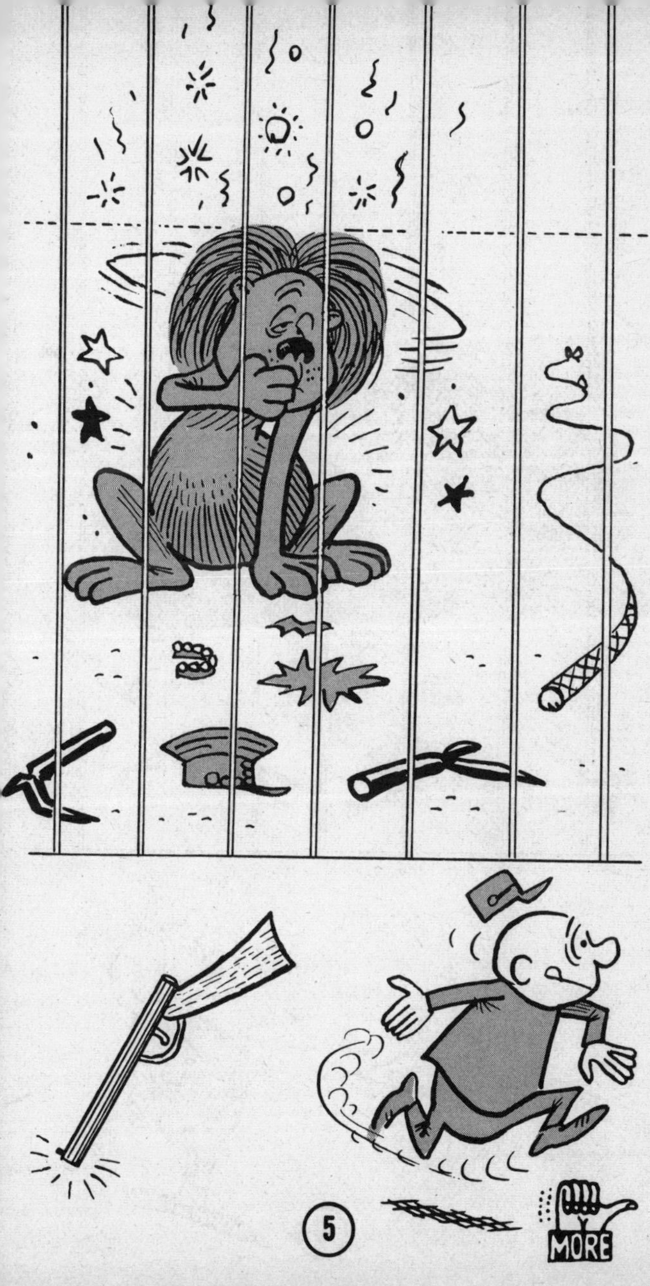
MORE

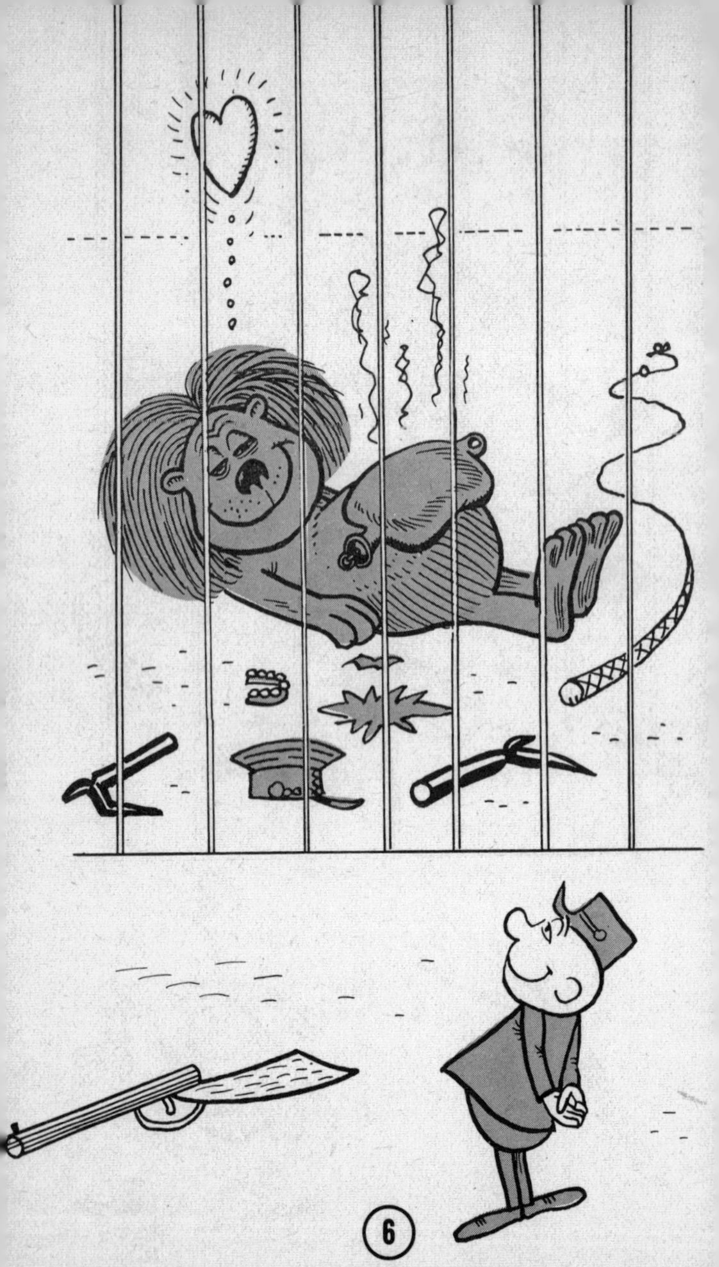

A Breathtaking Medley of Overripe Putrescences

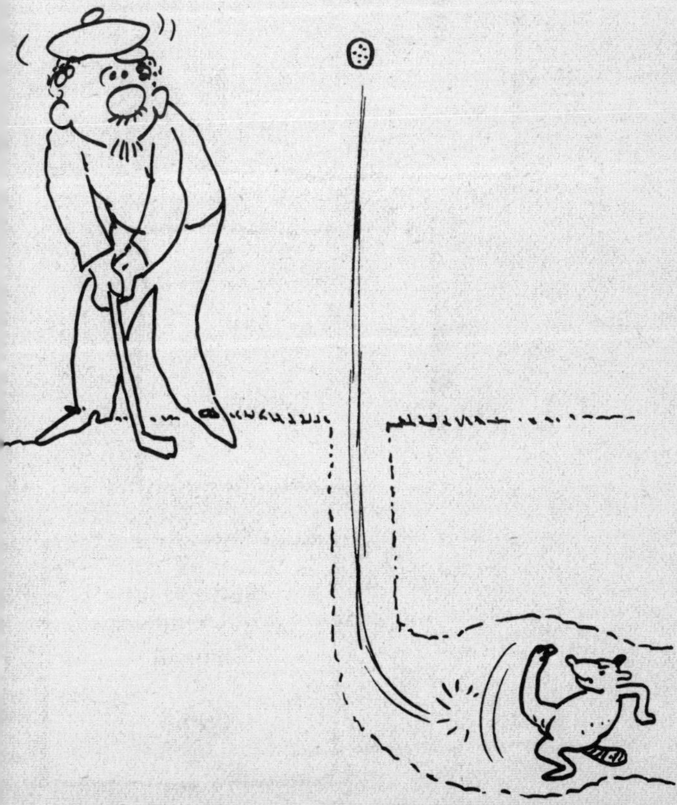

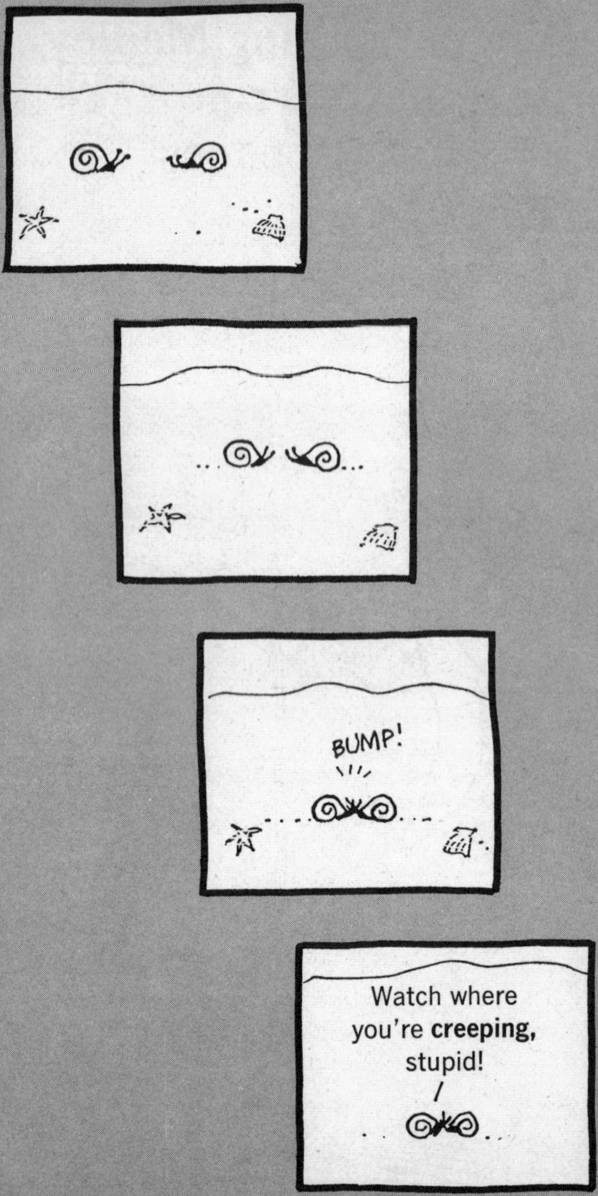

BUMP!
Watch where you're **creeping,** stupid!

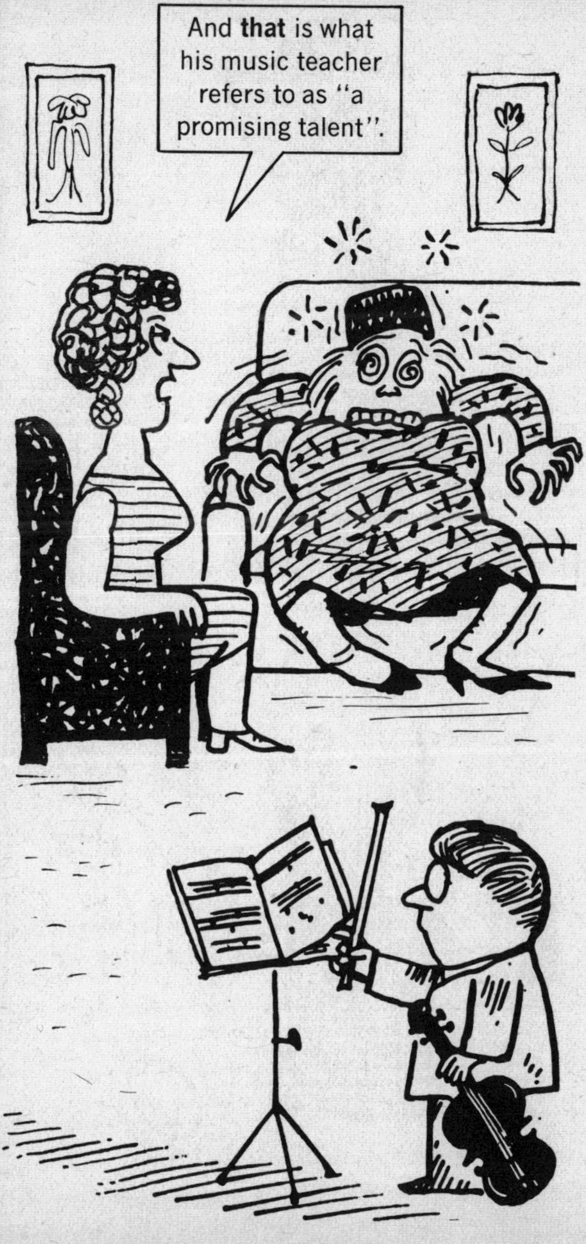
And **that** is what his music teacher refers to as "a promising talent".

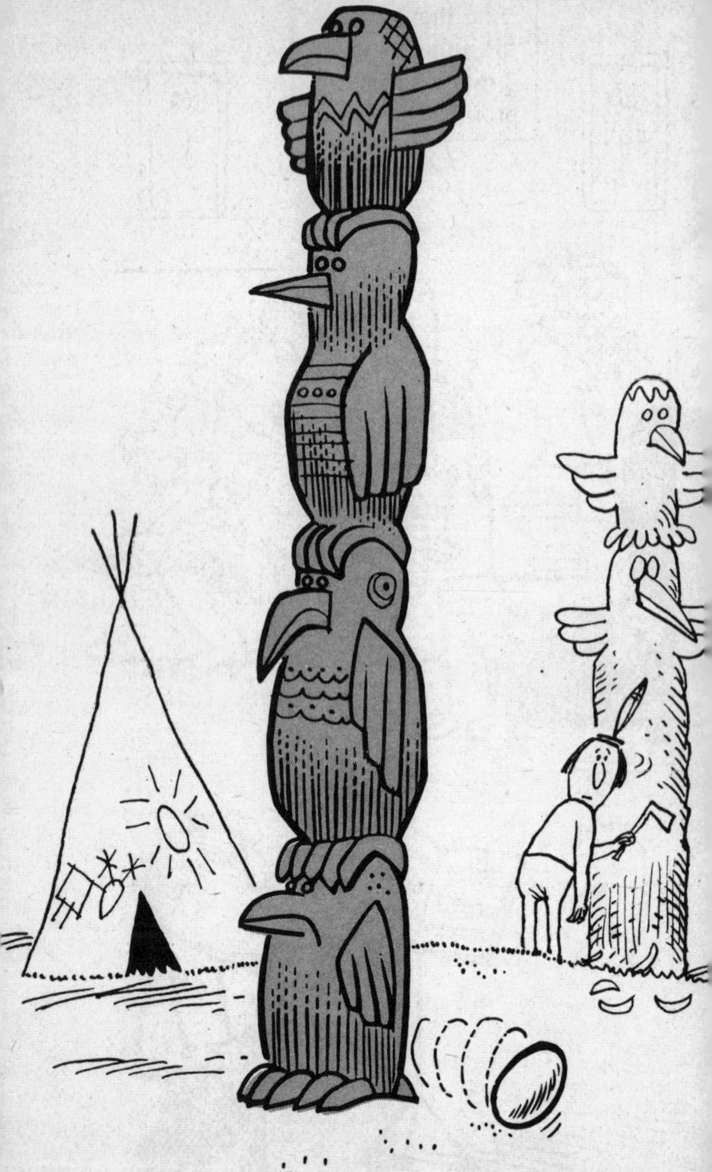

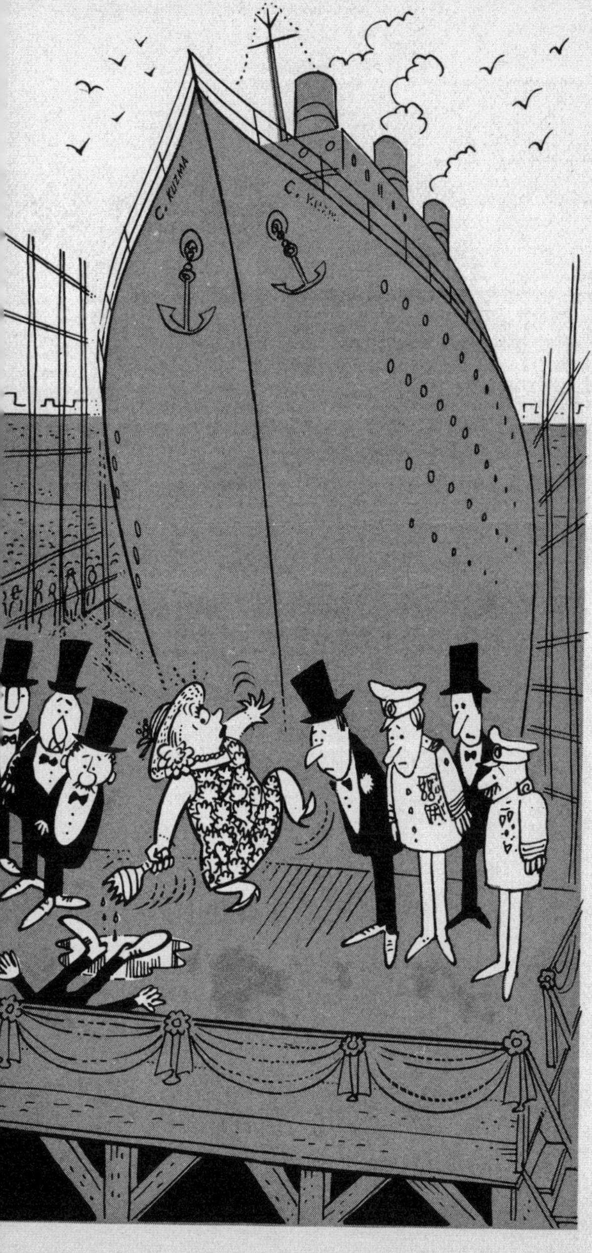
C. KUZMA

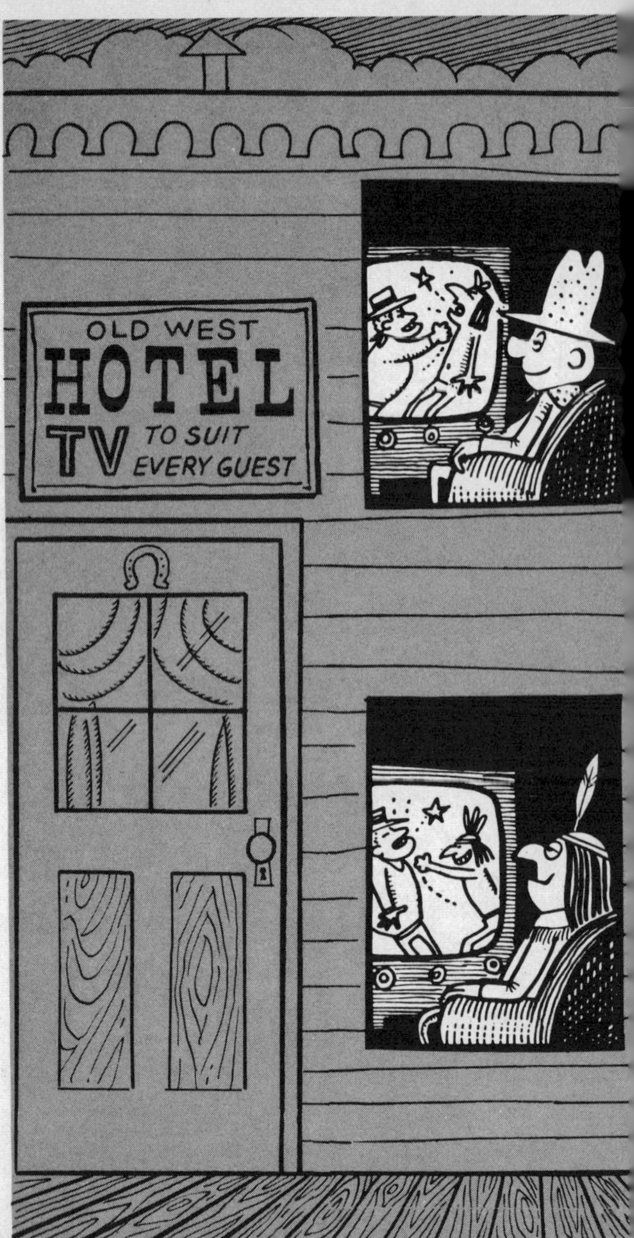
OLD WEST
HOTEL
TV TO SUIT EVERY GUEST

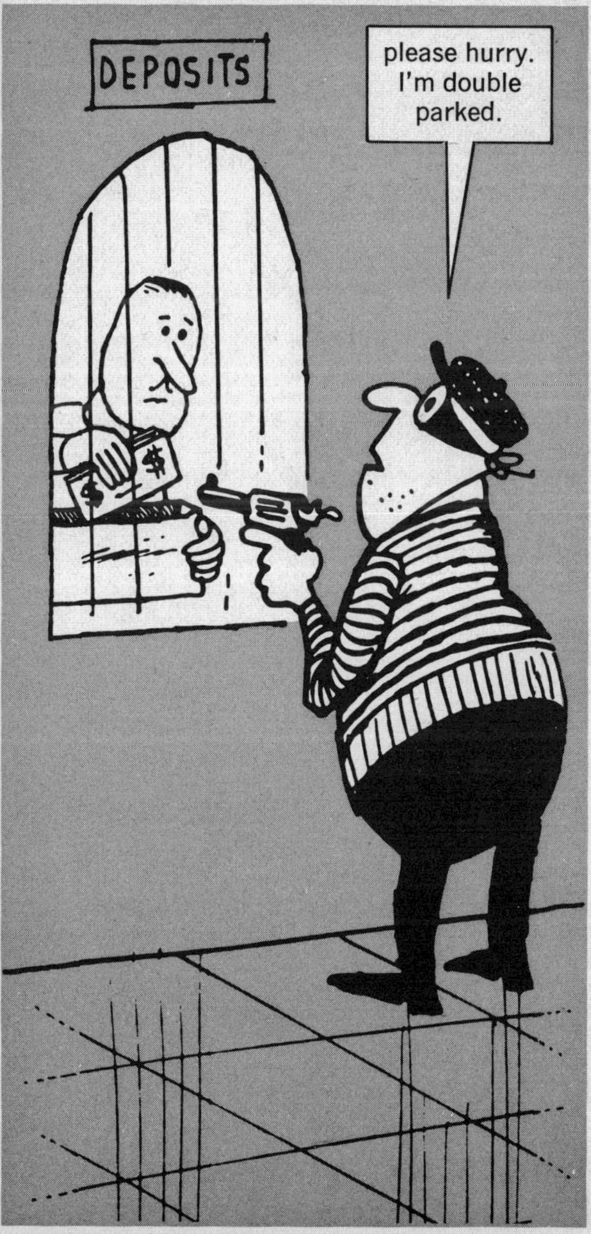
DEPOSITS
please hurry. I'm double parked.

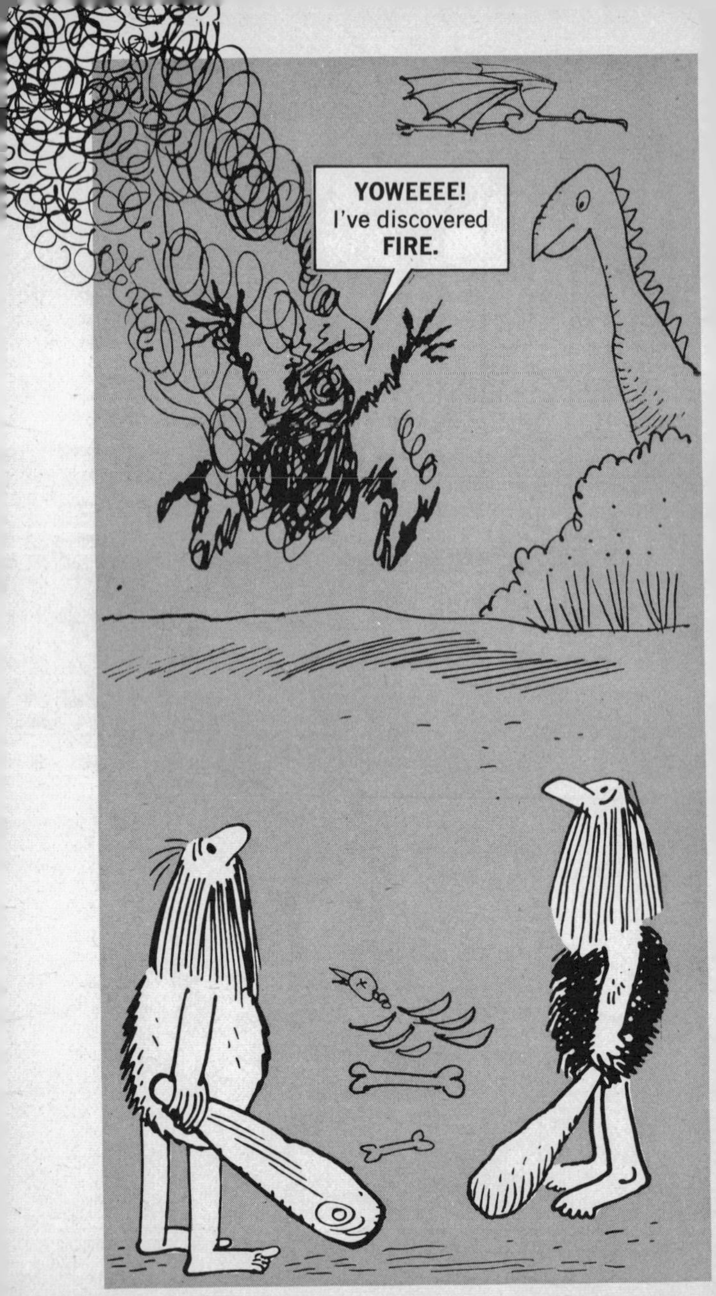
YOWEEEE!
I've discovered
FIRE.

A Titillatingly Tedious Tightrope Tale

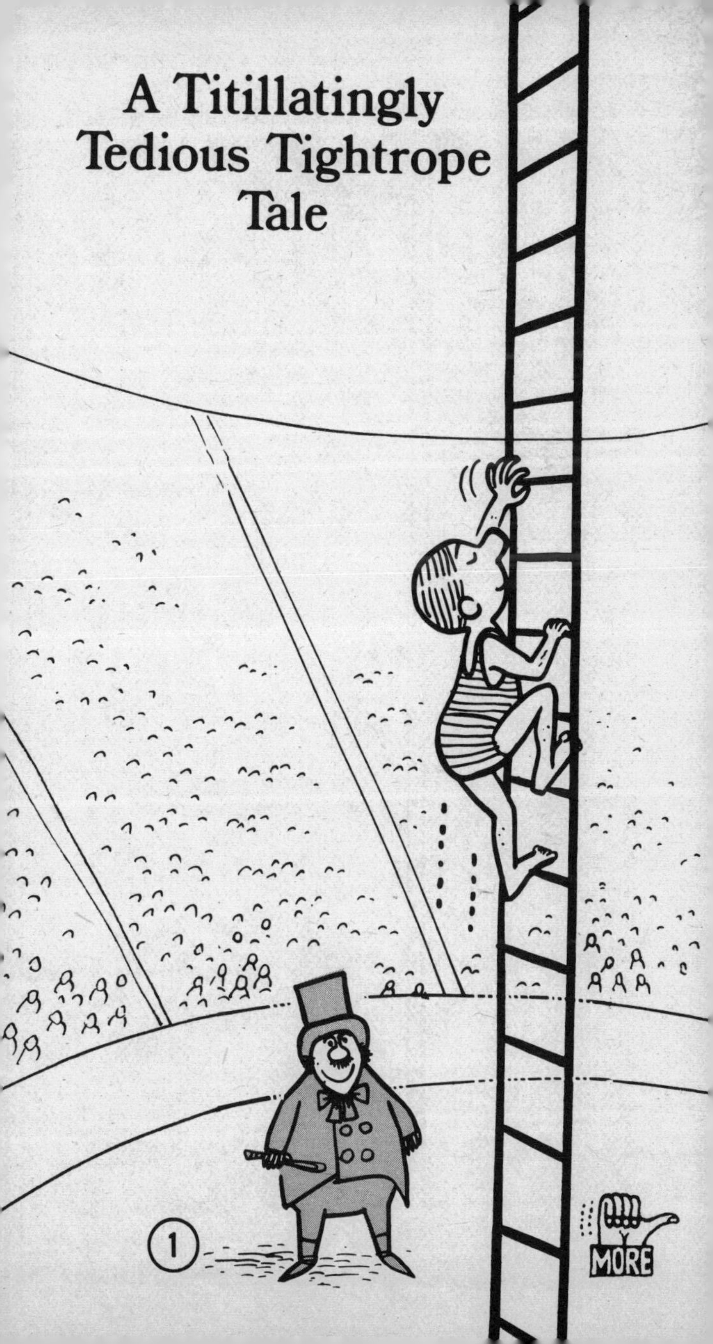
1
MORE

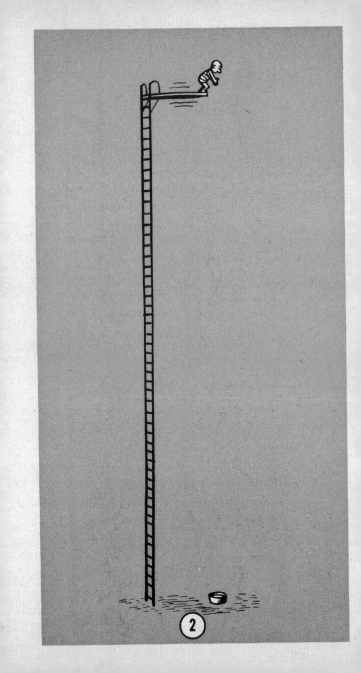

2

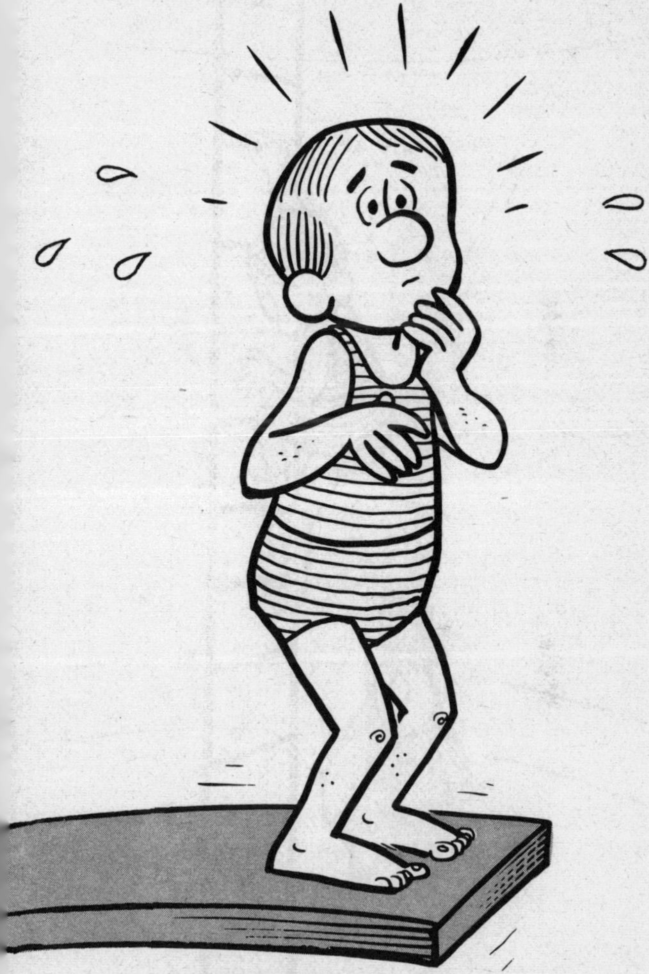

3

MORE

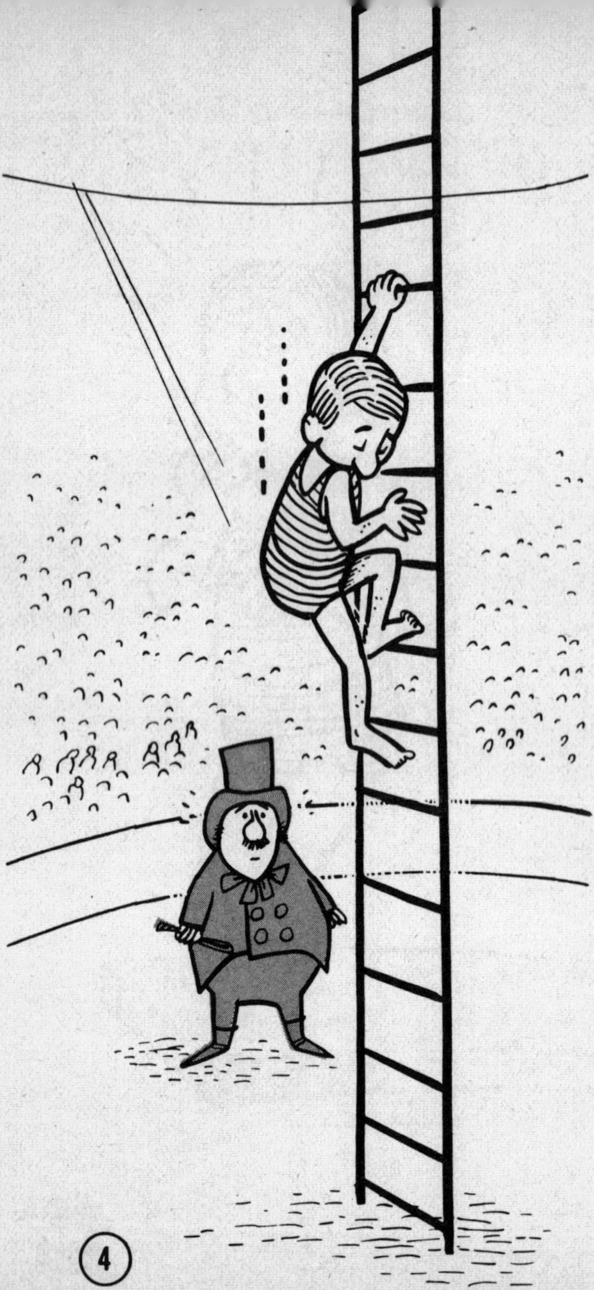

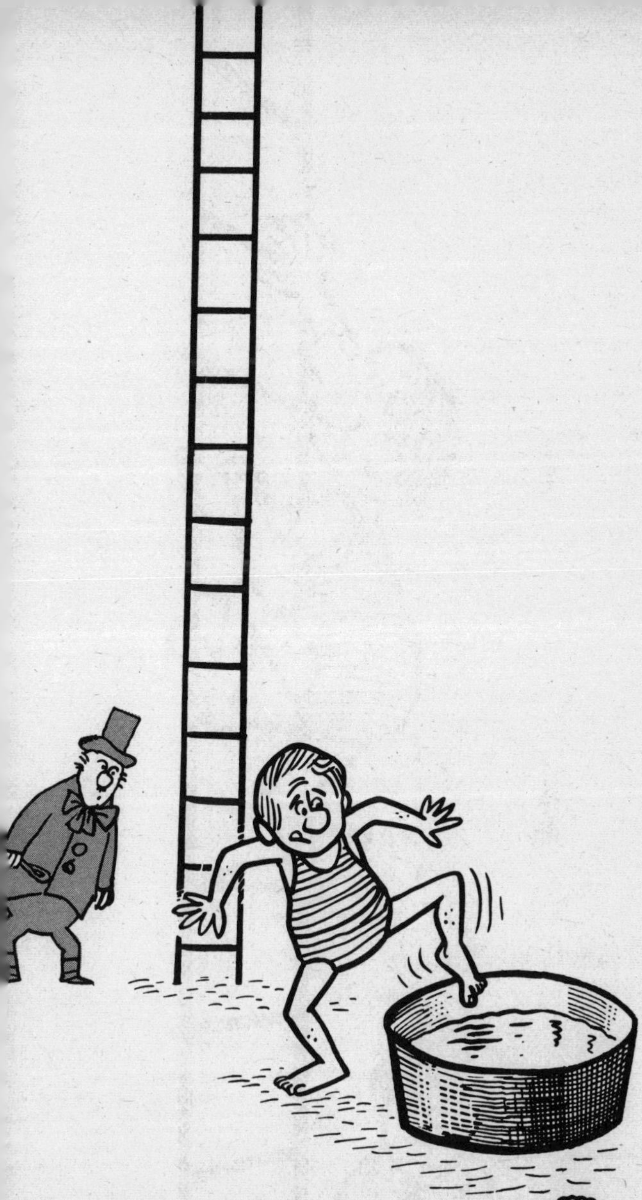
MORE

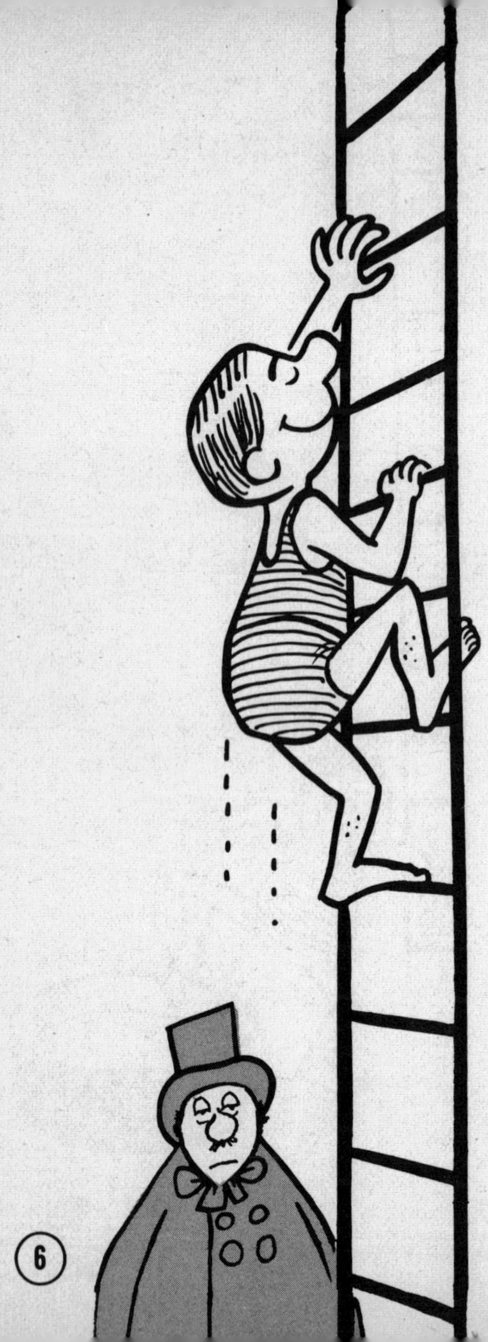
6

A Glorious Collection of Tightrope Trivialities

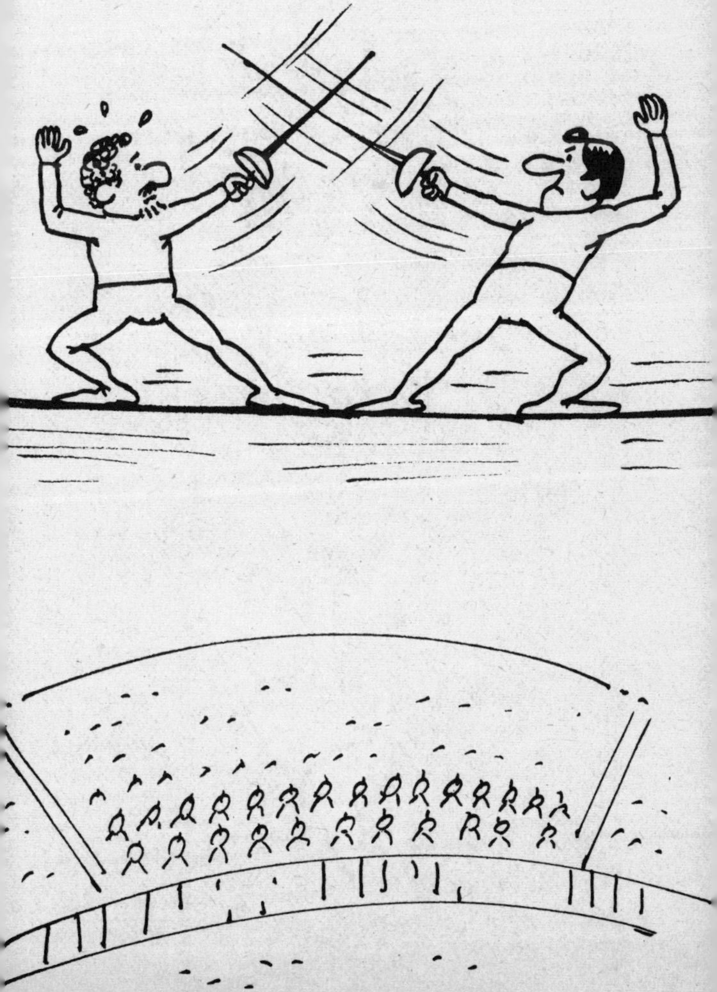

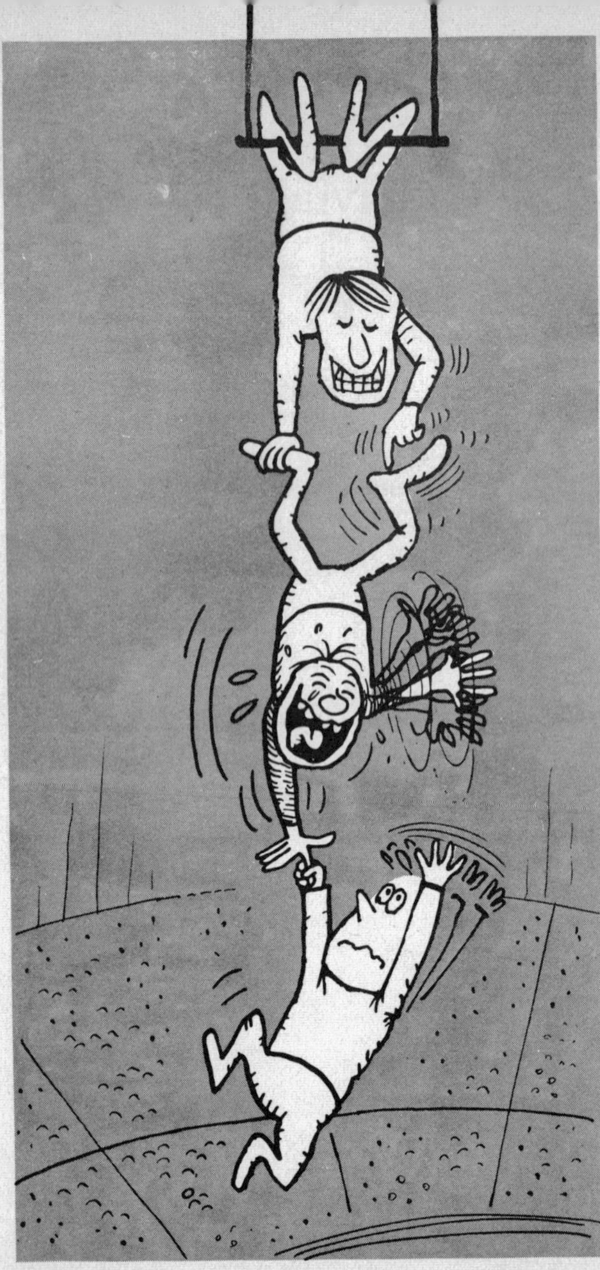

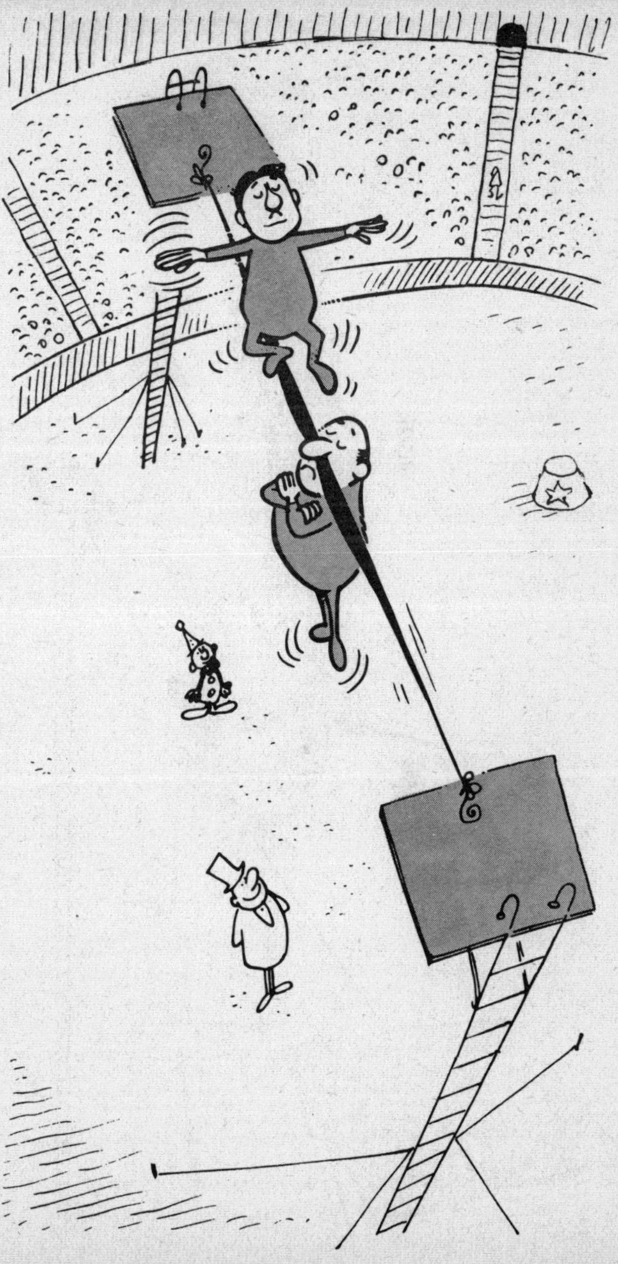

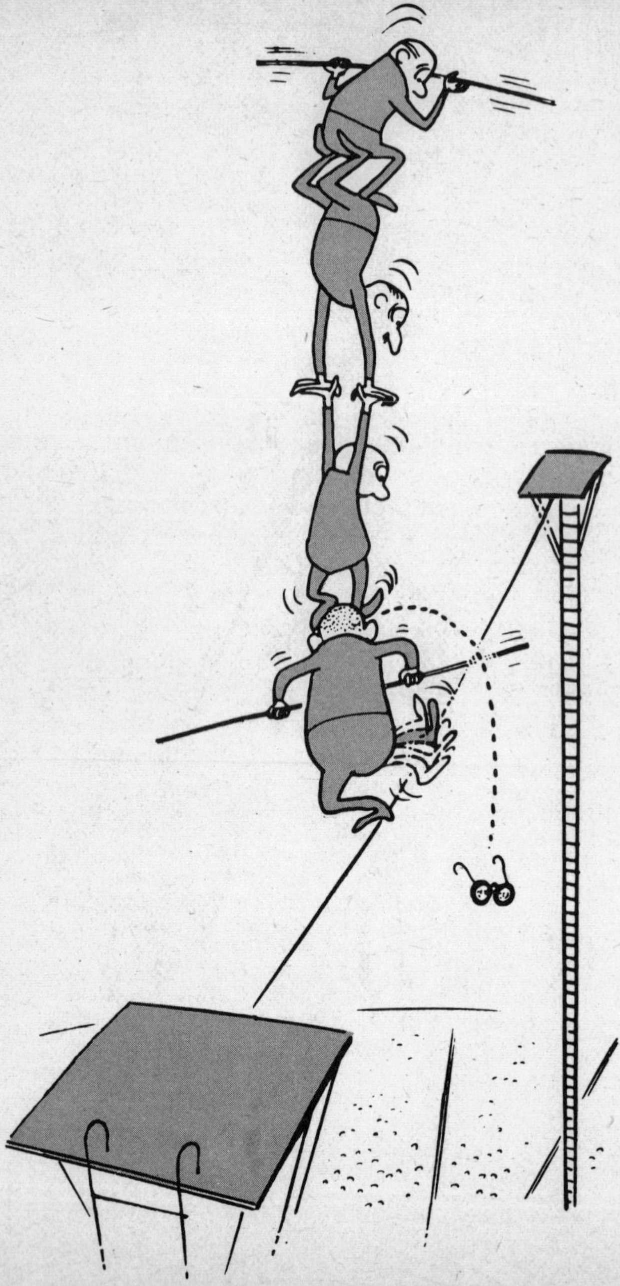

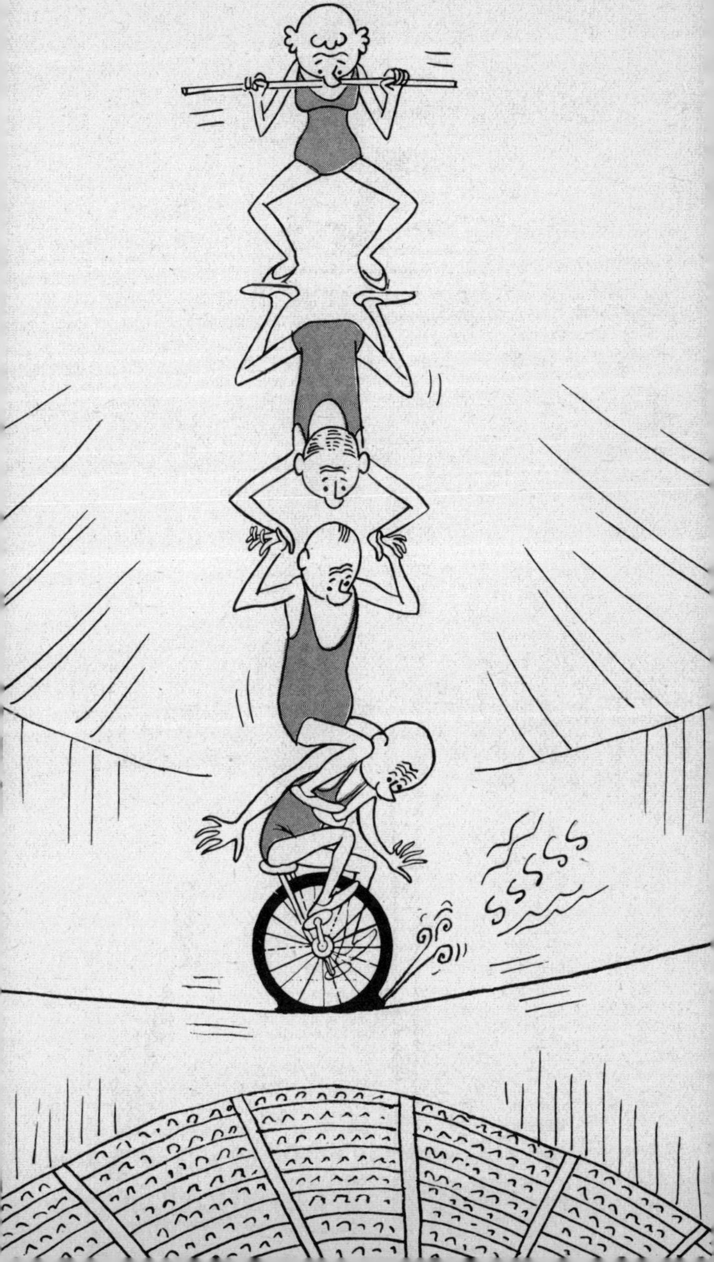
SSSSS

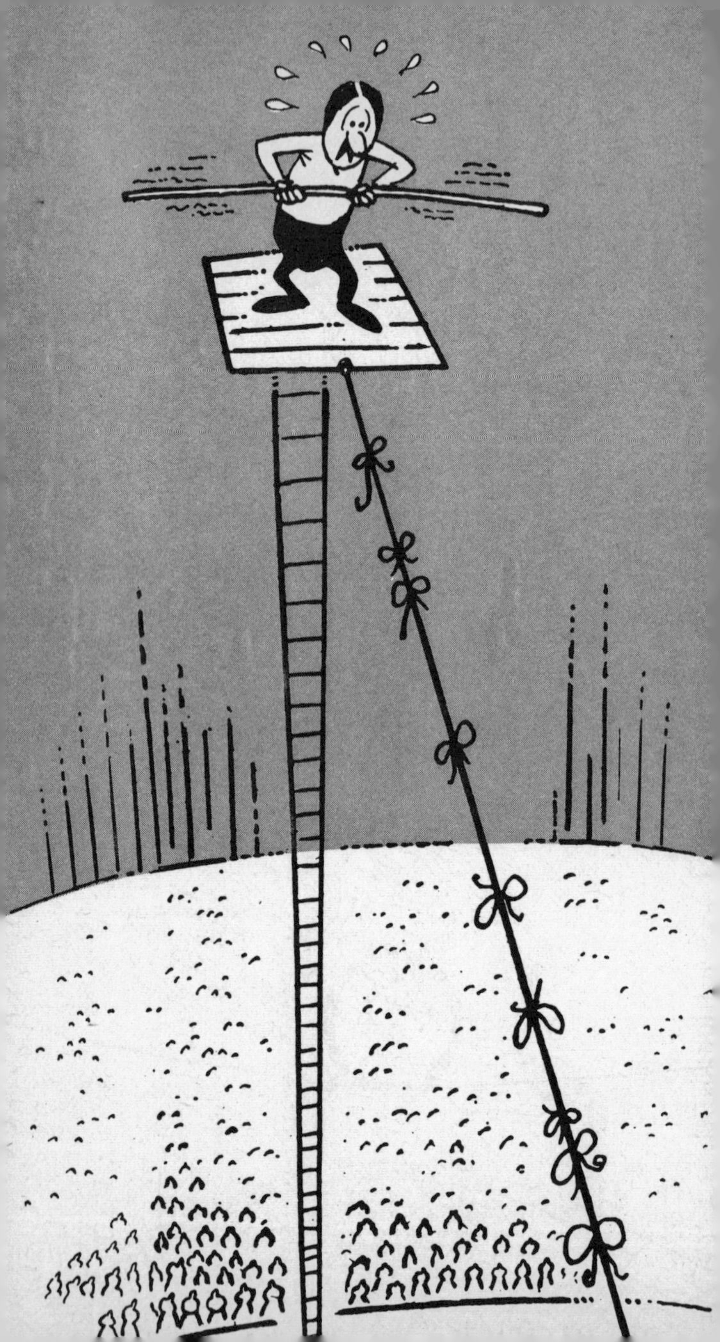

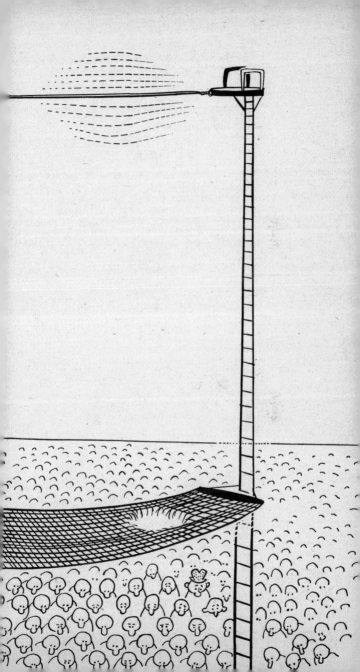

A Miraculously Miserable Mermaid Mishmash

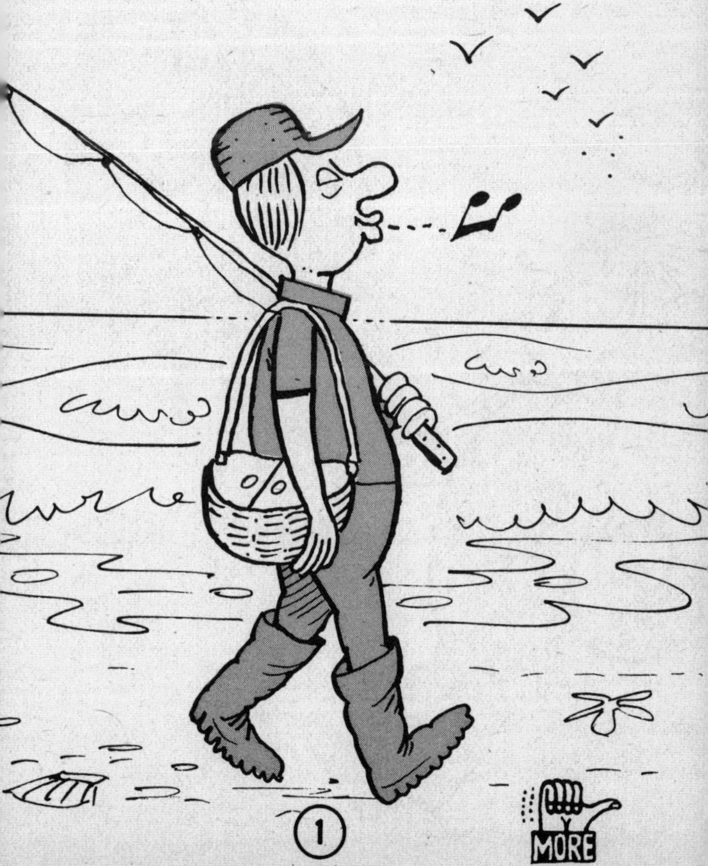
MORE

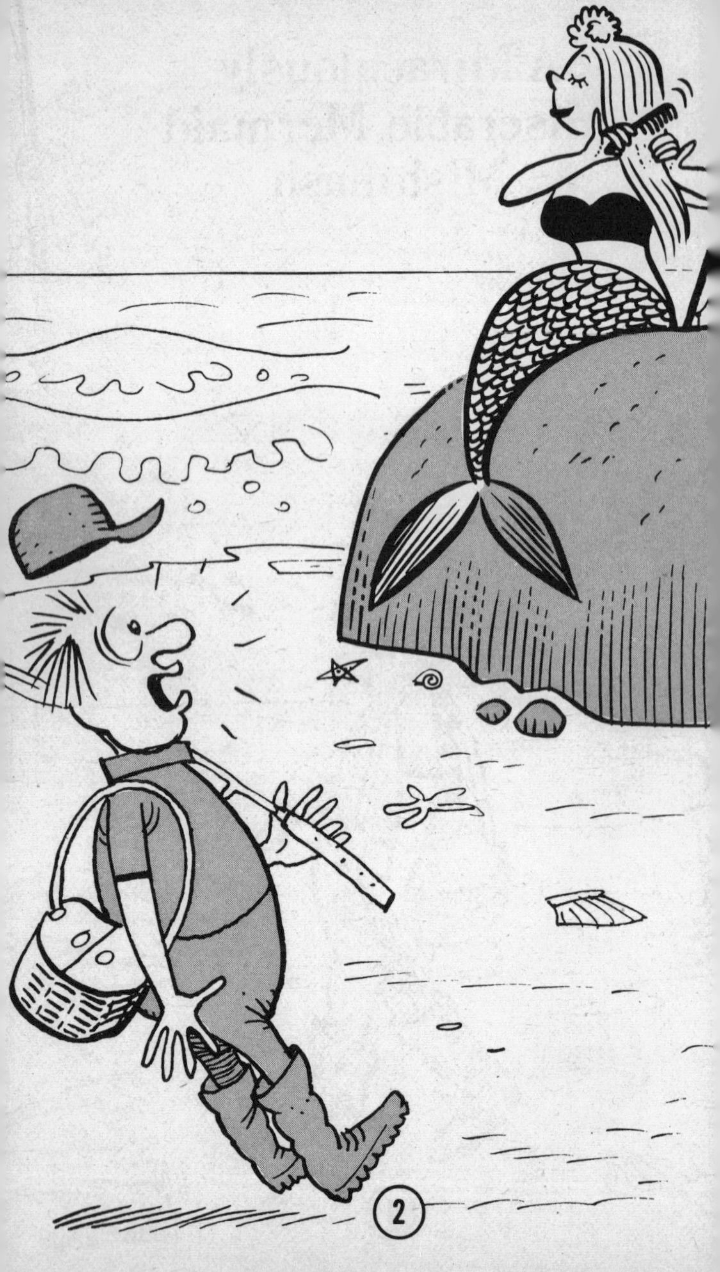
2

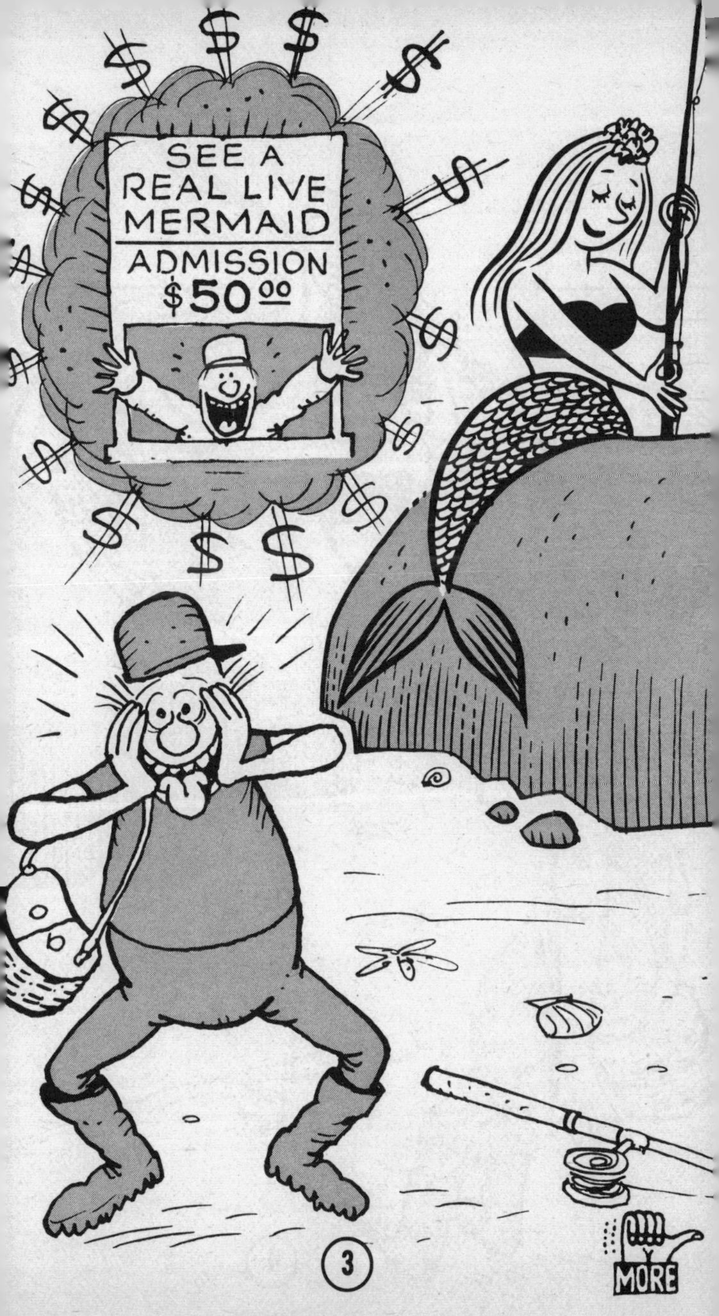
SEE A
REAL LIVE
MERMAID
ADMISSION
$50.00
MORE

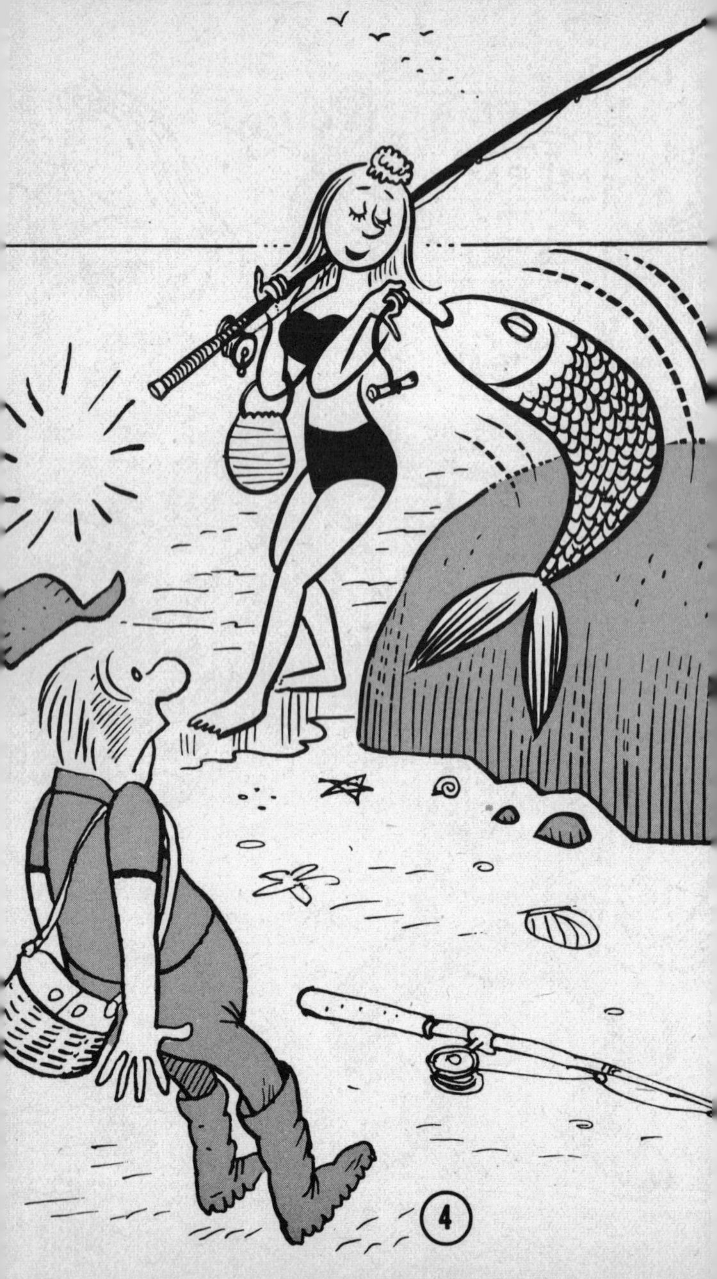
4

A Male Chauvinist Pig Section

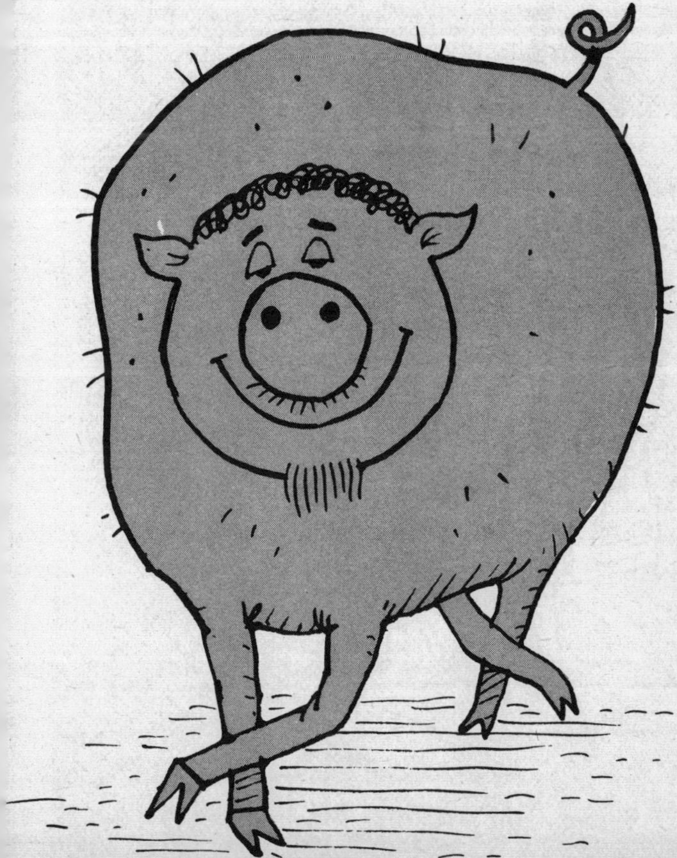

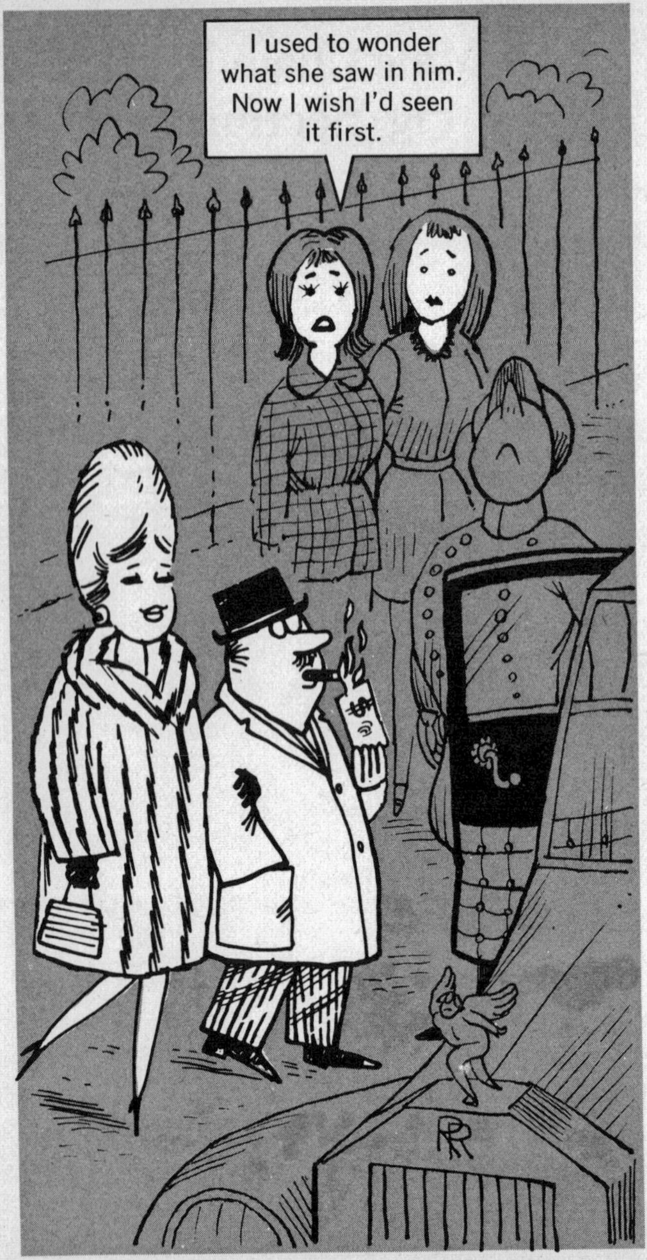
I used to wonder what she saw in him. Now I wish I'd seen it first.

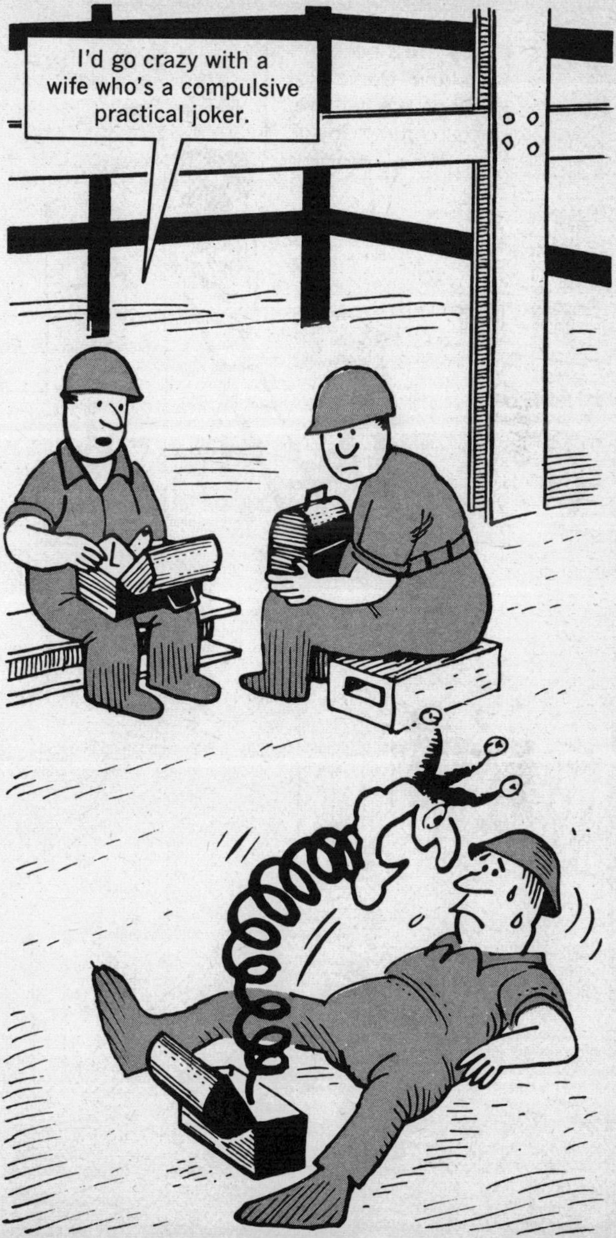
I'd go crazy with a wife who's a compulsive practical joker.

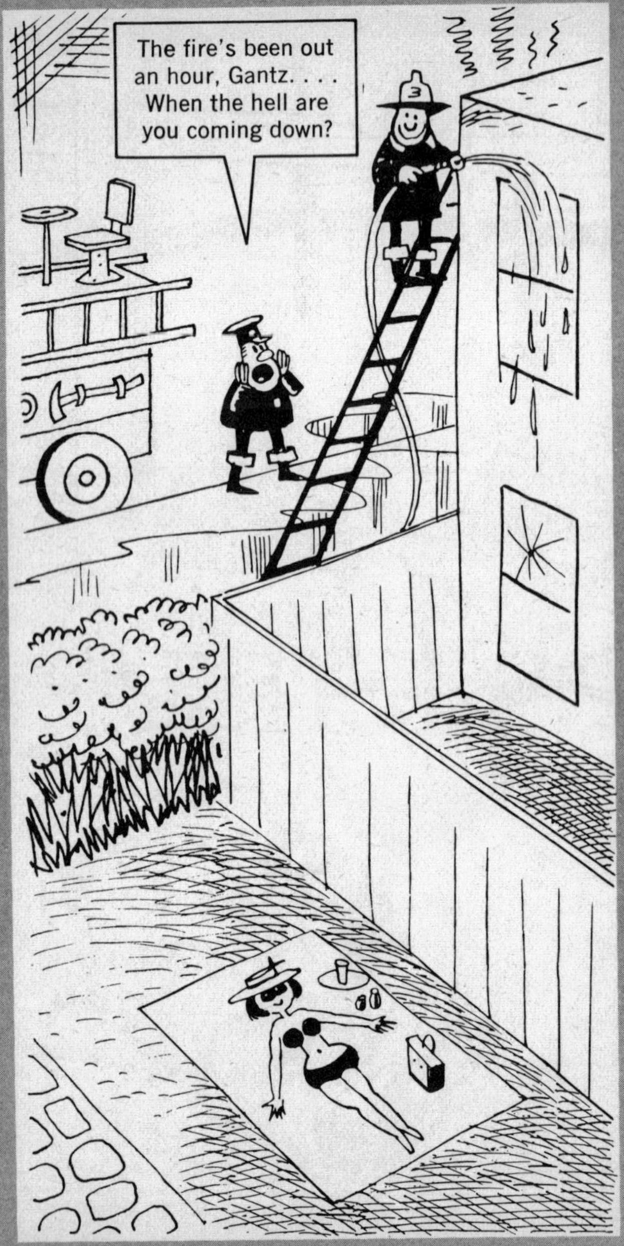
The fire's been out an hour, Gantz. . . . When the hell are you coming down?

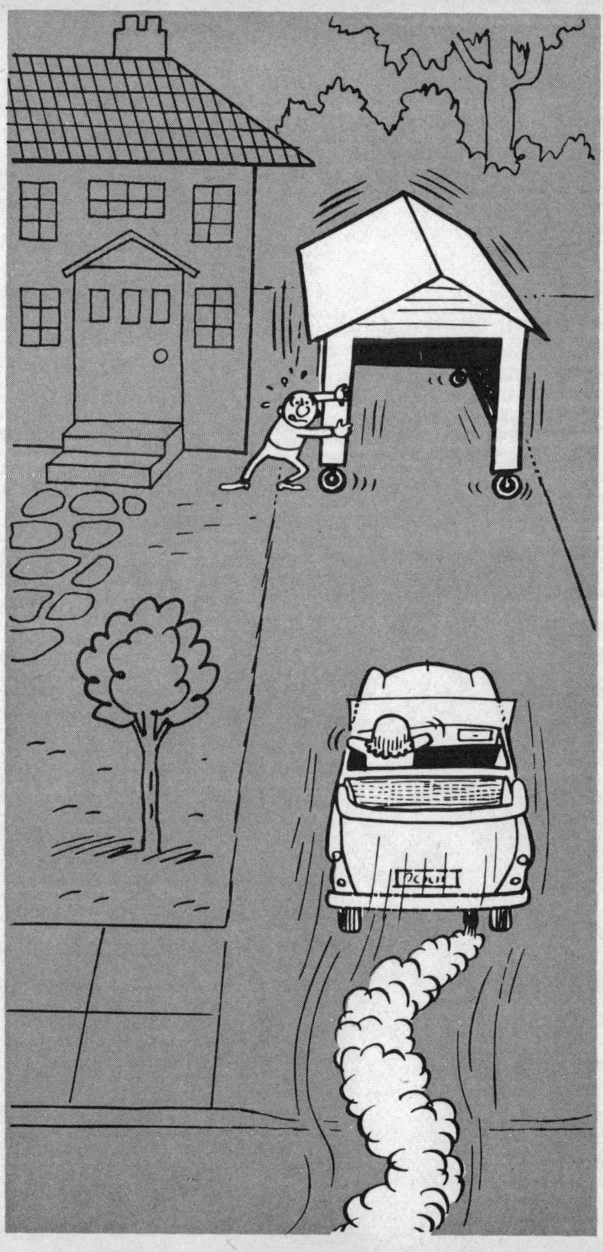

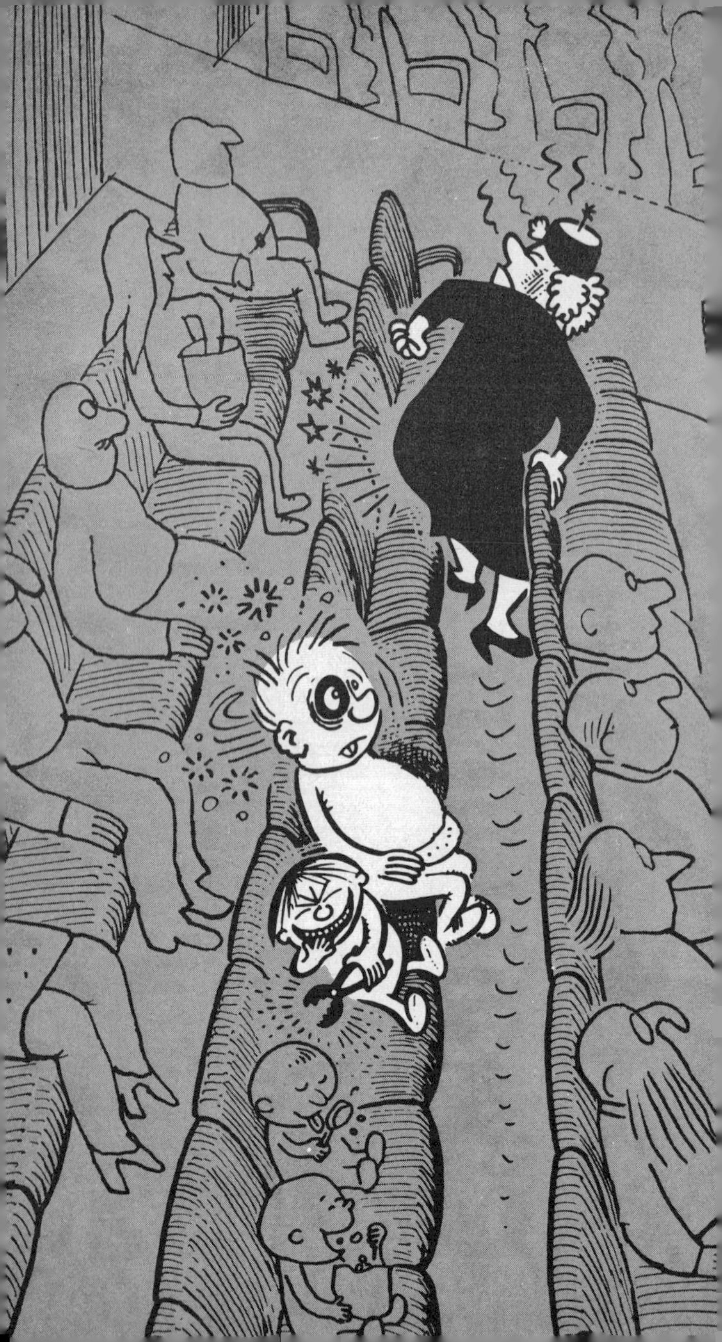

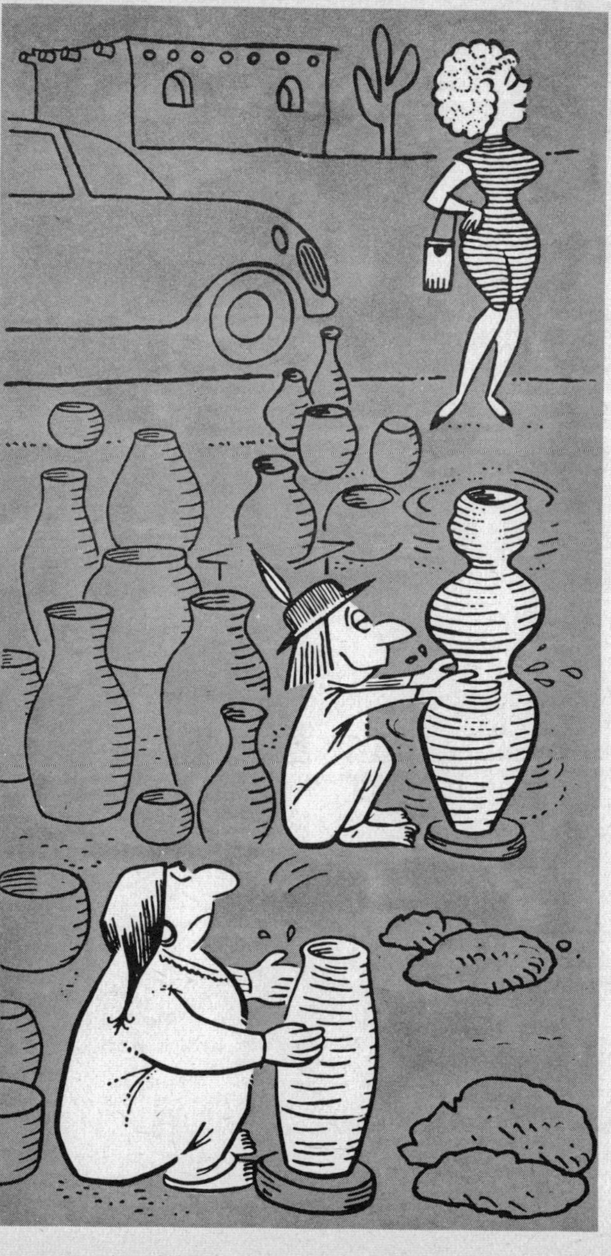

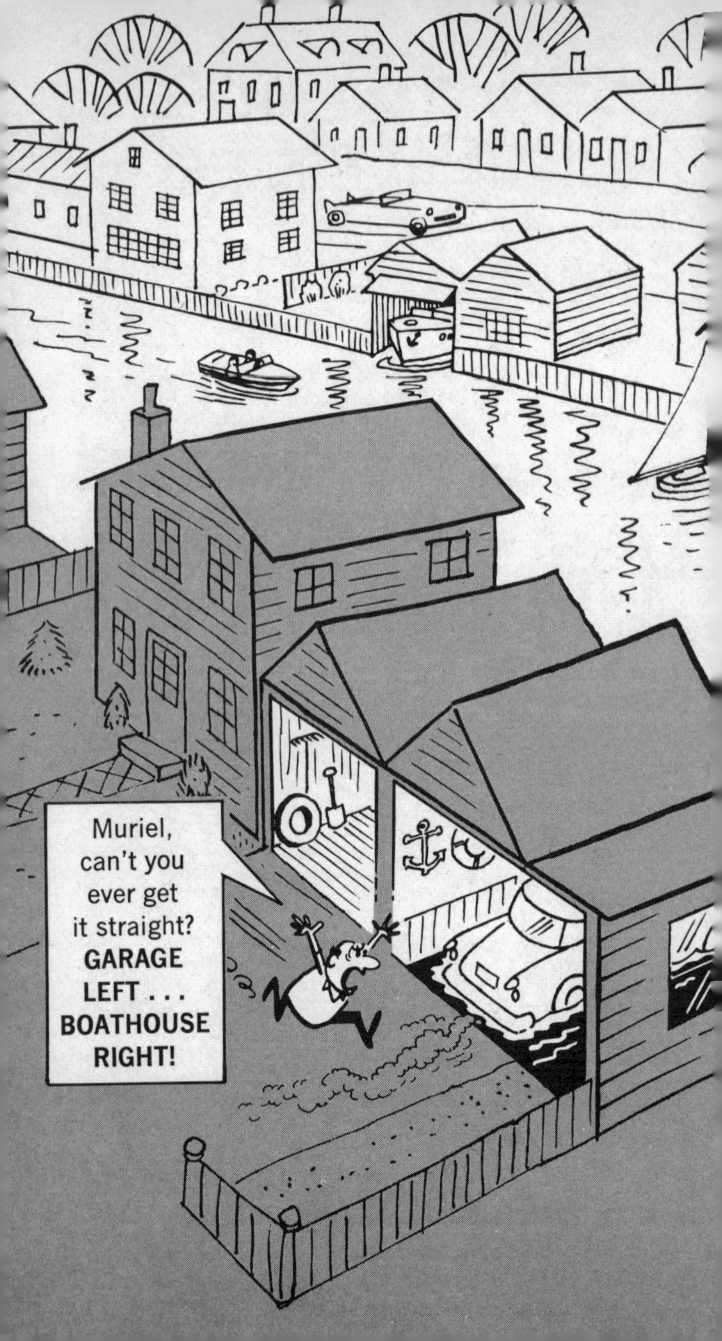
Muriel, can't you ever get it straight? GARAGE LEFT . . . BOATHOUSE RIGHT!

An Admirably Artless Artist's Arrangement

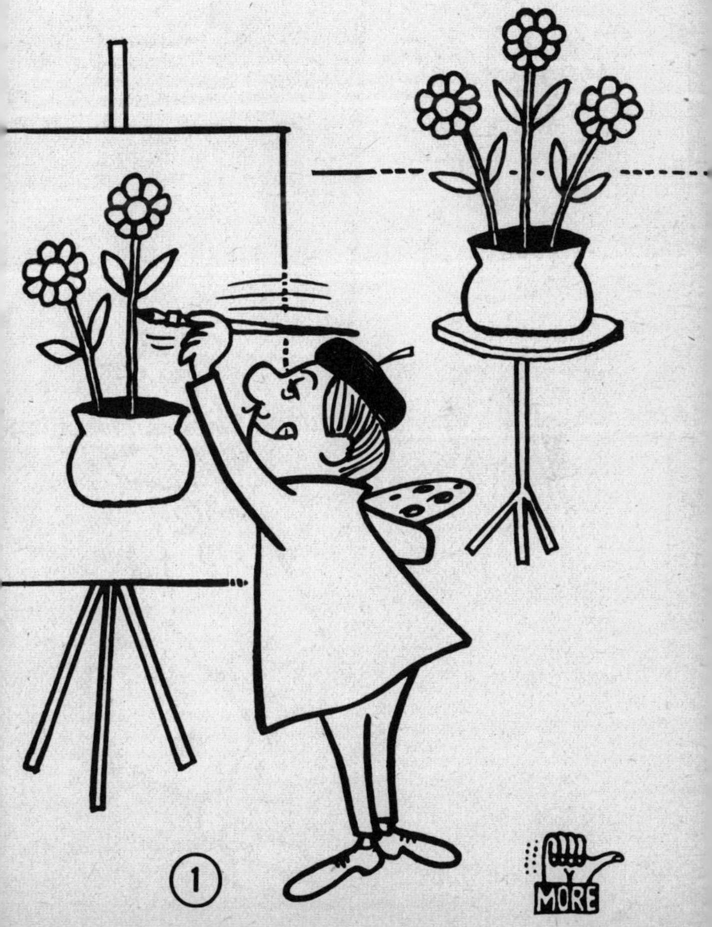
MORE

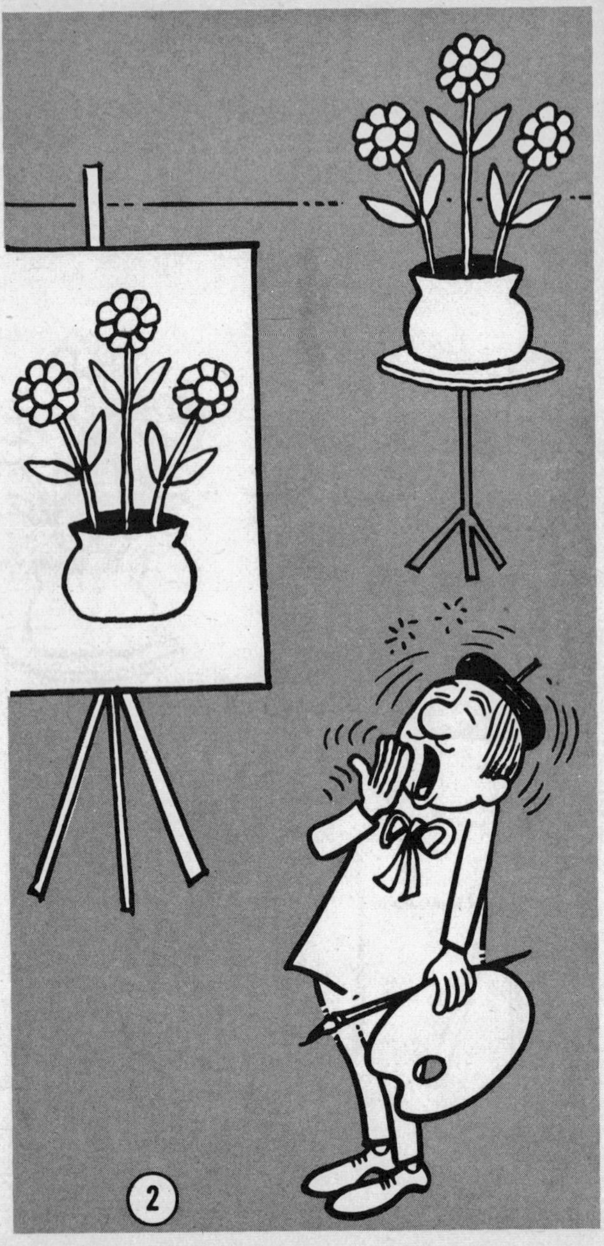
2

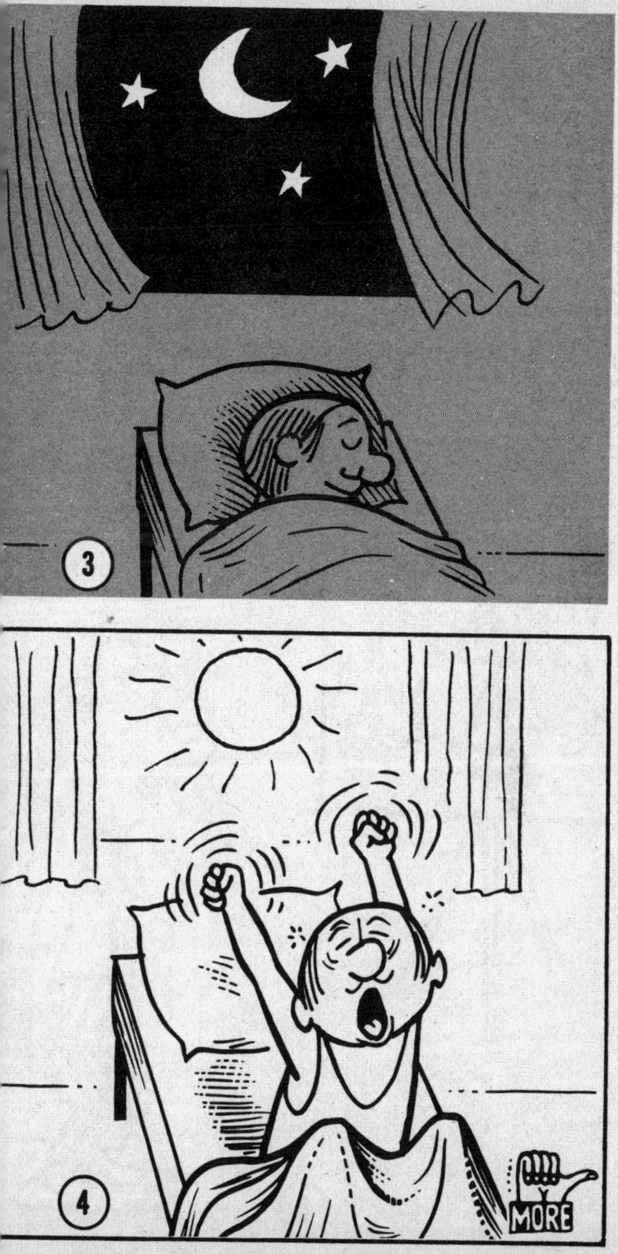
3
4
MORE

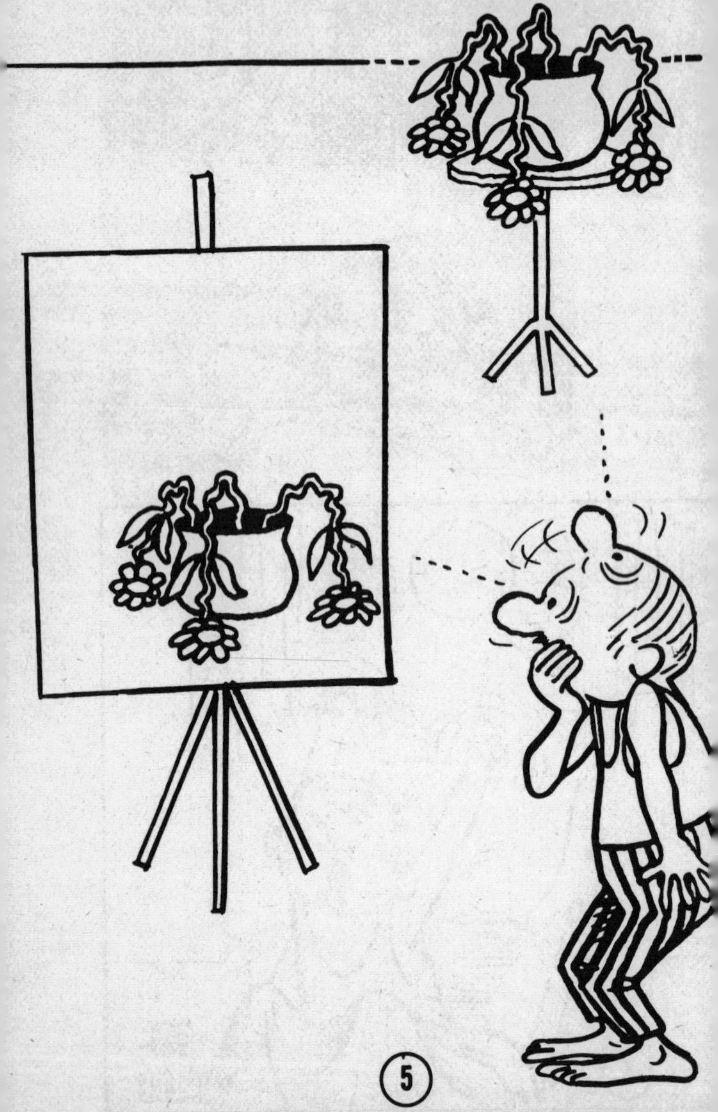

A Transcendent
Concentration of
Capricious Calamities

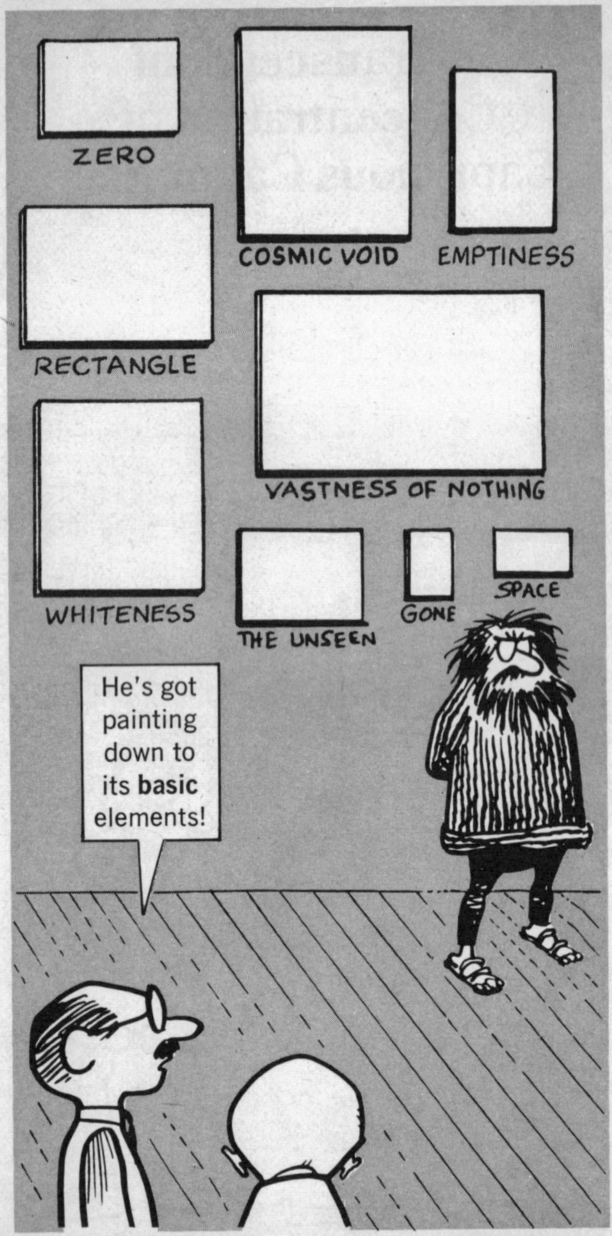
ZERO
COSMIC VOID
EMPTINESS
RECTANGLE
VASTNESS OF NOTHING
WHITENESS
THE UNSEEN
GONE
SPACE
He's got painting down to its **basic** elements!

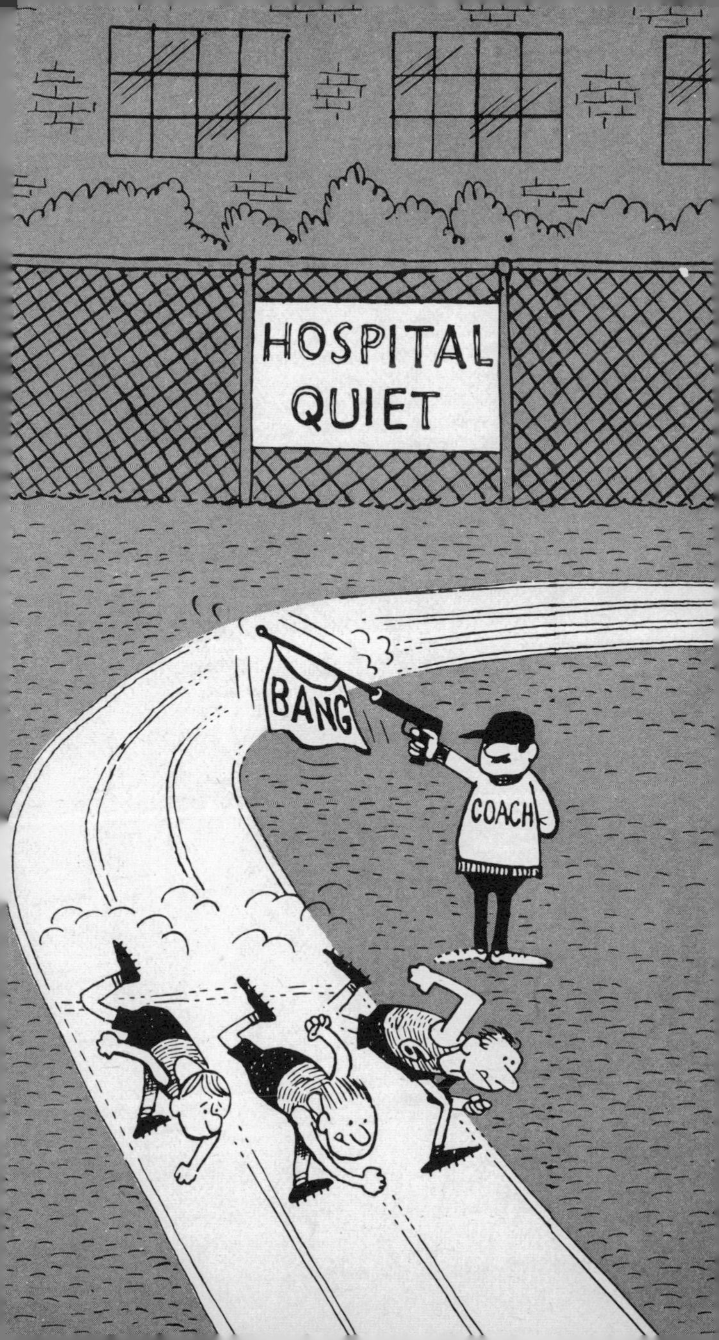
HOSPITAL
QUIET
BANG
COACH

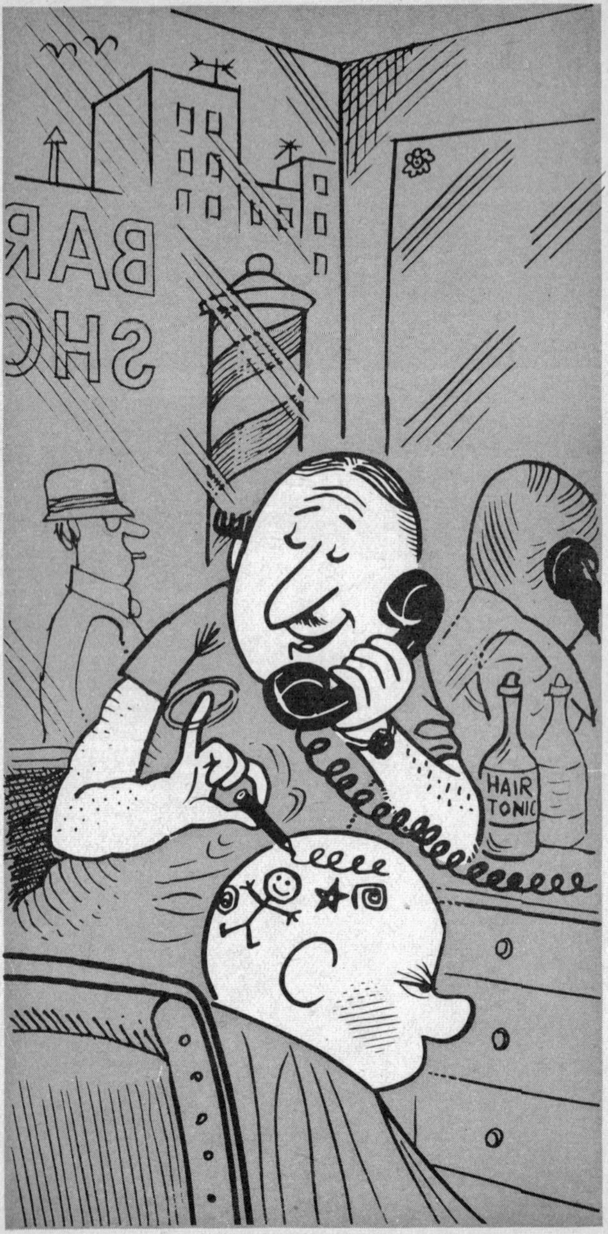
HAIR TONIC

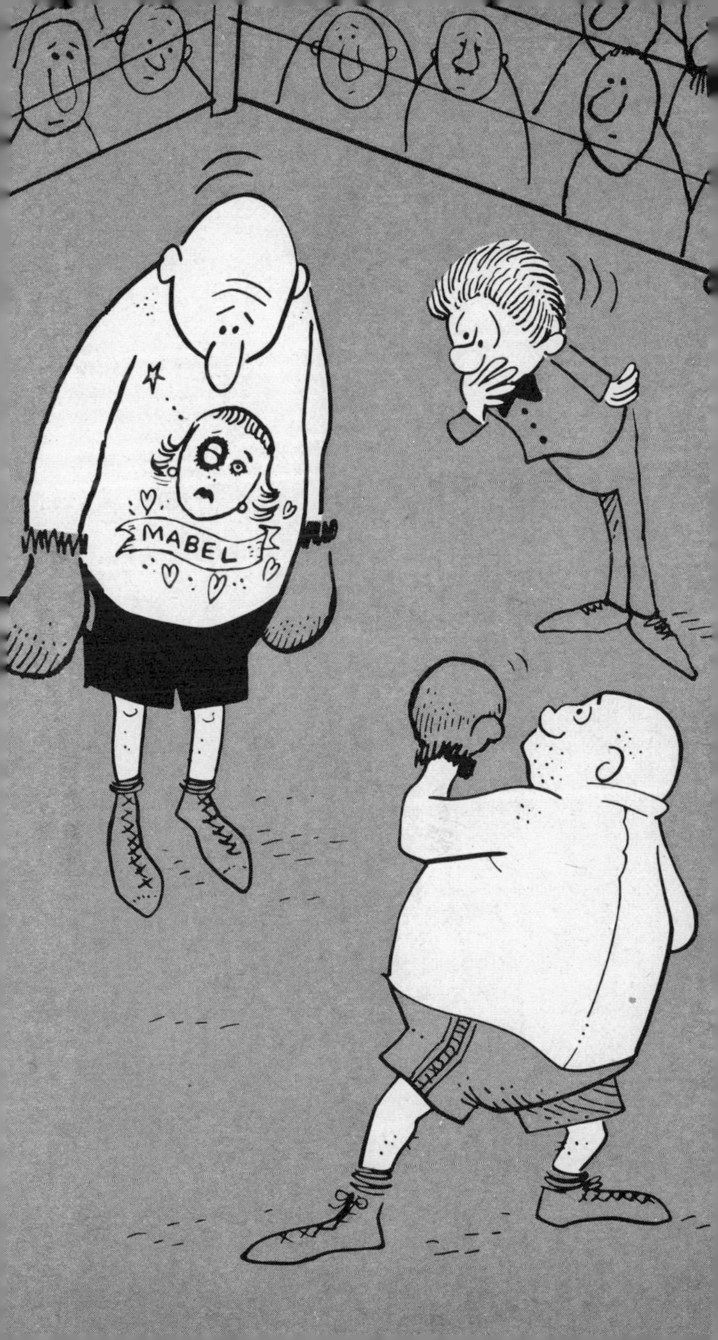
MABEL

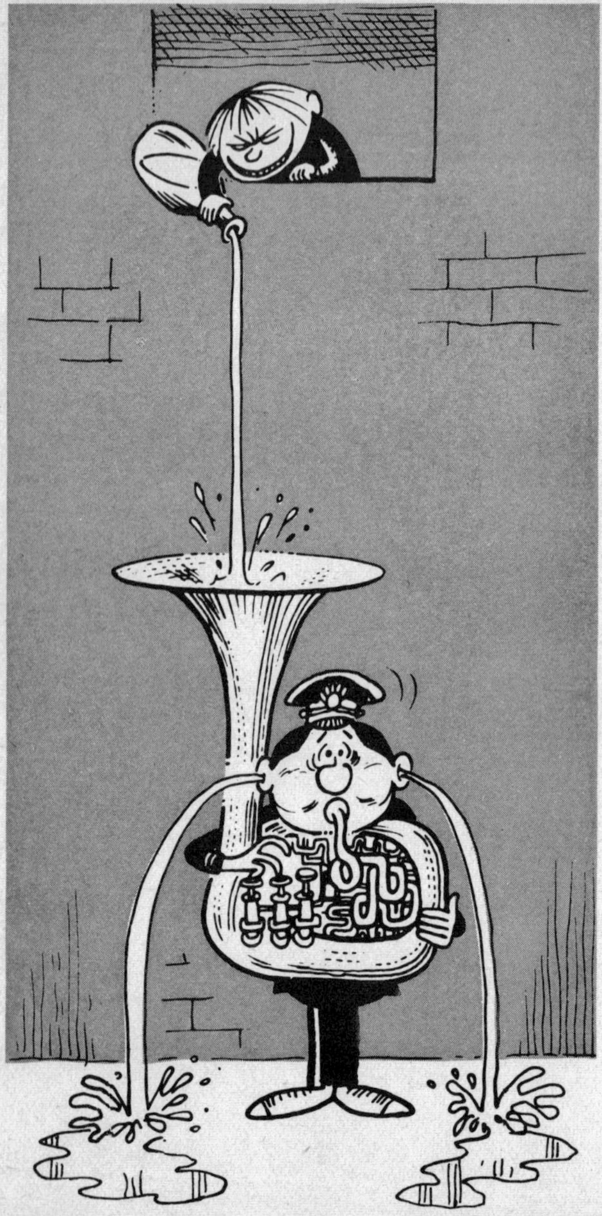

A Creatively Confusing Cop Caper

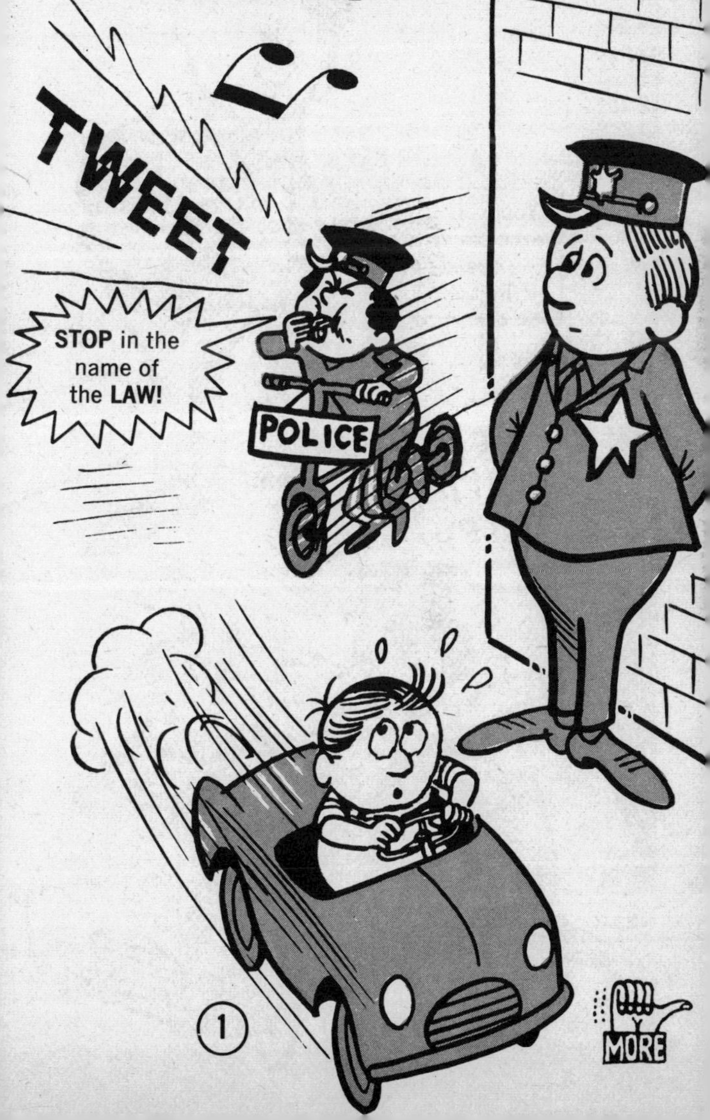
TWEET
STOP in the name of the LAW!
POLICE
1
MORE

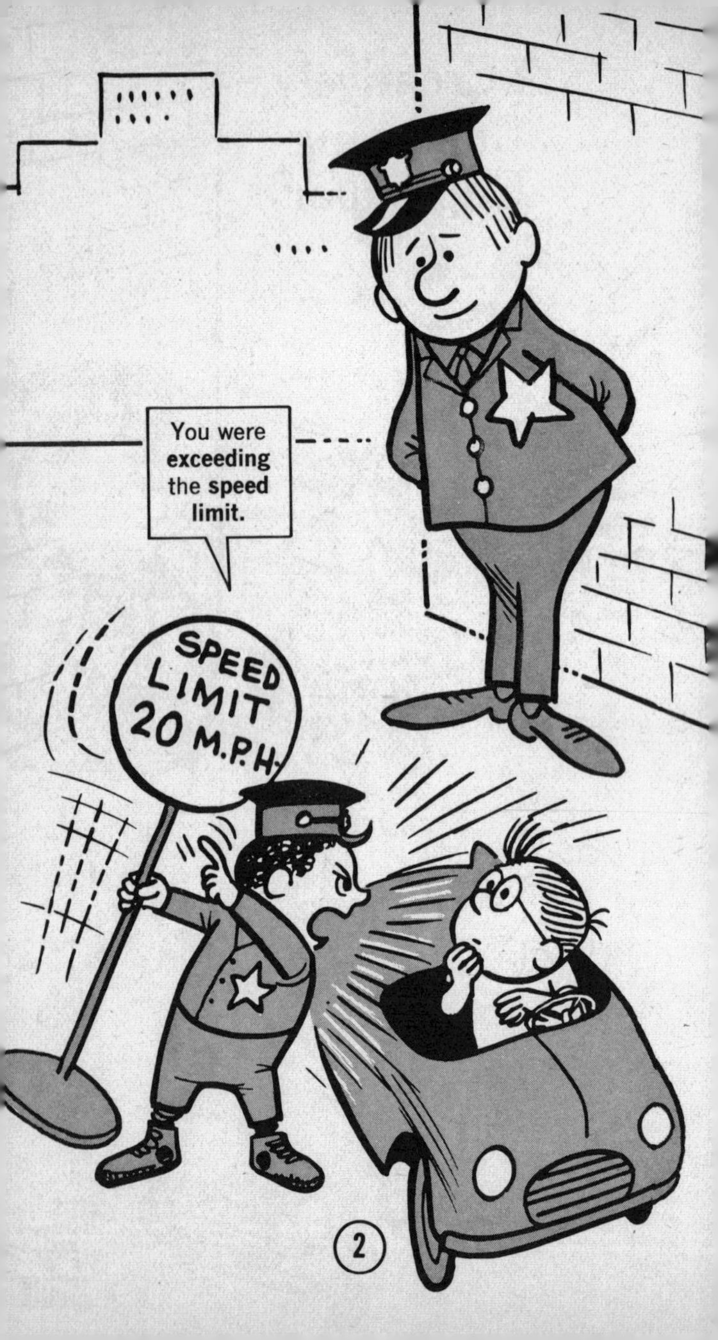

You were exceeding the speed limit.
SPEED LIMIT 20 M.P.H.

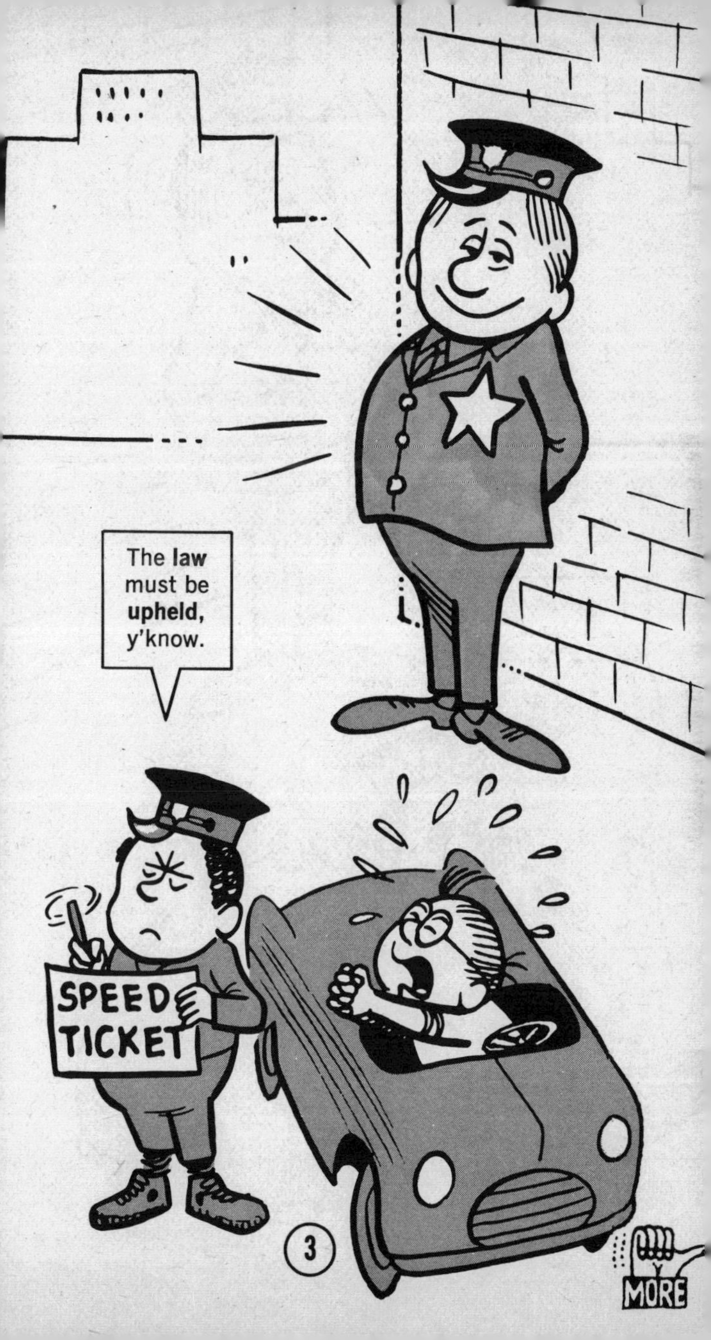
The law must be upheld, y'know.
SPEED TICKET
3
MORE

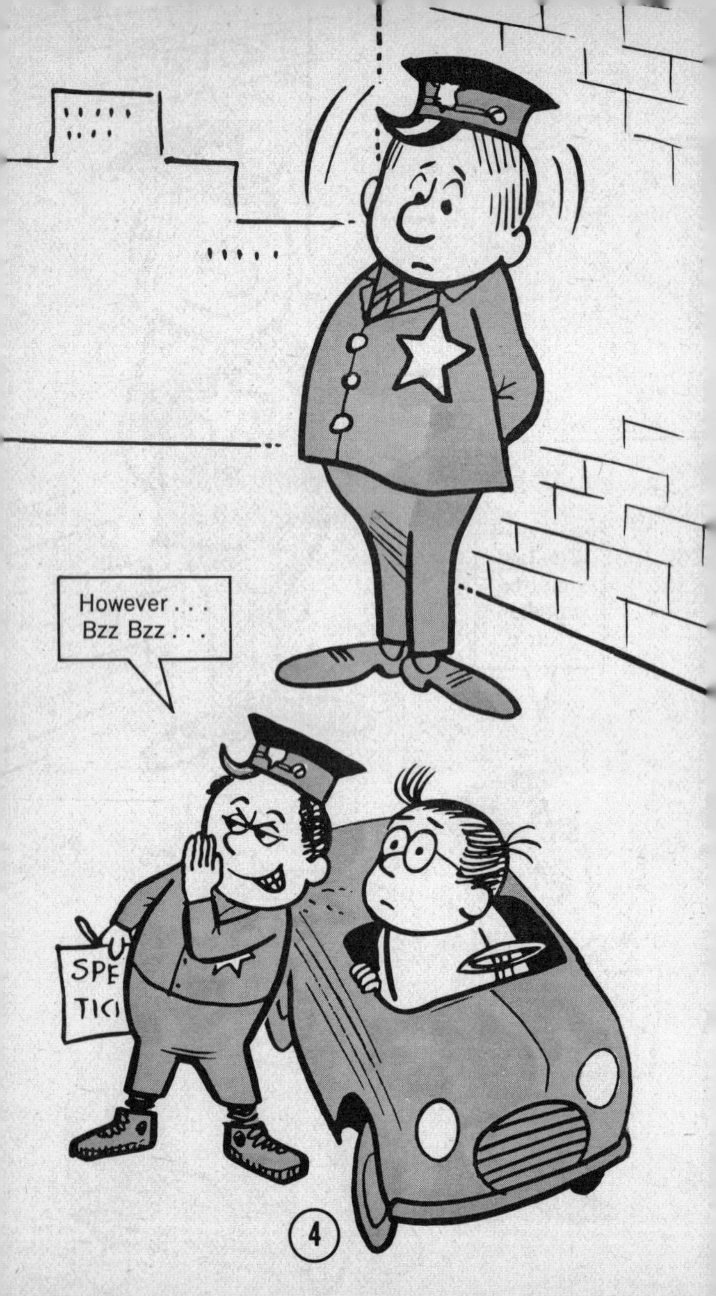
However . . .
Bzz Bzz . . .
SPE
TICI
4

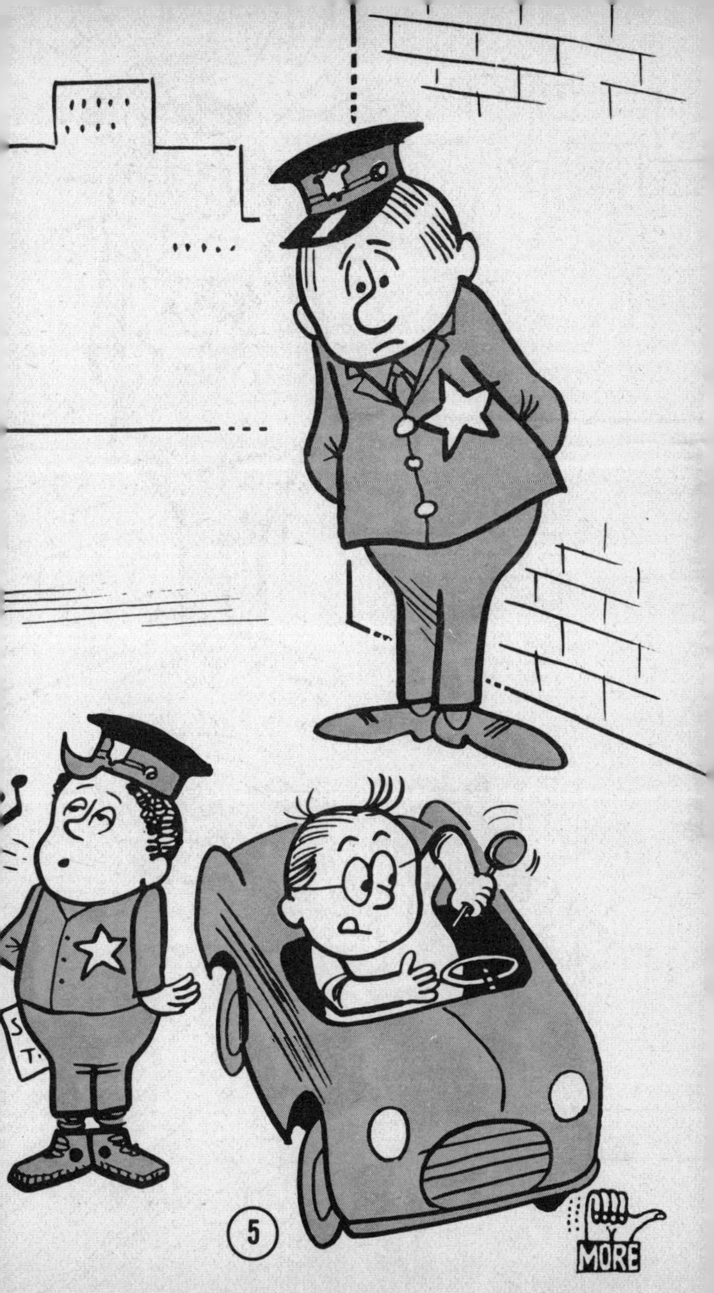
S
T.
5
MORE

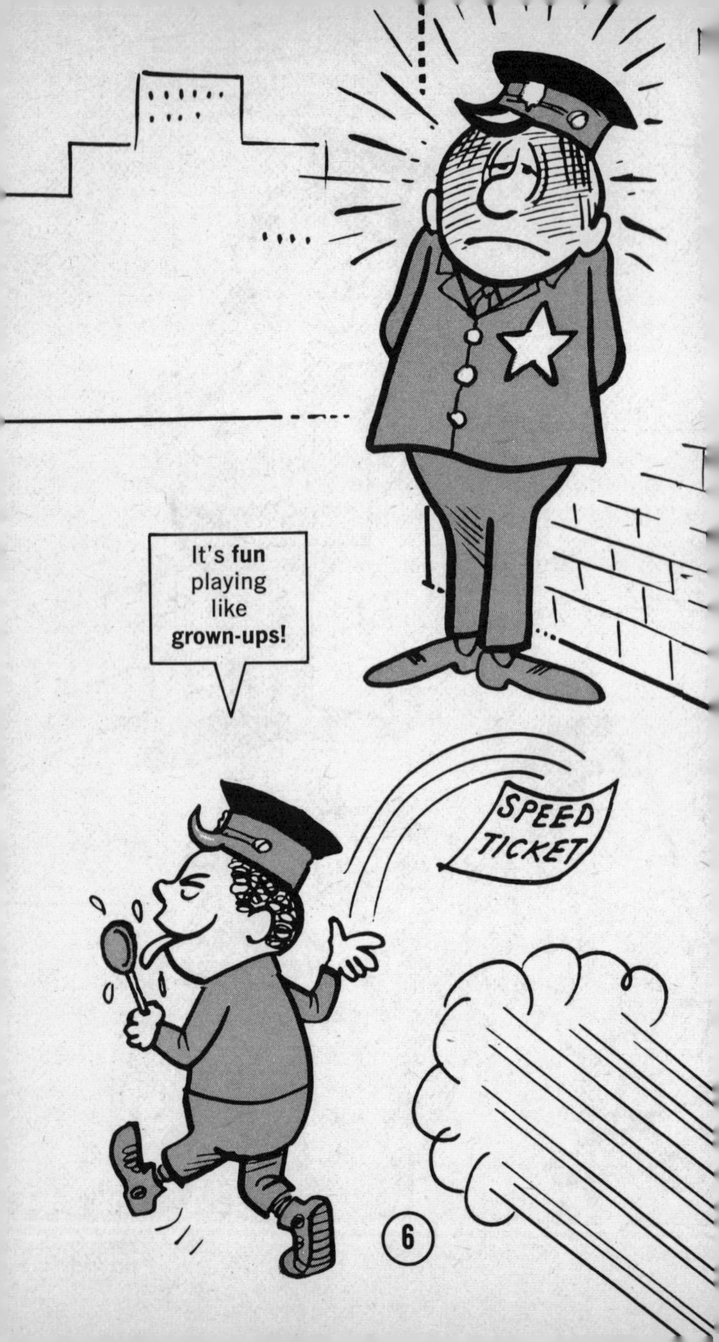
It's fun playing like grown-ups!
SPEED TICKET

A Heartwarming Amassment of Substandard Banalities

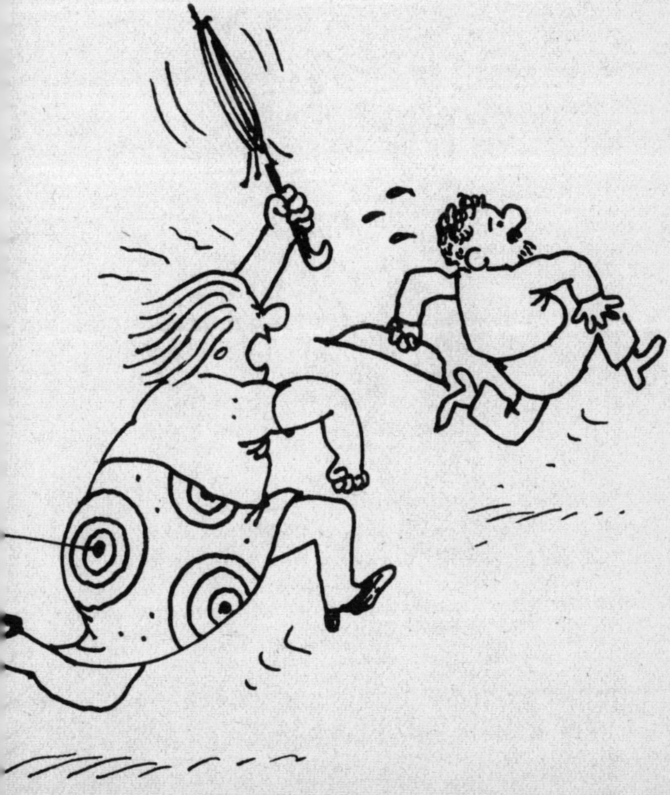

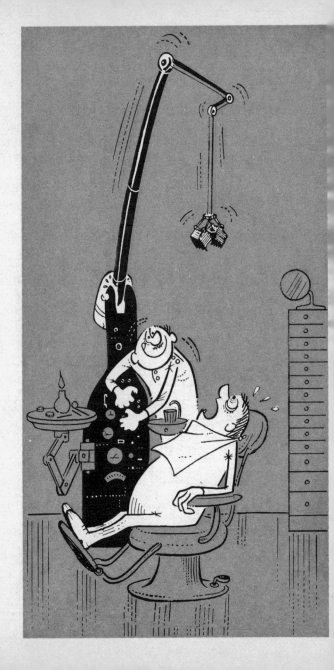

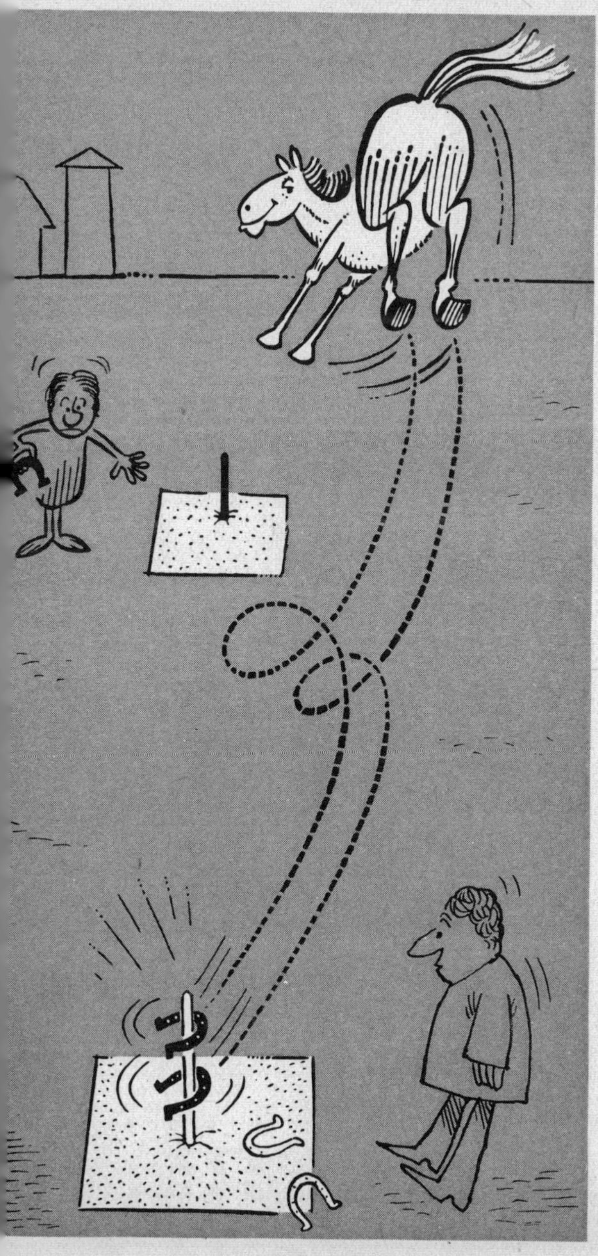

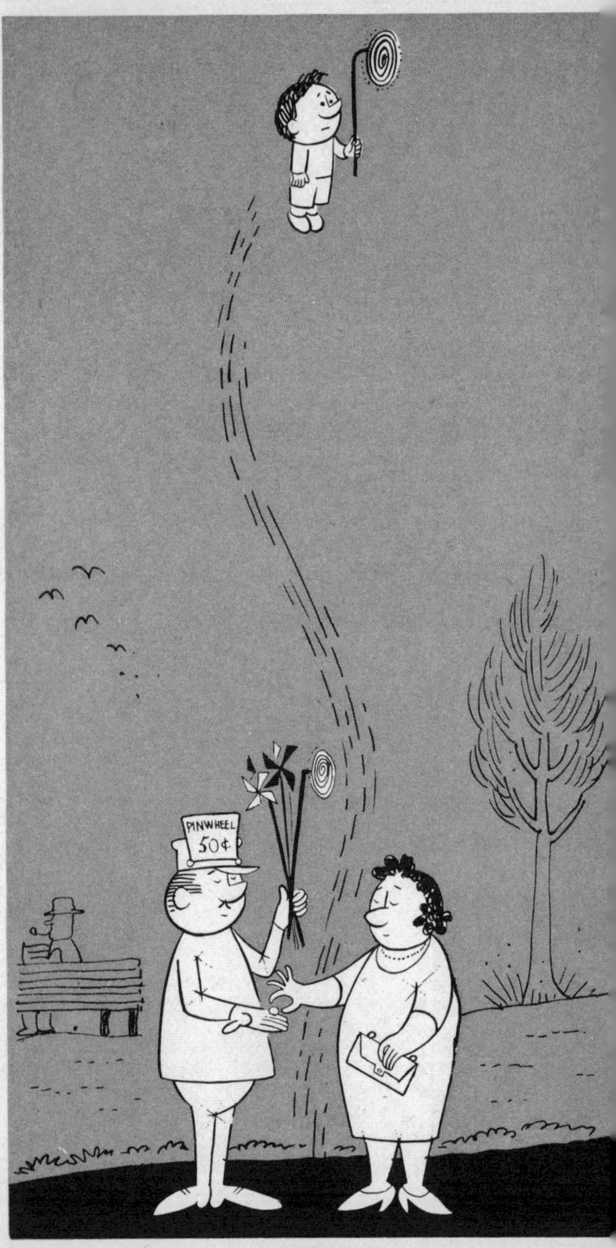
PINWHEEL
50¢

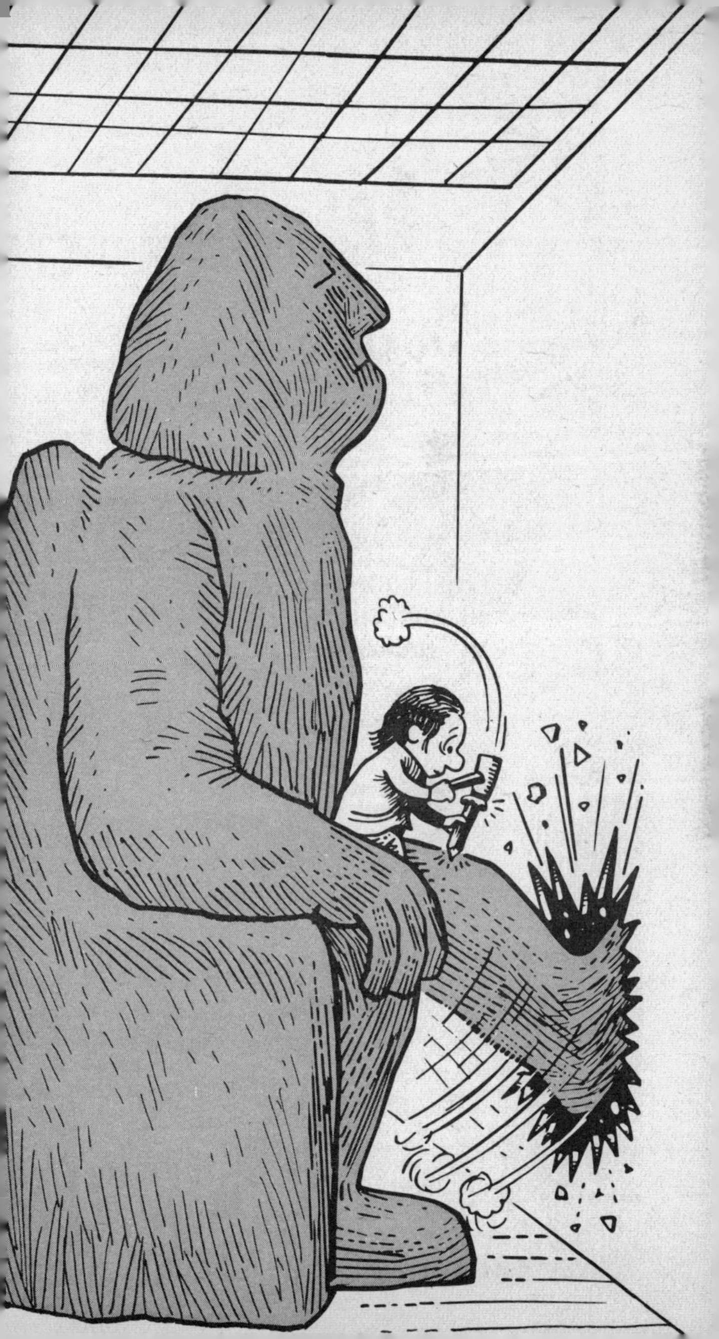

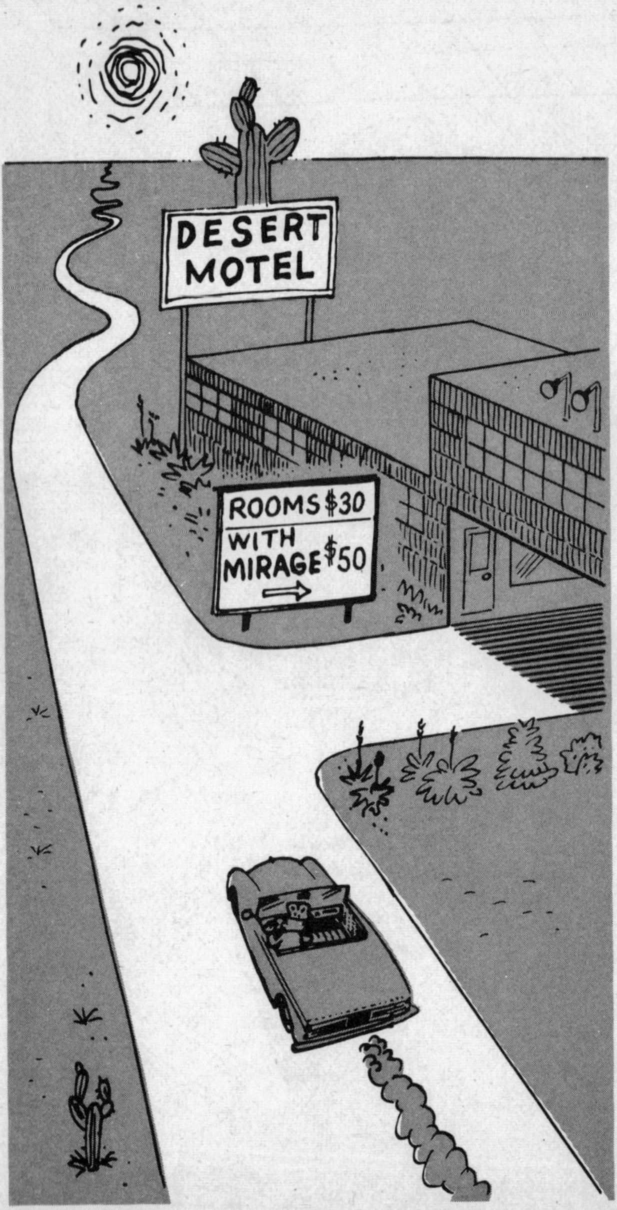
DESERT
MOTEL
ROOMS $30
WITH
MIRAGE $50

A Passionately Poor Painting Program

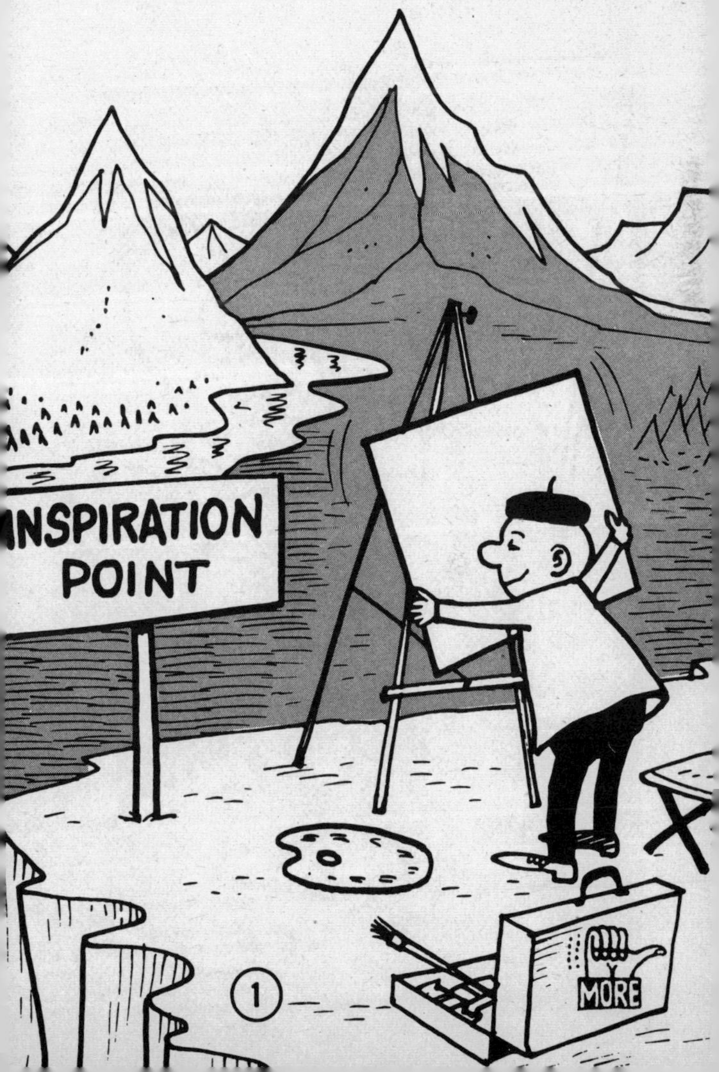
INSPIRATION
POINT
MORE
1

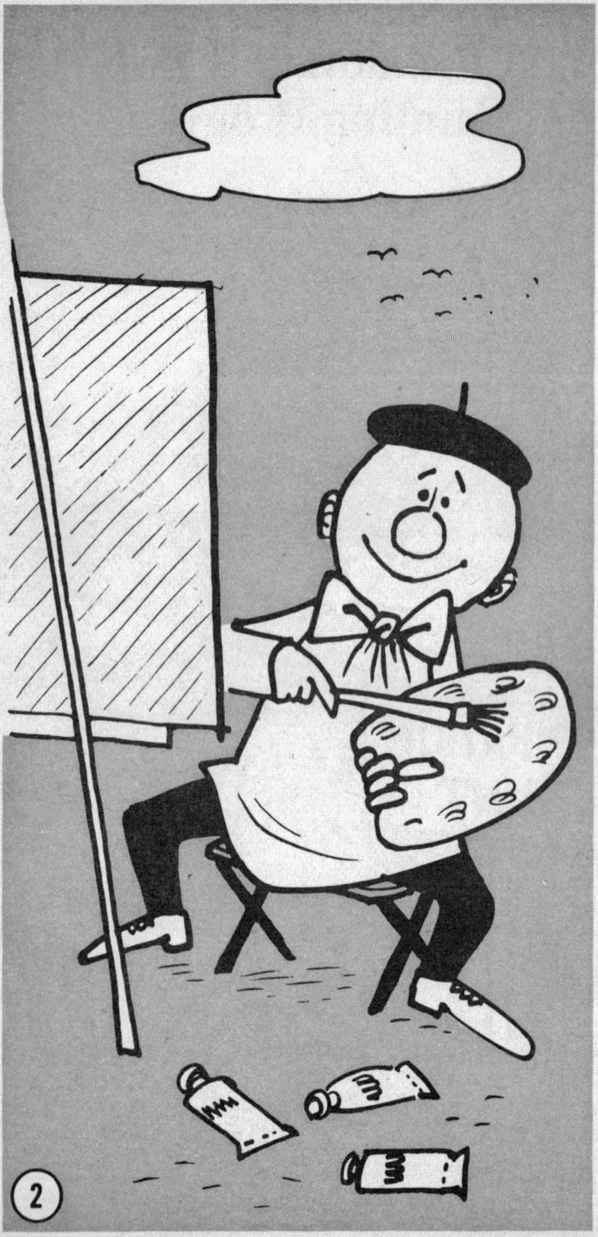
2

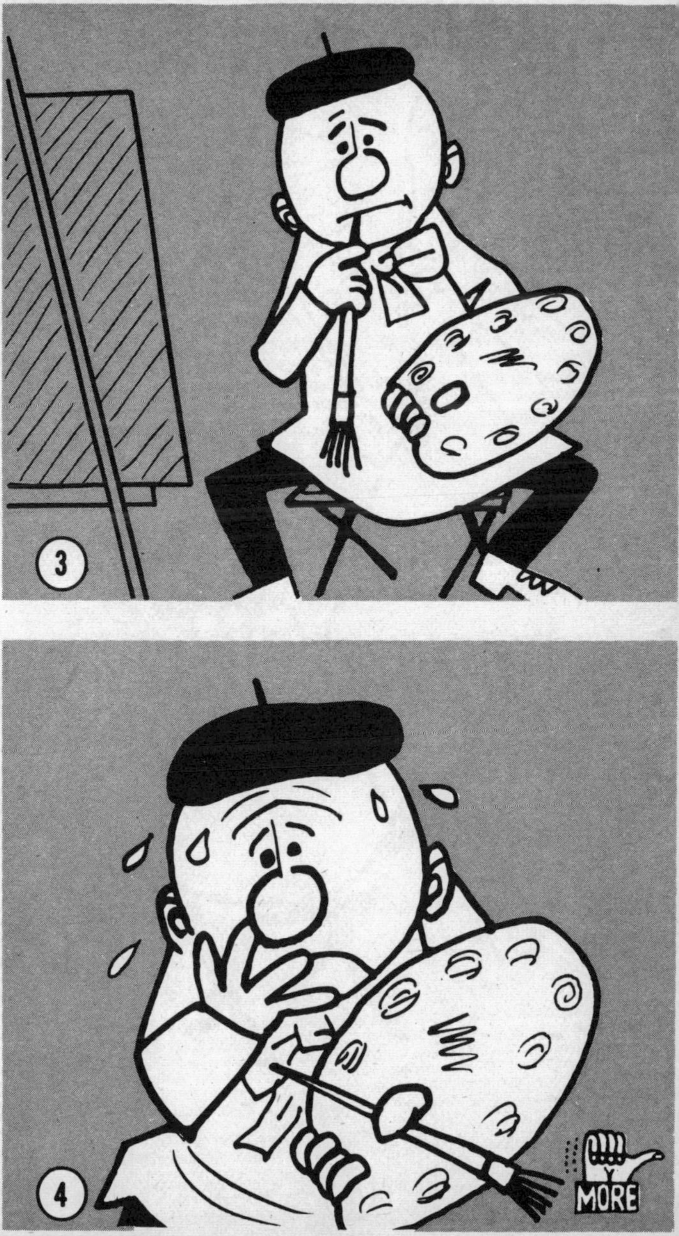
3
4
MORE

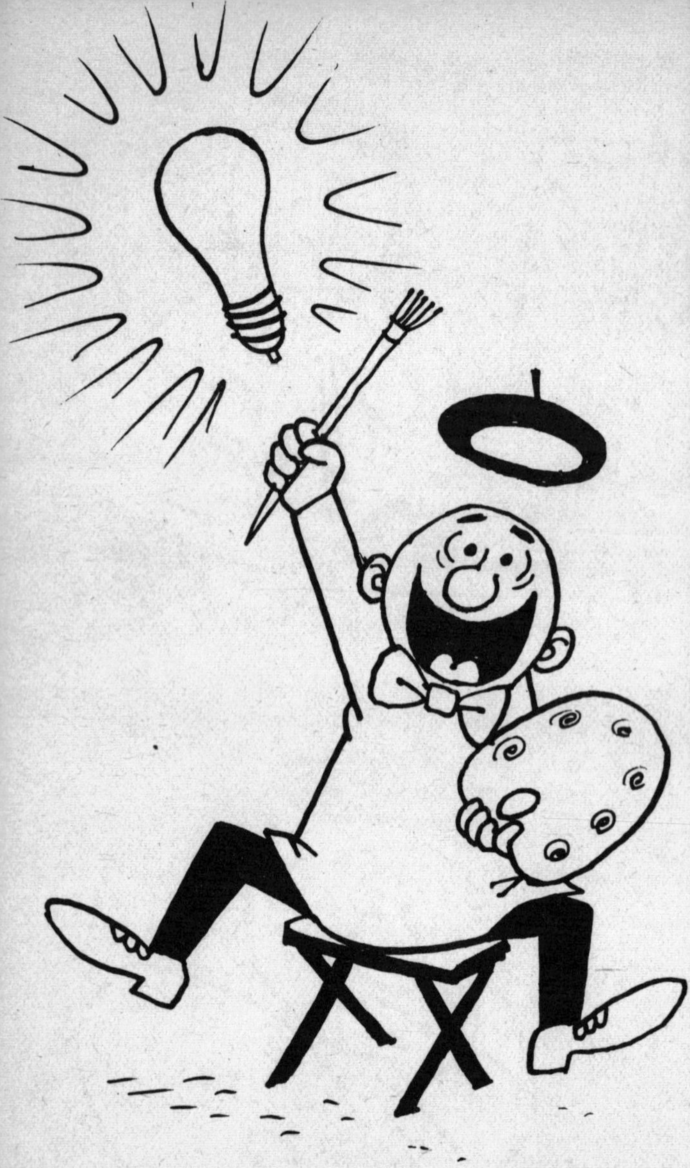

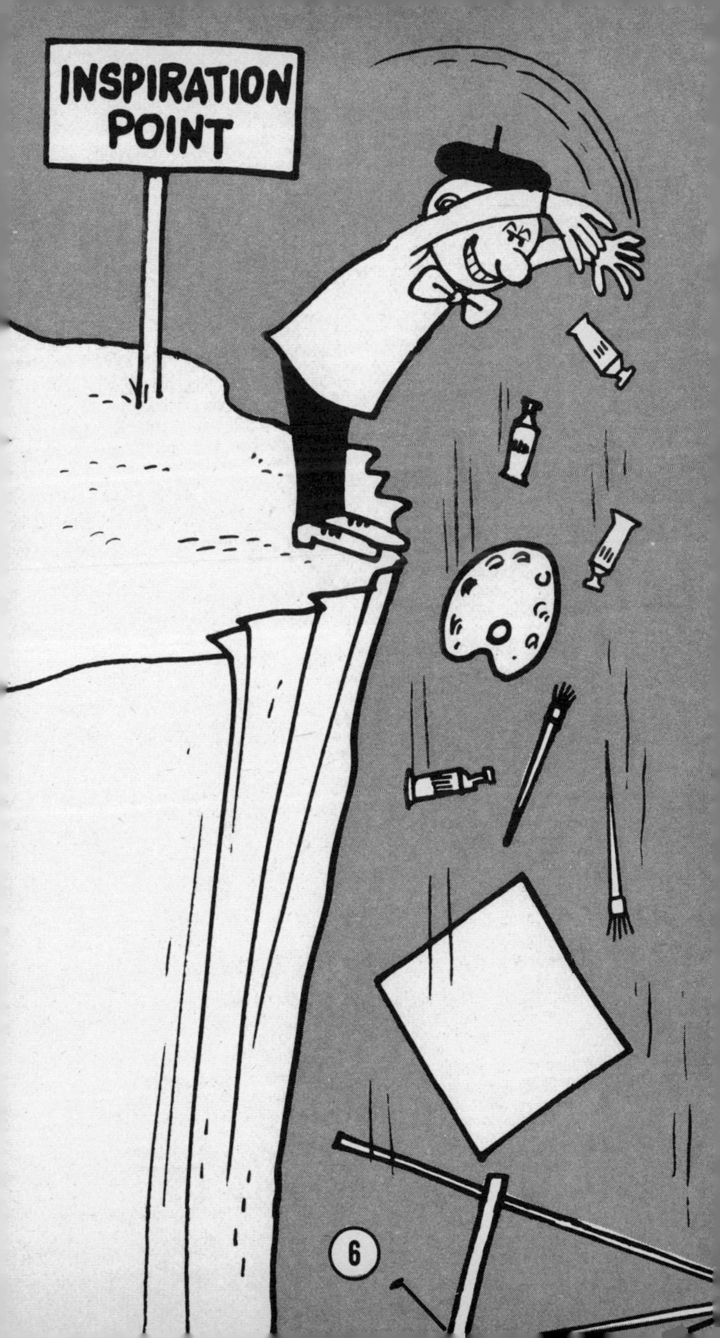
INSPIRATION POINT
6

A
Spectacular Assortment
of Burdensome
Frivolities

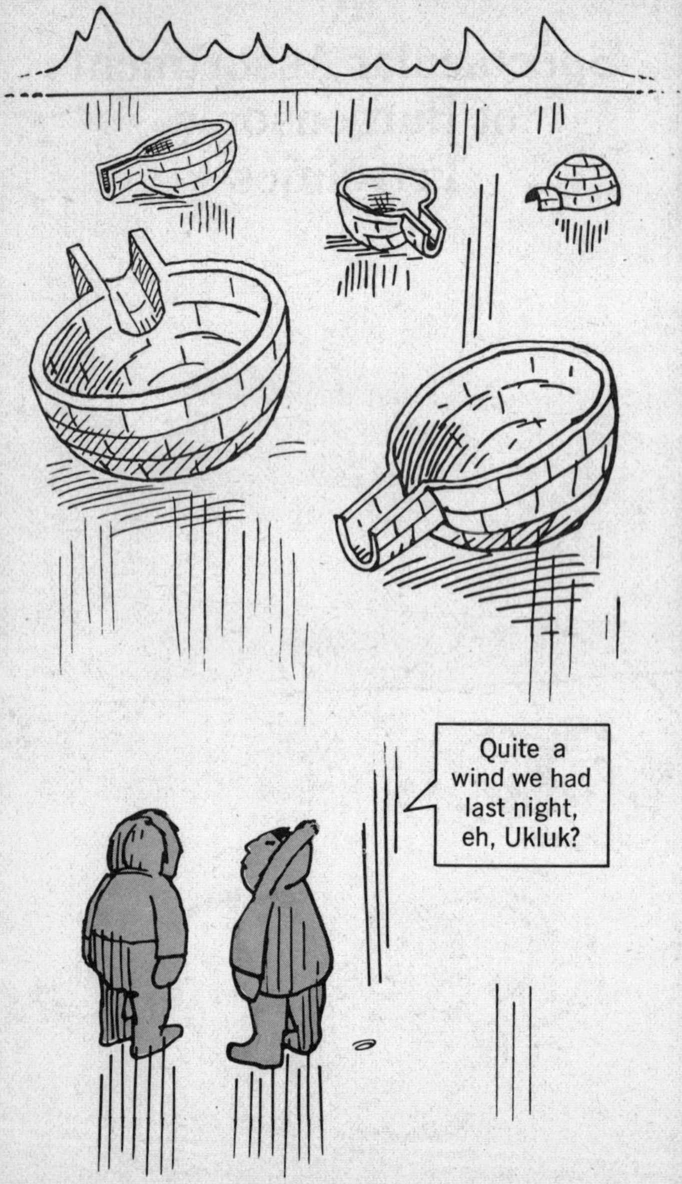
Quite a wind we had last night, eh, Ukluk?

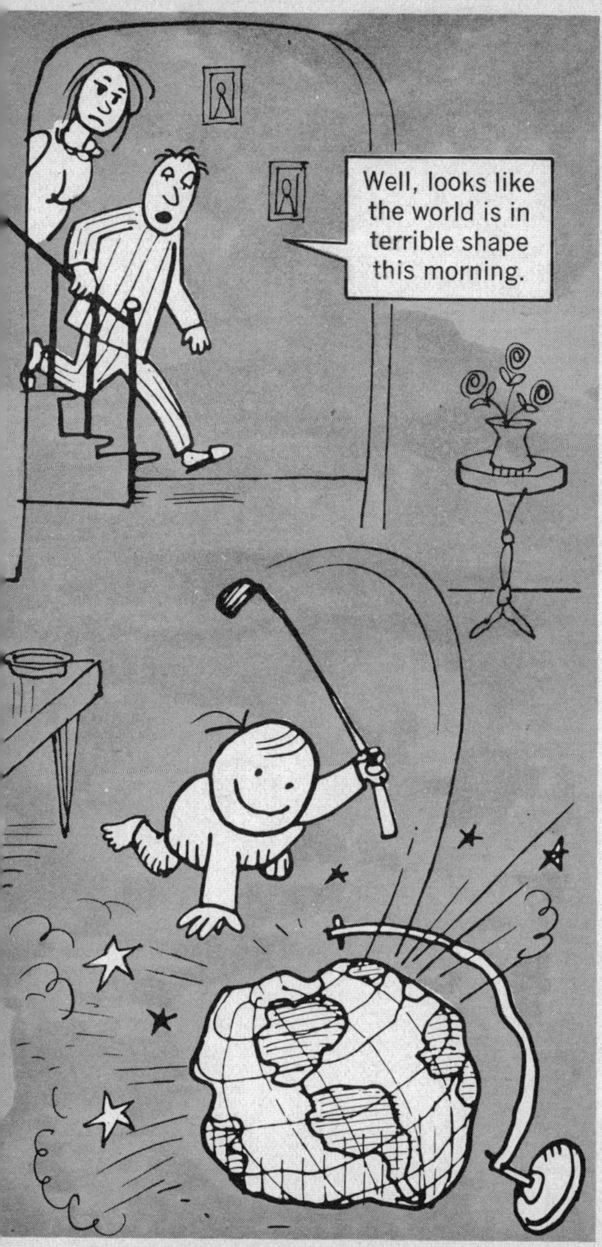
Well, looks like the world is in terrible shape this morning.

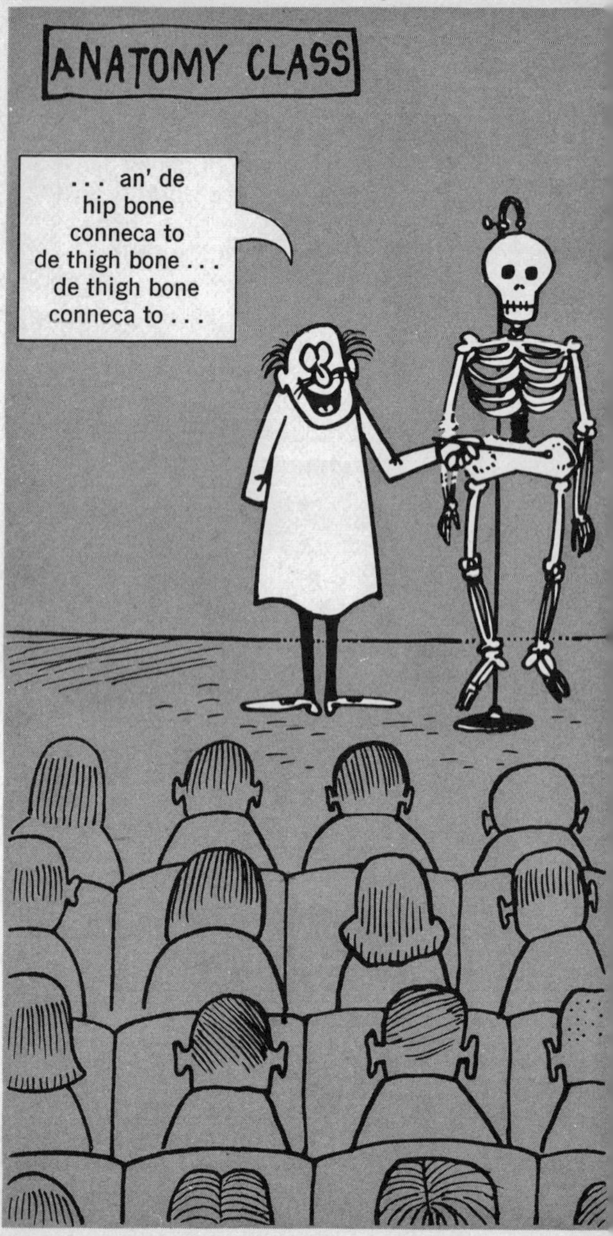
ANATOMY CLASS
. . . an' de hip bone conneca to de thigh bone . . . de thigh bone conneca to . . .

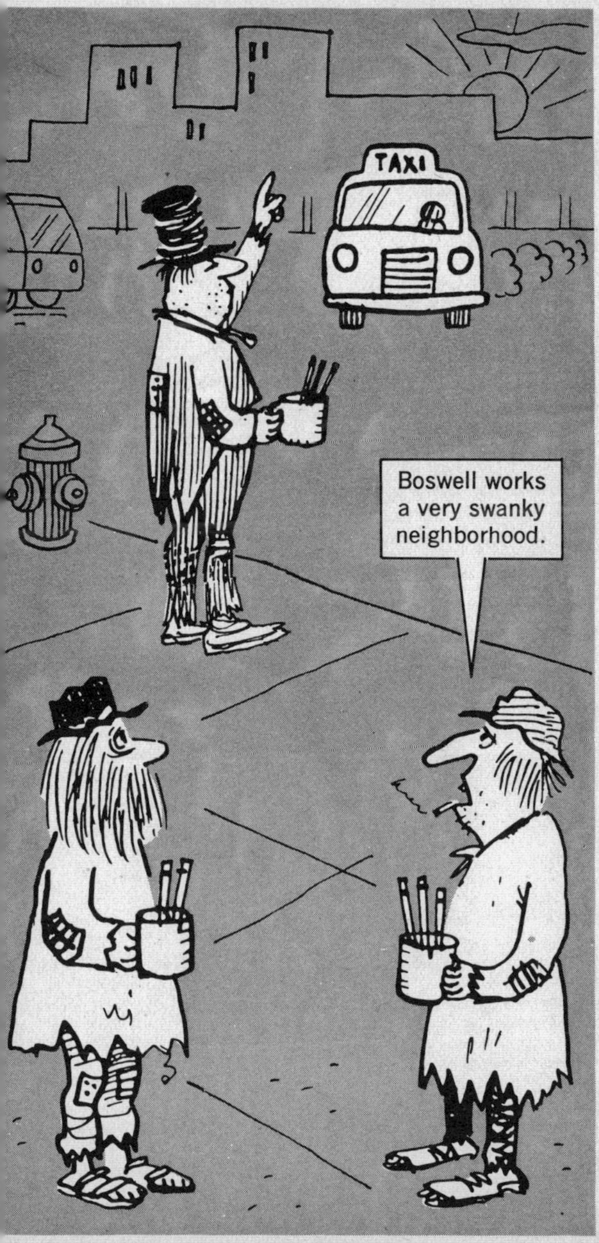
TAXI
Boswell works a very swanky neighborhood.

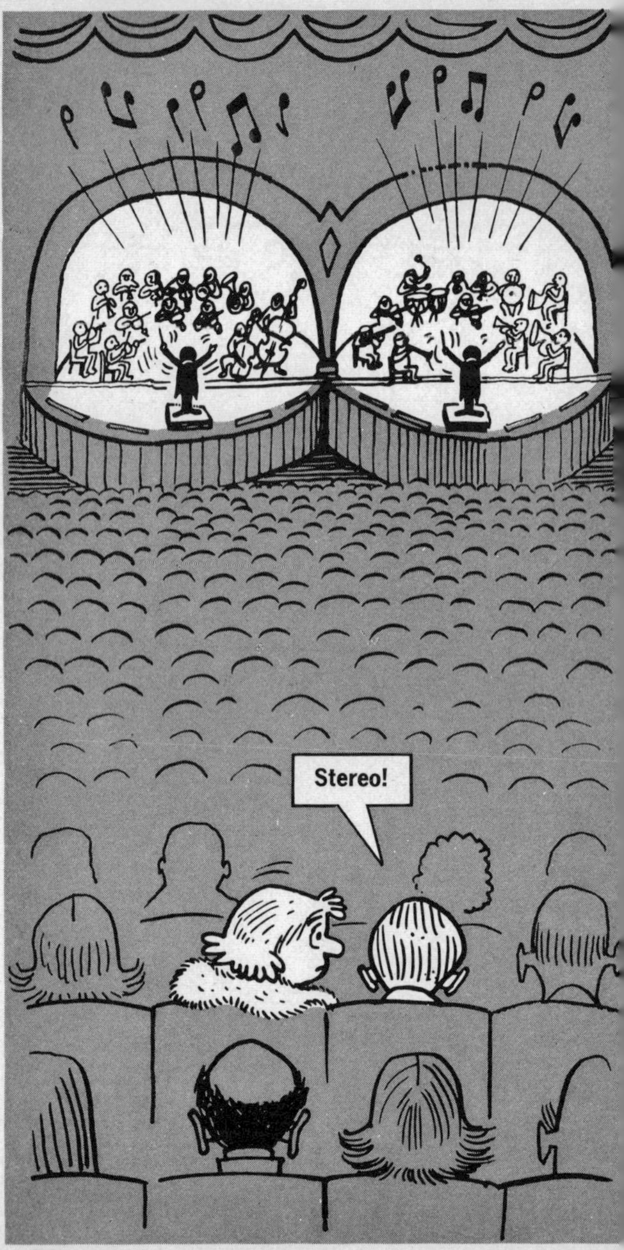
Stereo!

A Bedazzlingly Boring Bird Bafflement

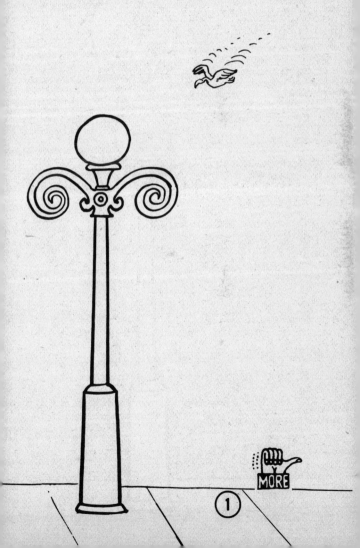

MORE

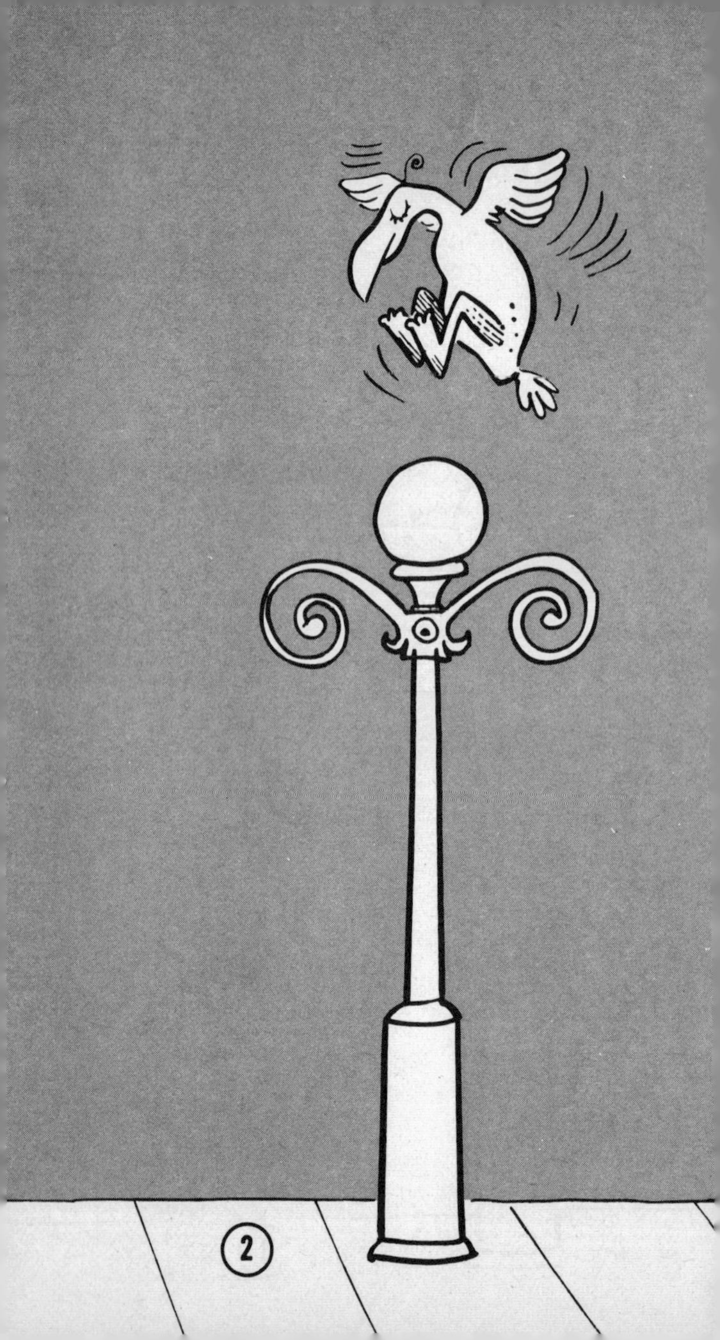
2

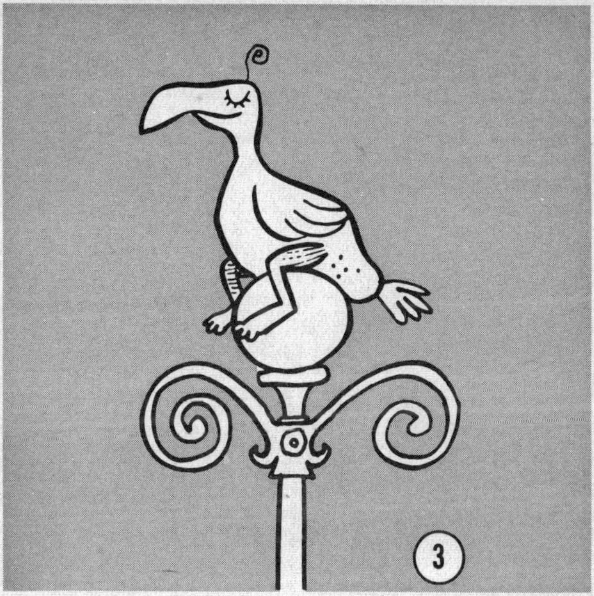
3

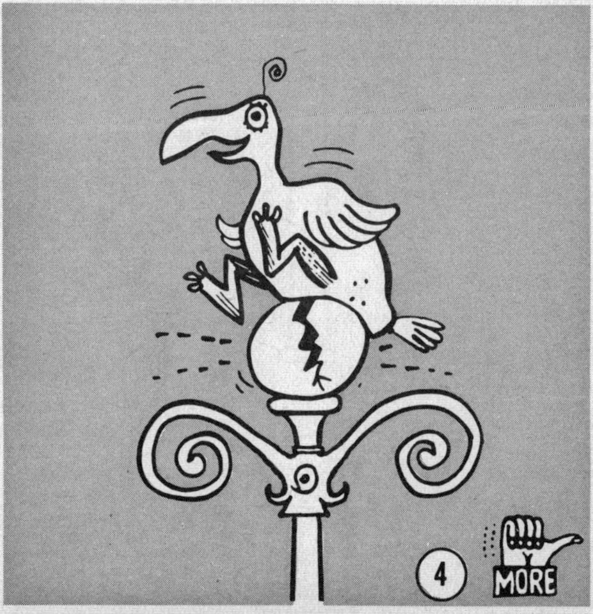
4
MORE

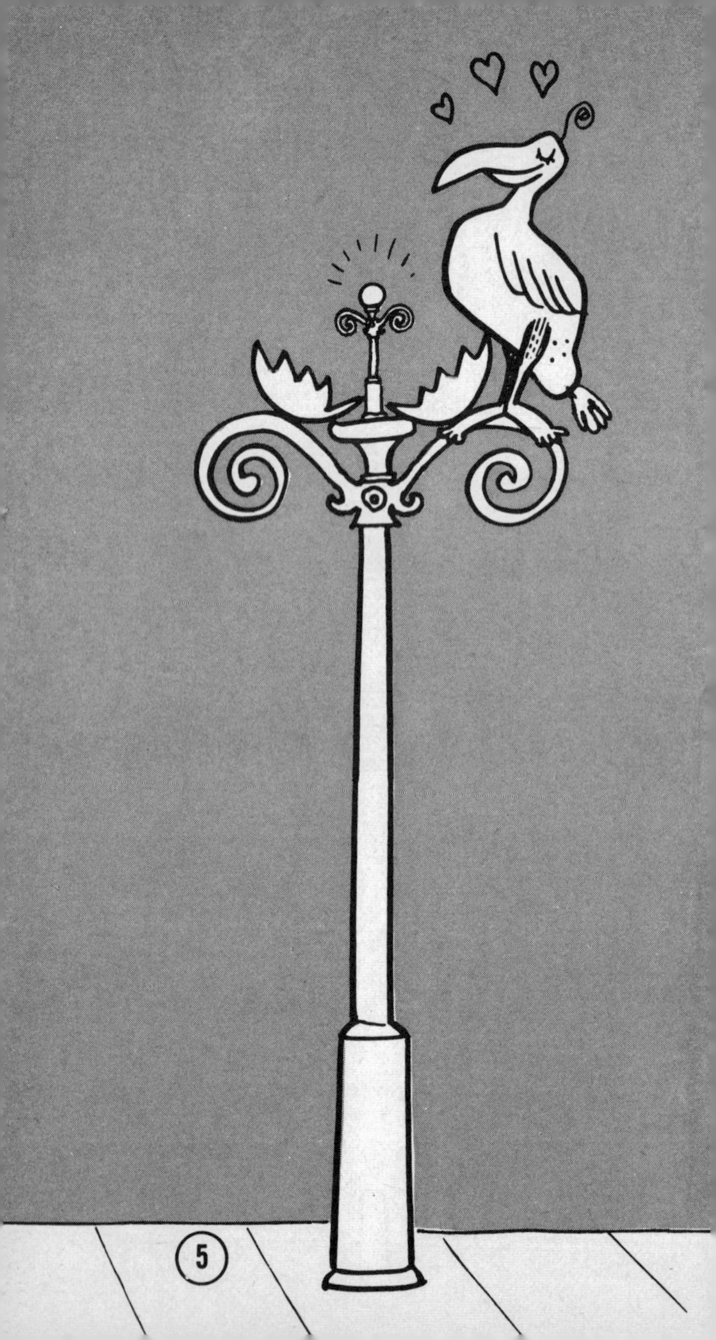
5

An Excellent Arrangement of Depressing Drivel

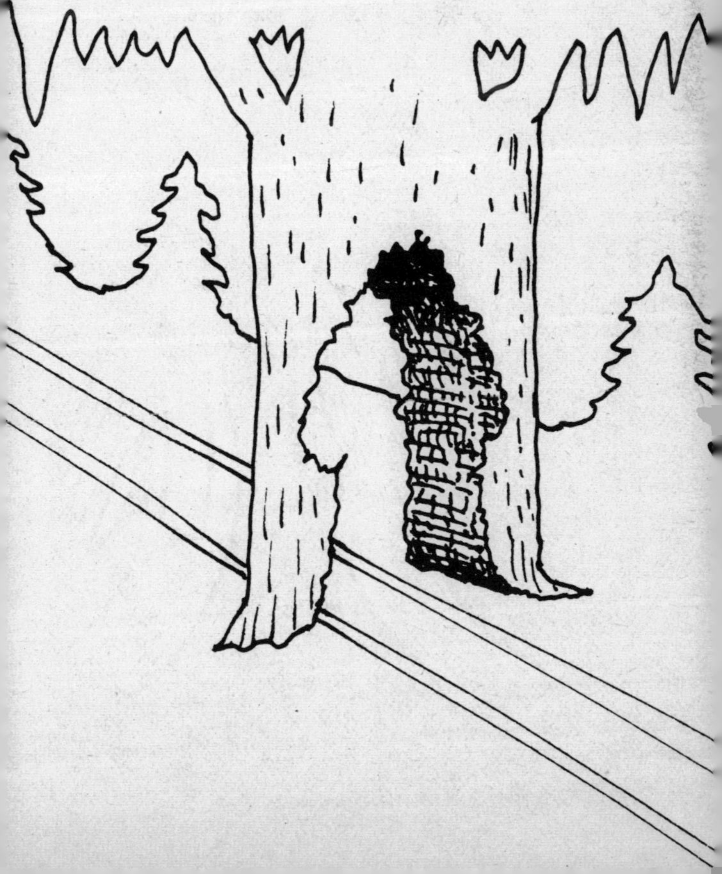

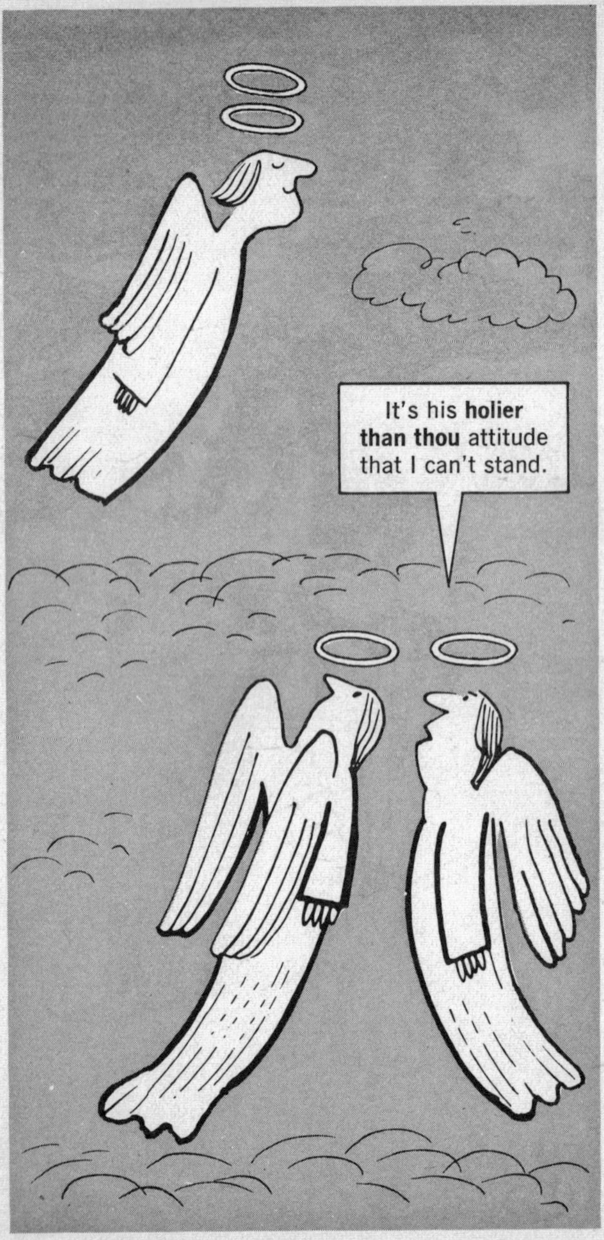
It's his **holier than thou** attitude that I can't stand.

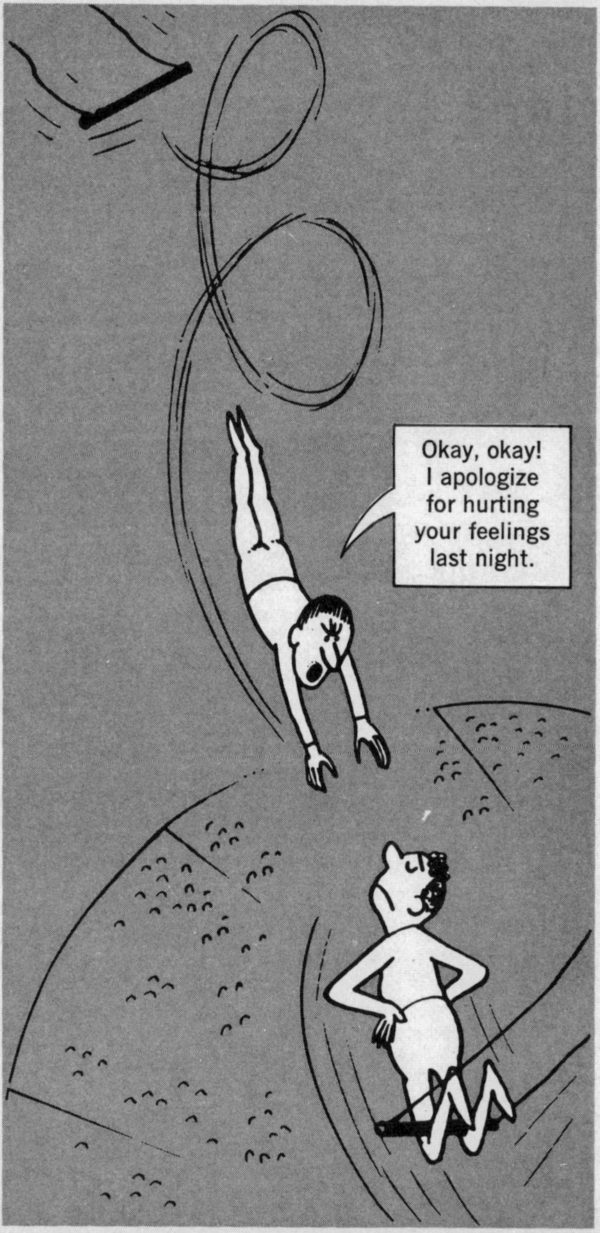
Okay, okay! I apologize for hurting your feelings last night.

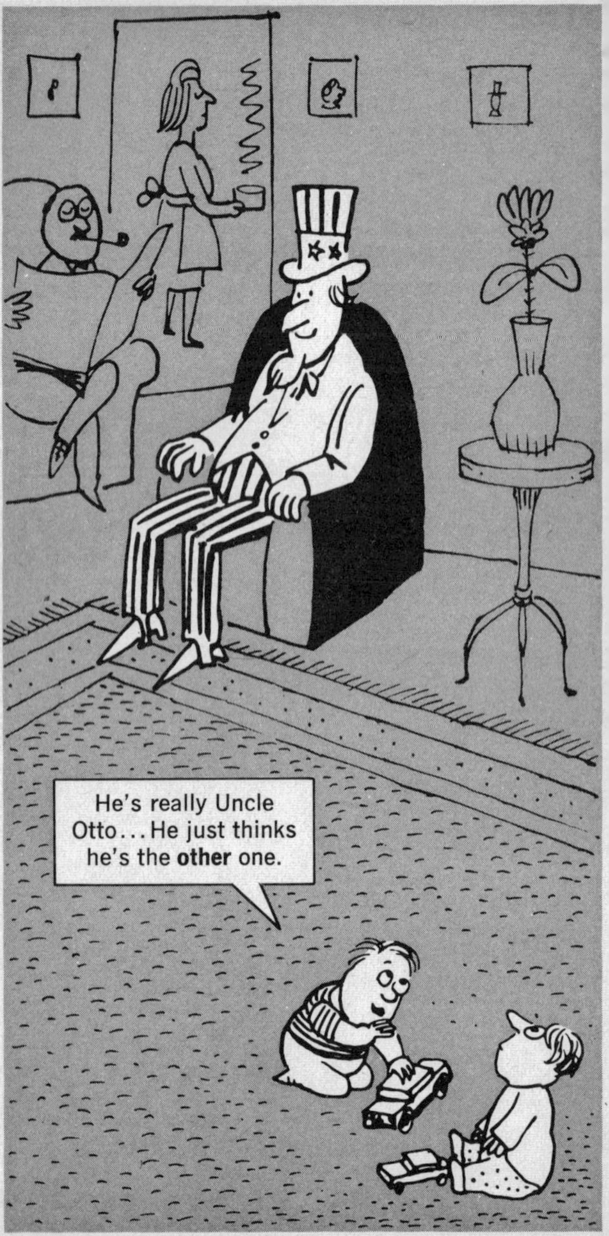
He's really Uncle Otto...He just thinks he's the **other** one.

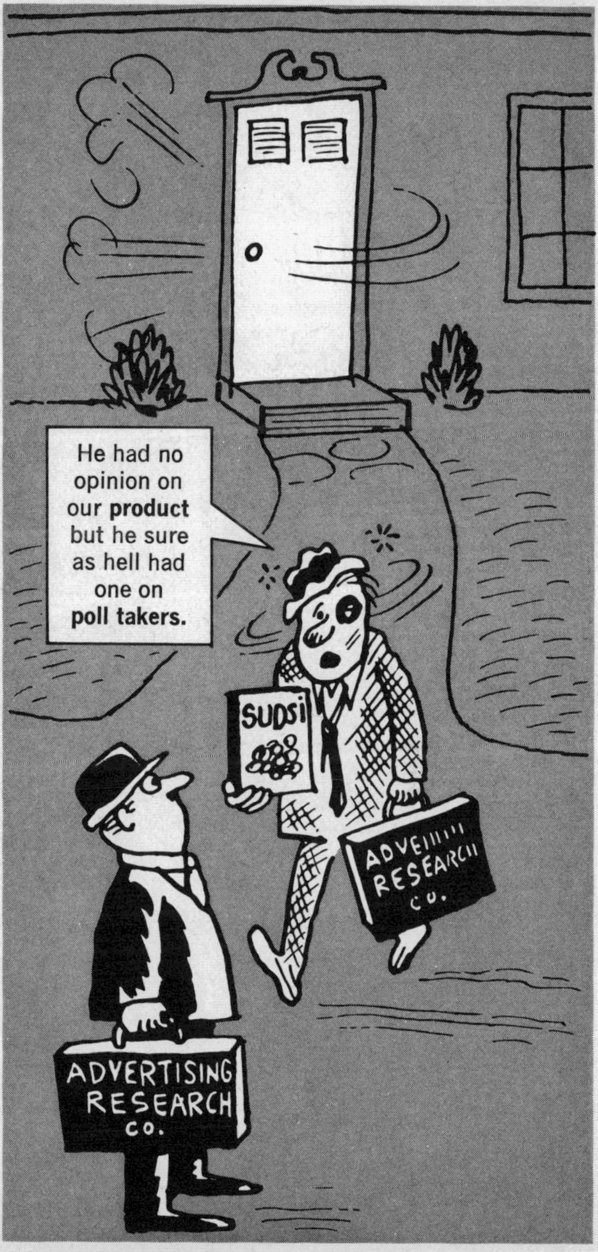
He had no opinion on our **product** but he sure as hell had one on **poll takers.**
SUDSI
ADVERTISING
RESEARCH
CO.

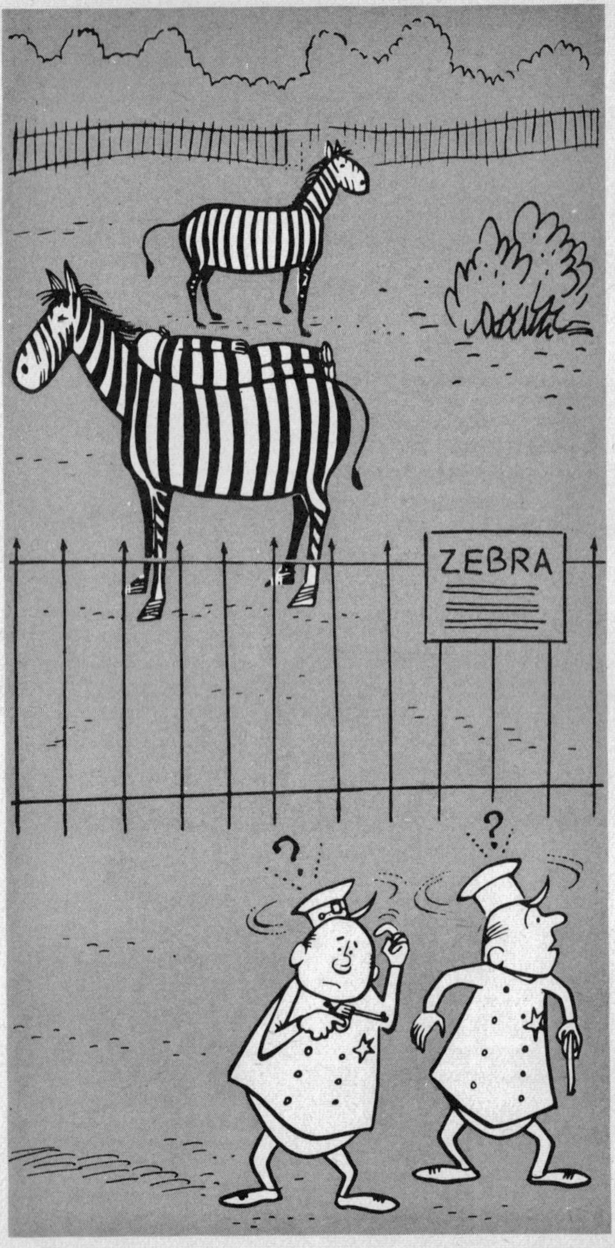
ZEBRA

A Magnificently Monotonous Mover's Machination

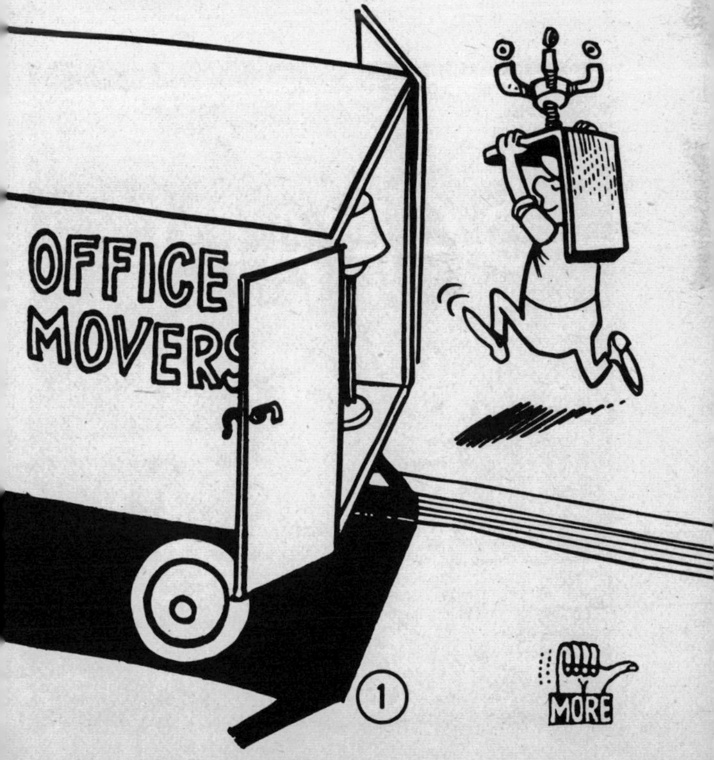
OFFICE
MOVERS
MORE

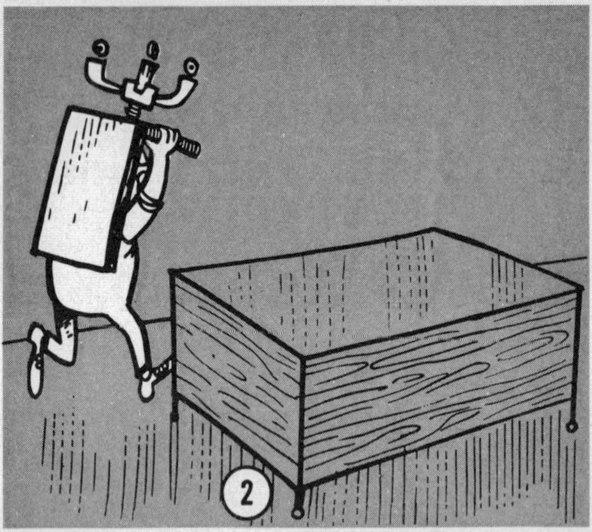
2

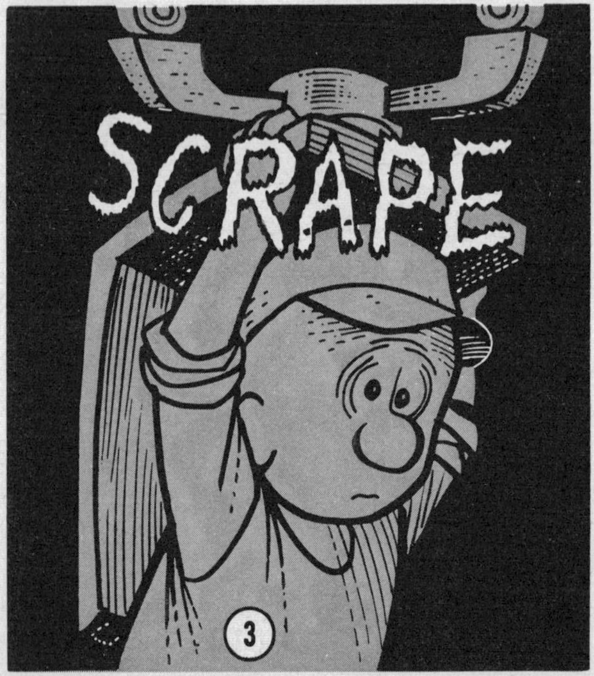
SCRAPE
3

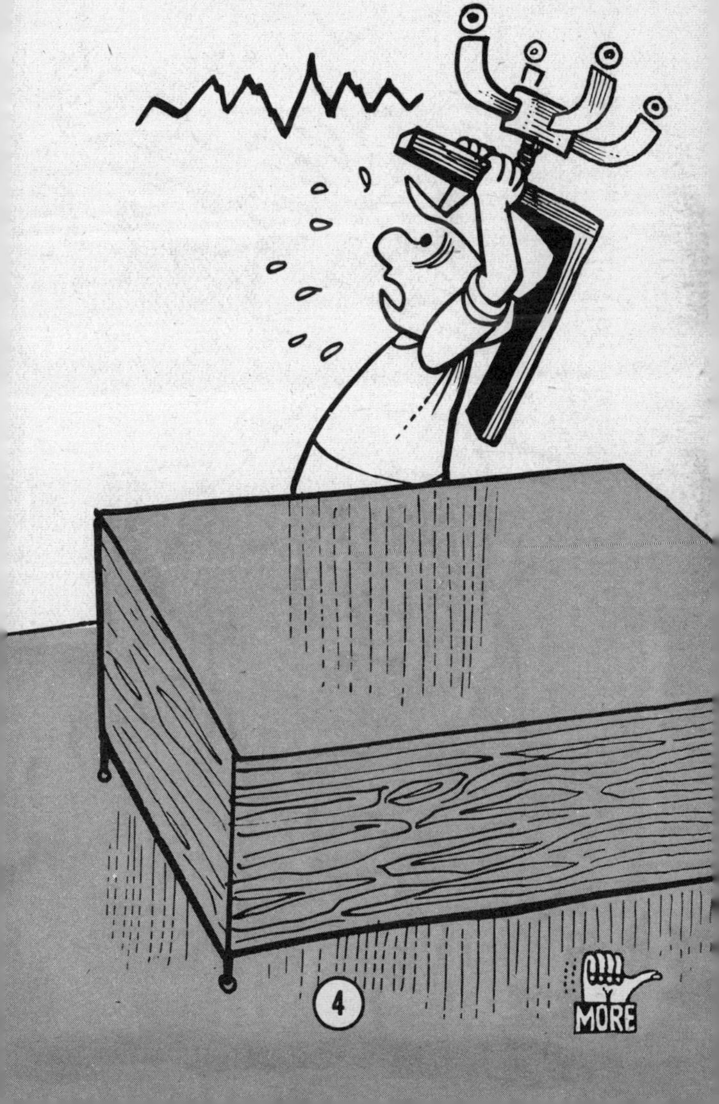
4
MORE

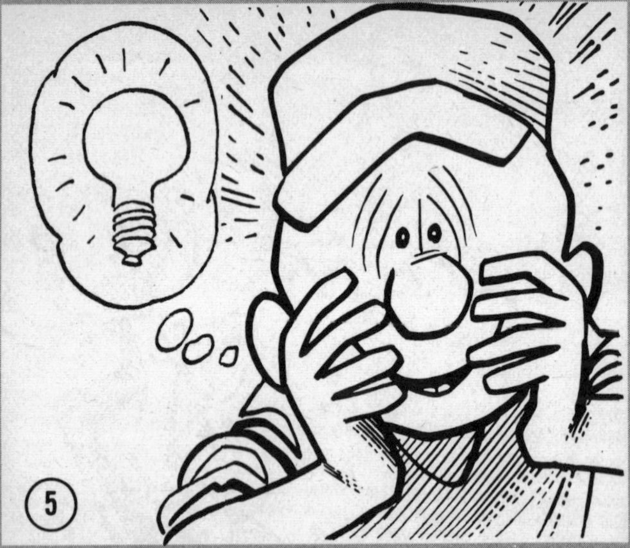
5

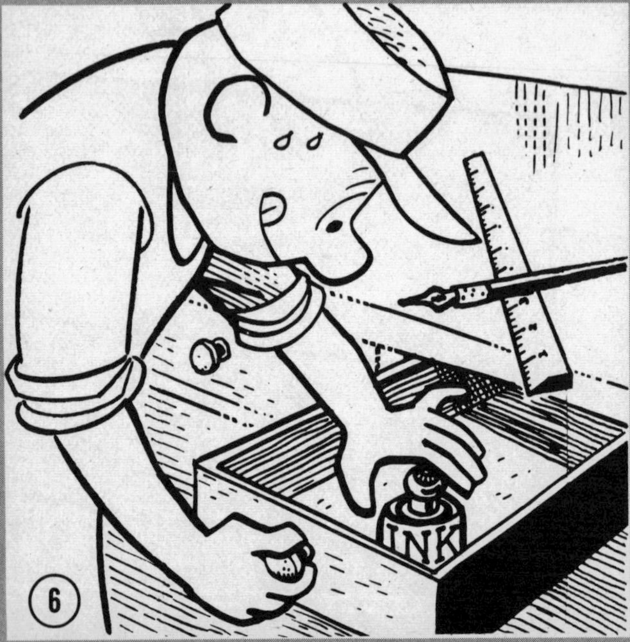
INK
6

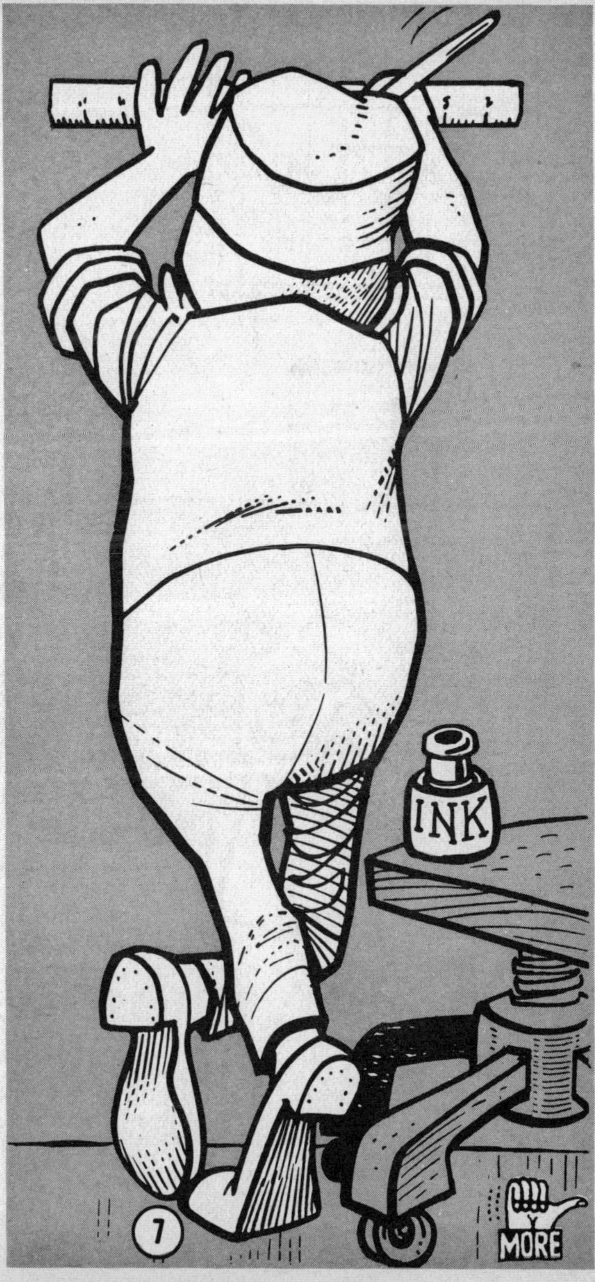
INK
7
MORE

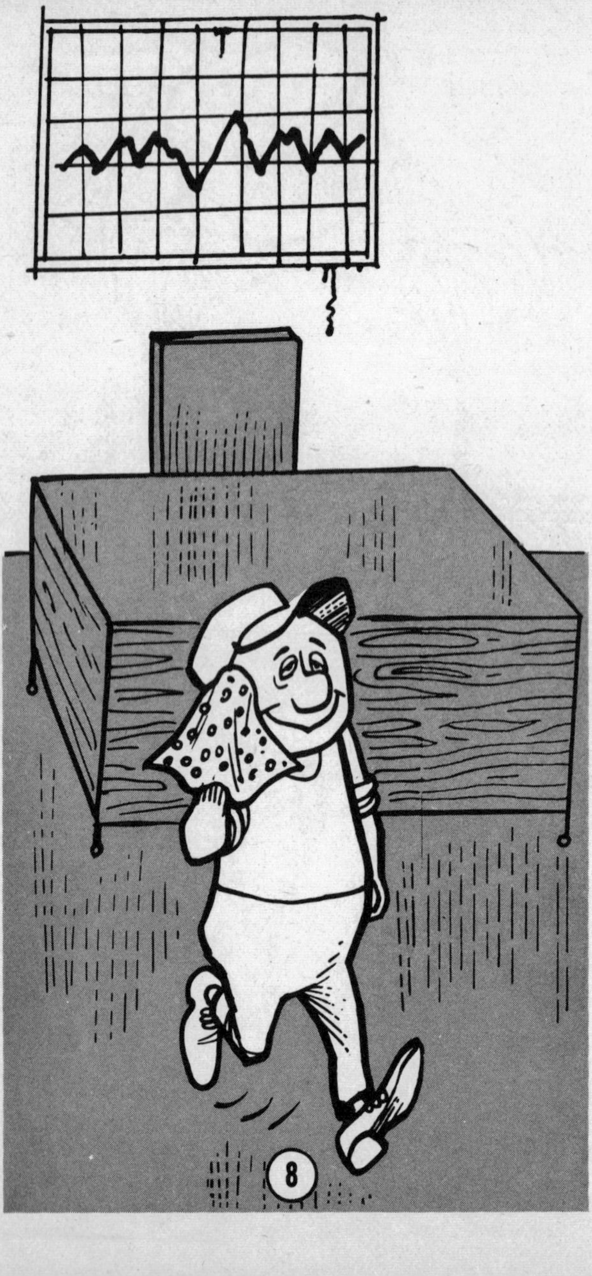
8

A Sensational Accumulation of Needless Nonentities

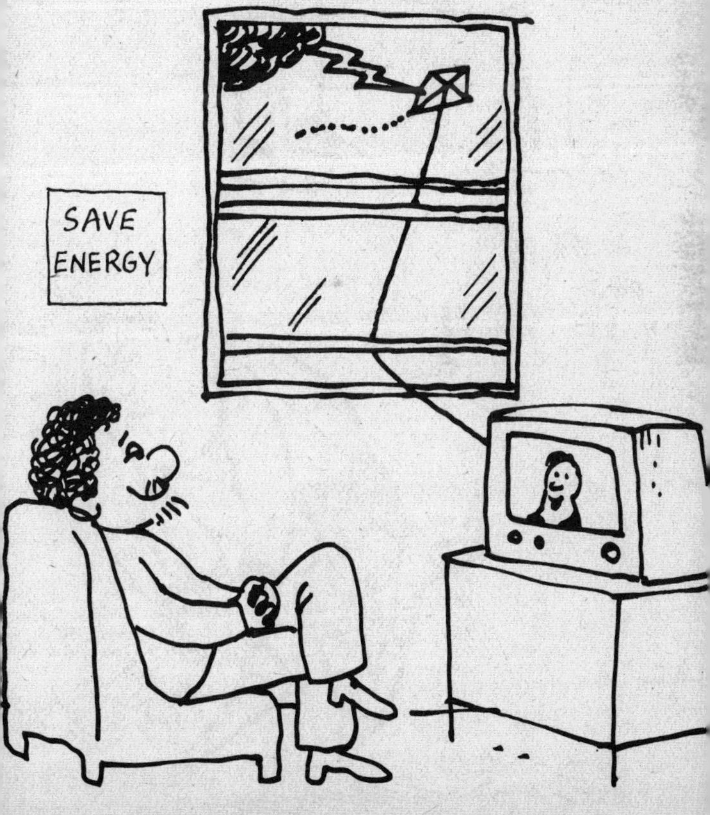
SAVE
ENERGY

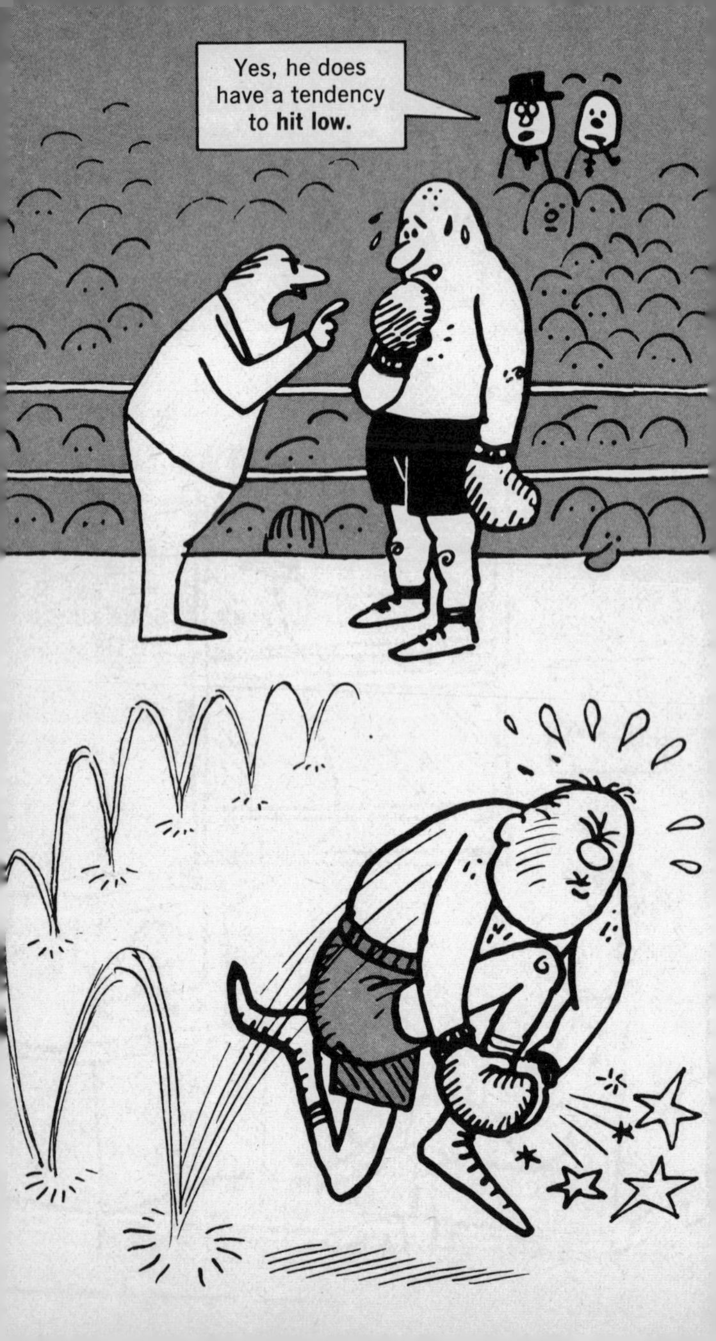
Yes, he does have a tendency to **hit low.**

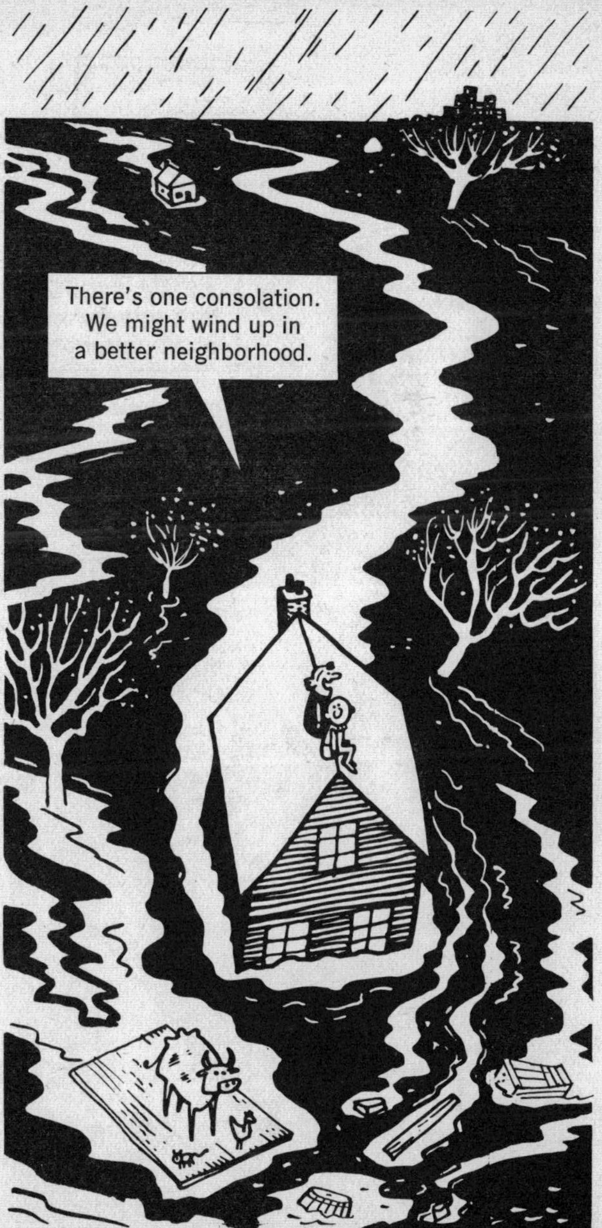
There's one consolation. We might wind up in a better neighborhood.

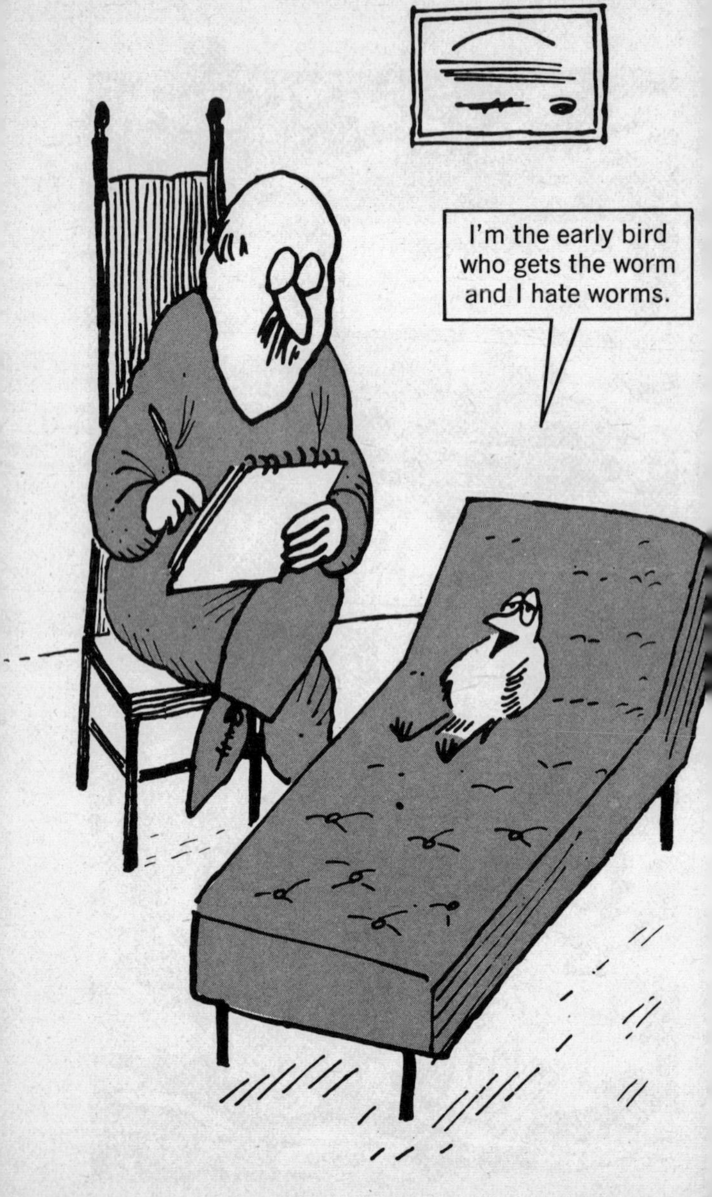
I'm the early bird who gets the worm and I hate worms.

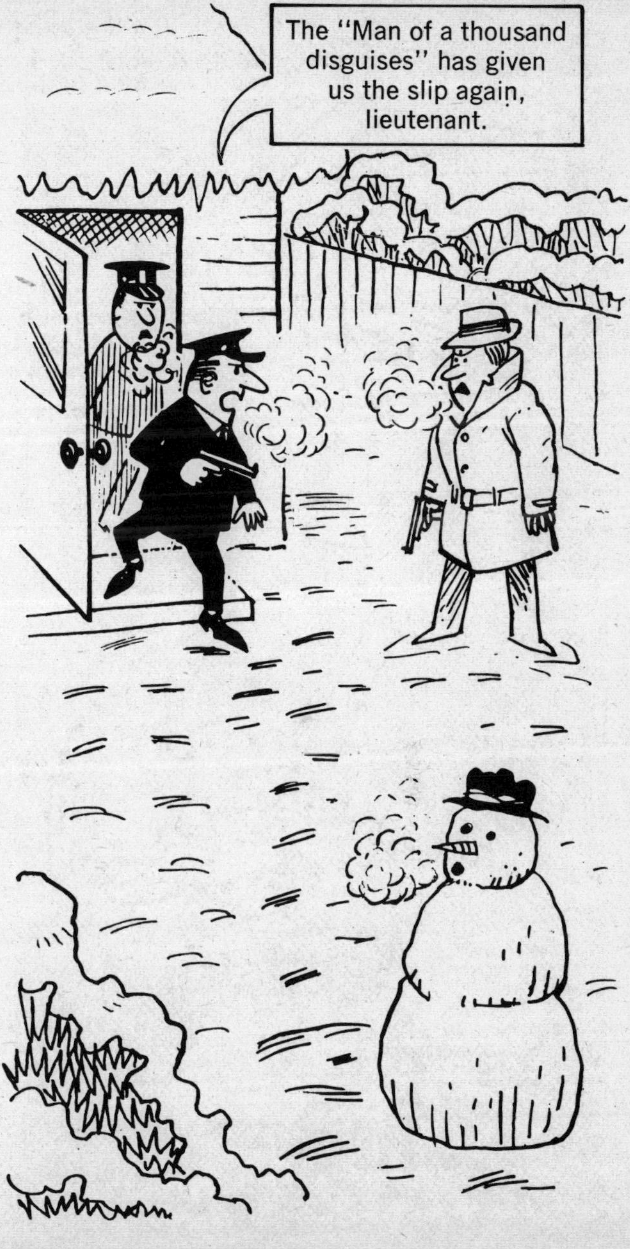
The "Man of a thousand disguises" has given us the slip again, lieutenant.

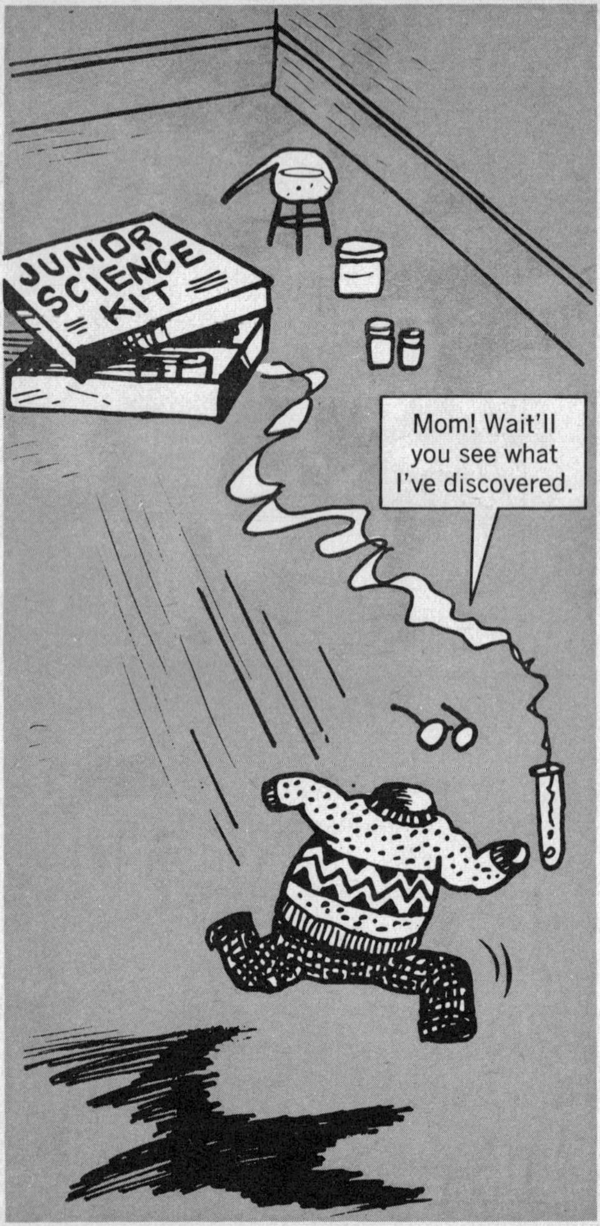
JUNIOR SCIENCE KIT
Mom! Wait'll you see what I've discovered.

A Delightfully Dull Dueling Dilemma

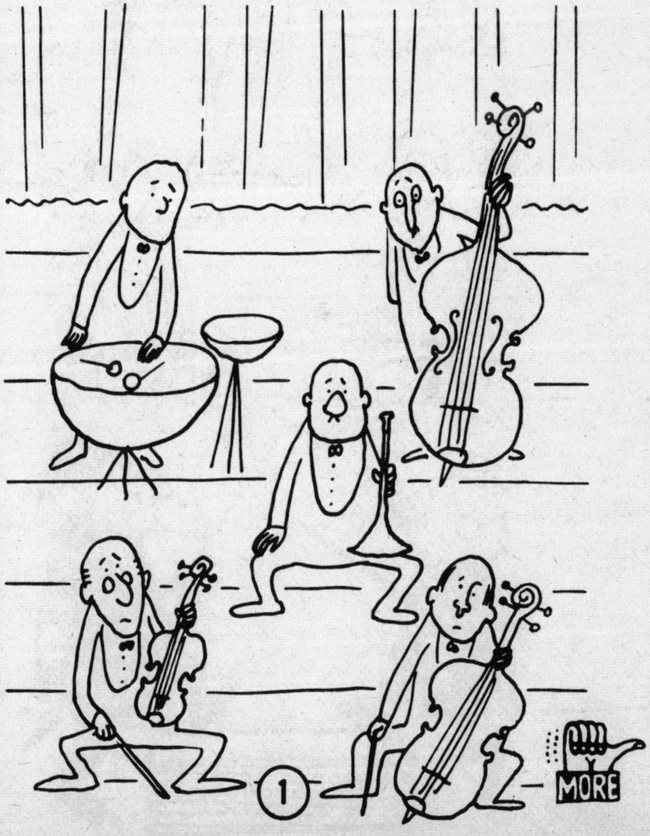
MORE

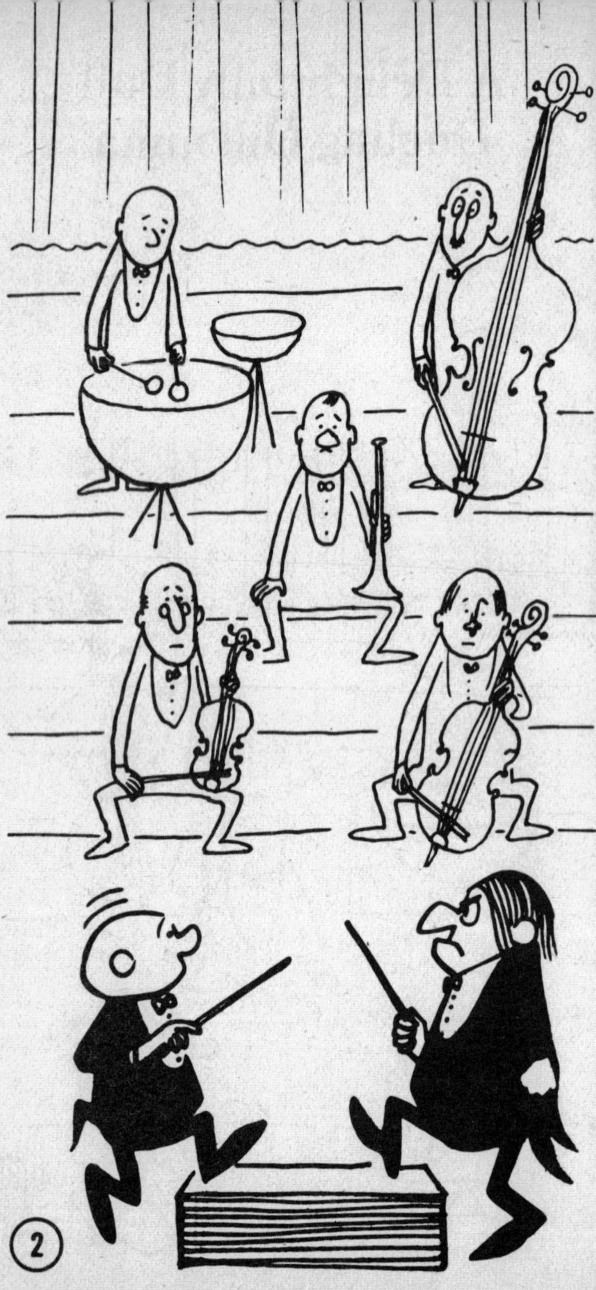

2

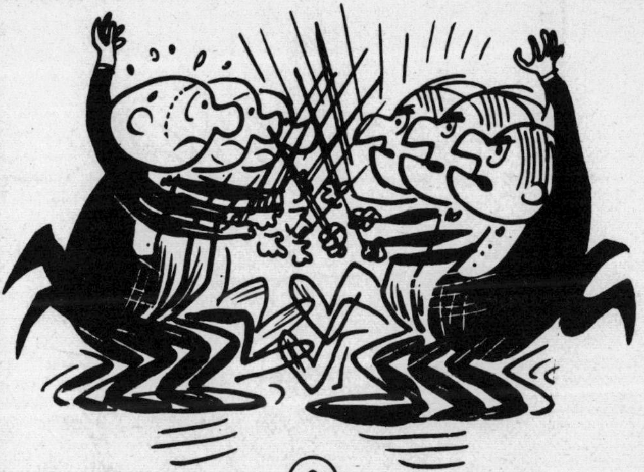

3

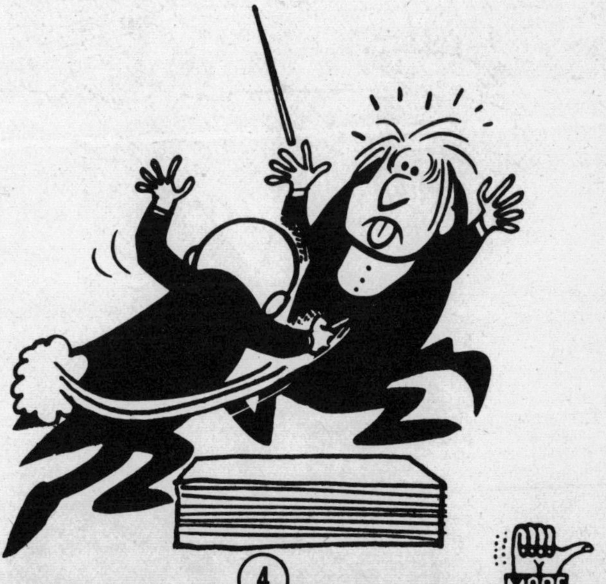

4

MORE

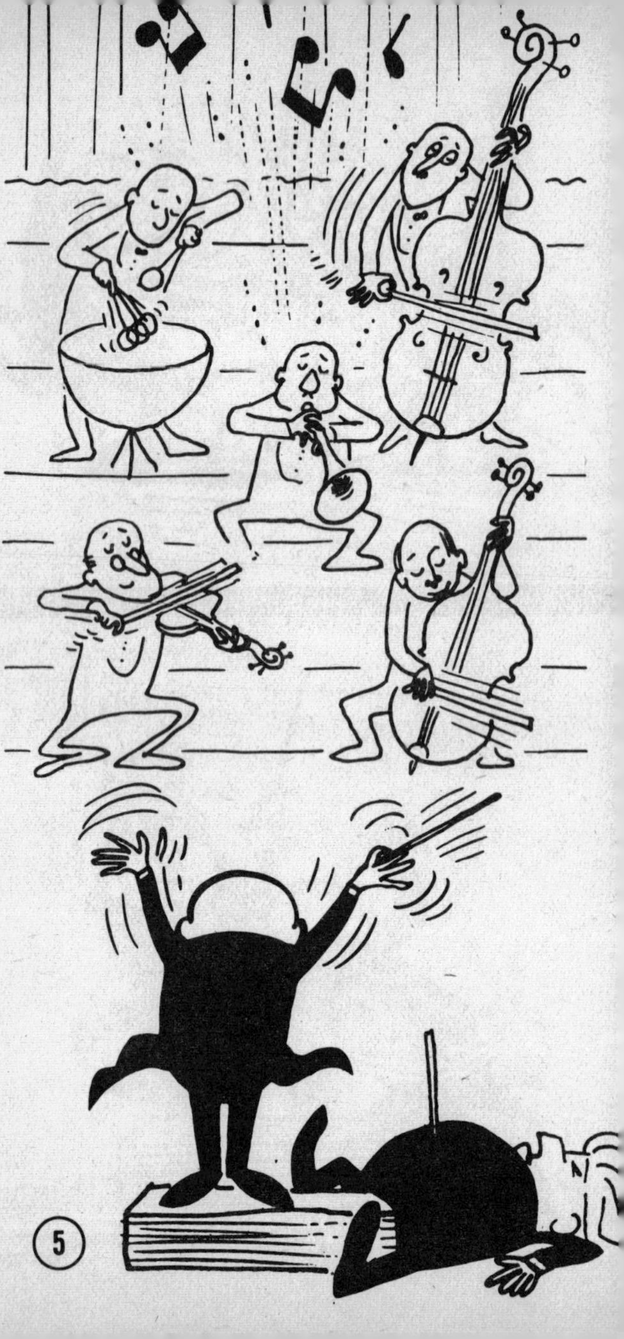
5

A Divine Quantity of Objectionable Tritenesses

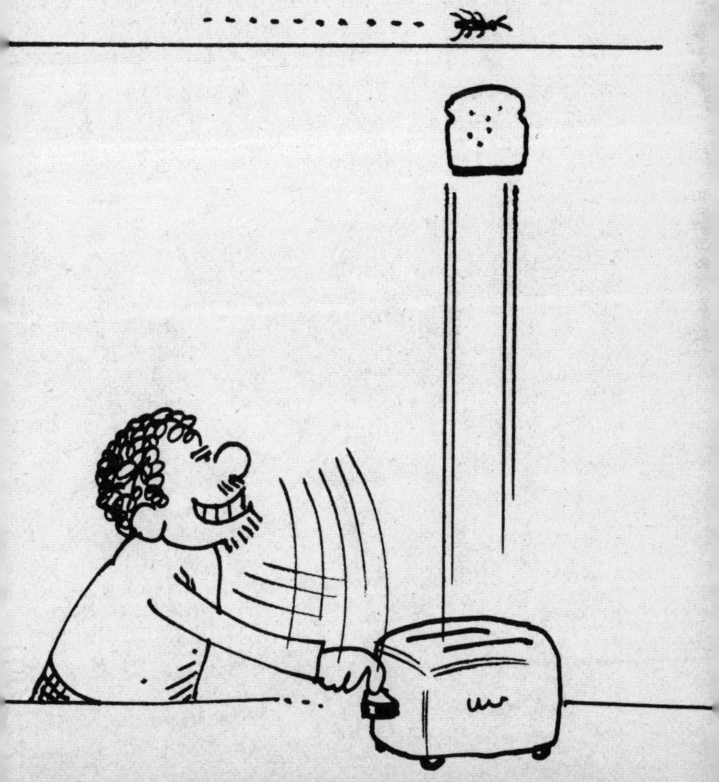

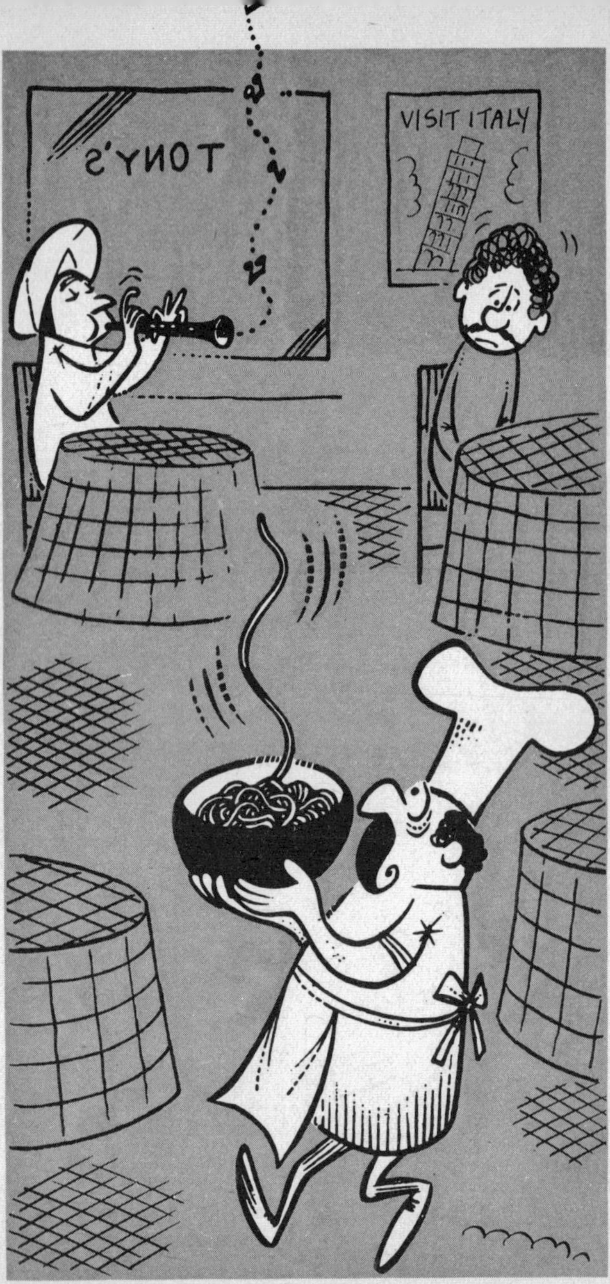
TONY'S
VISIT ITALY

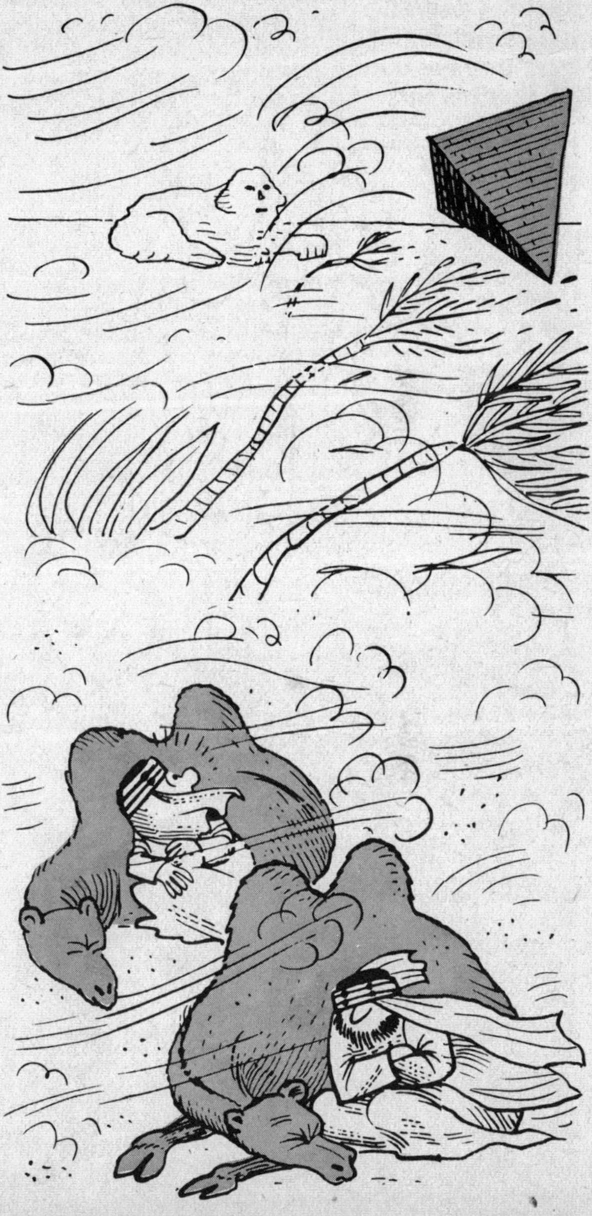

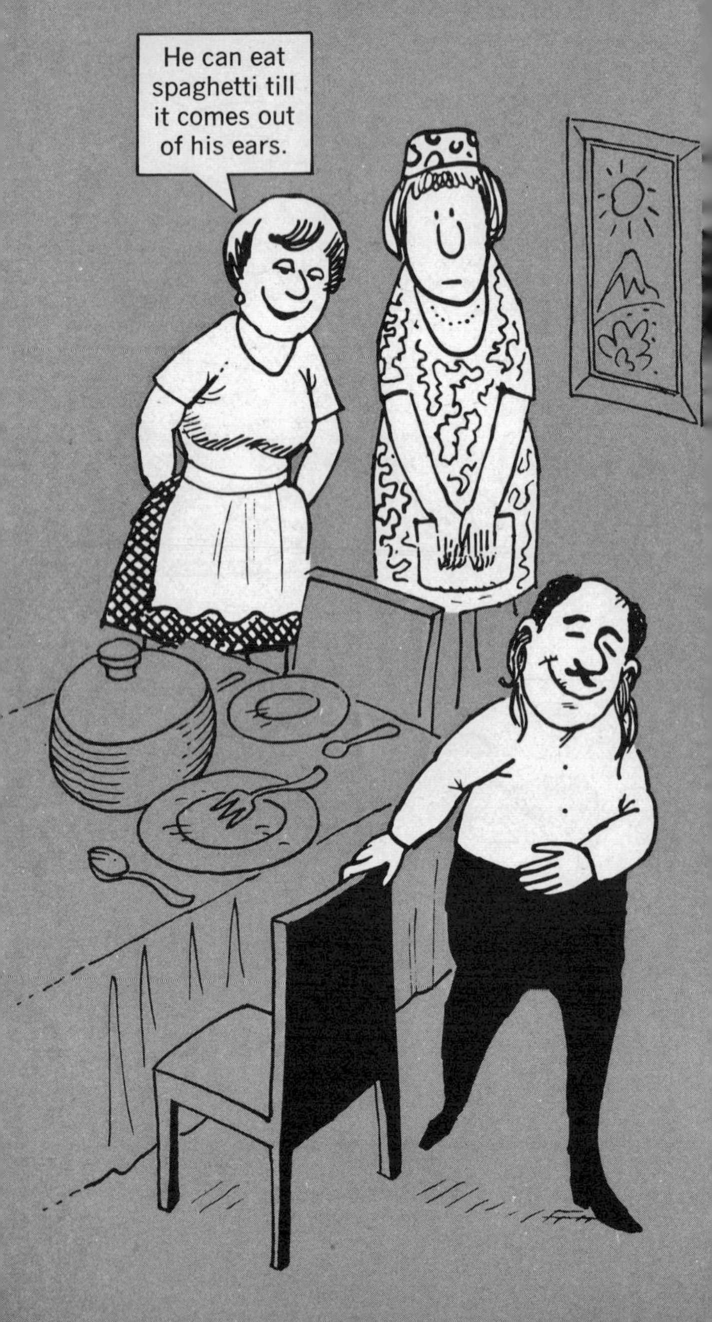
He can eat spaghetti till it comes out of his ears.

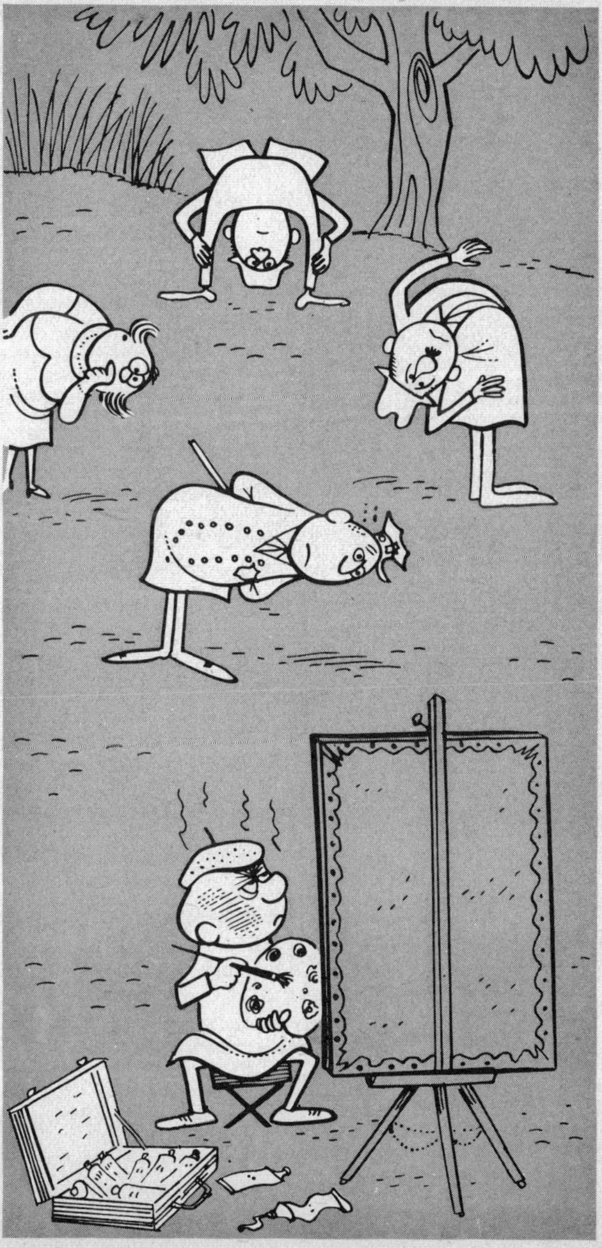

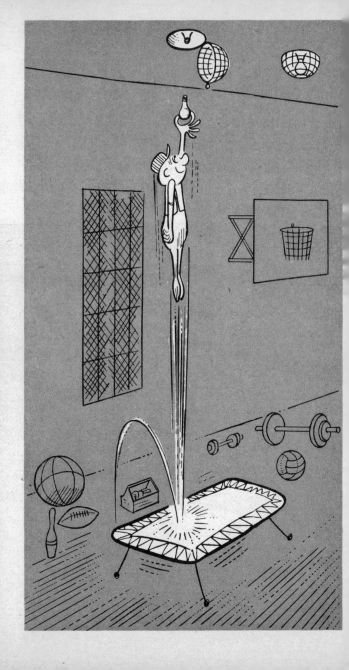

A Fantastically Foolish Flood Fantasy

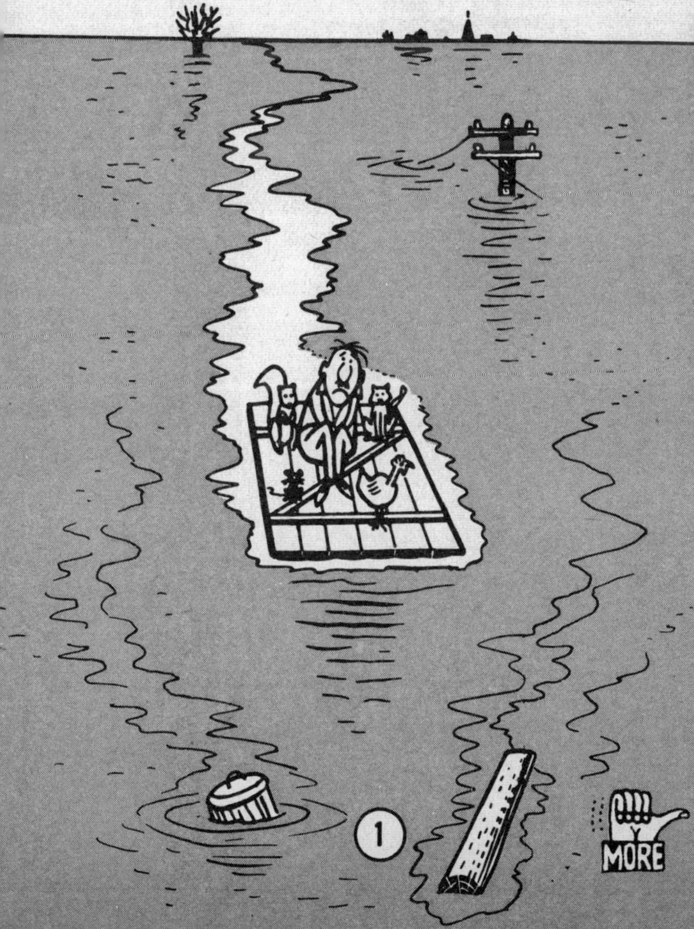
1
MORE

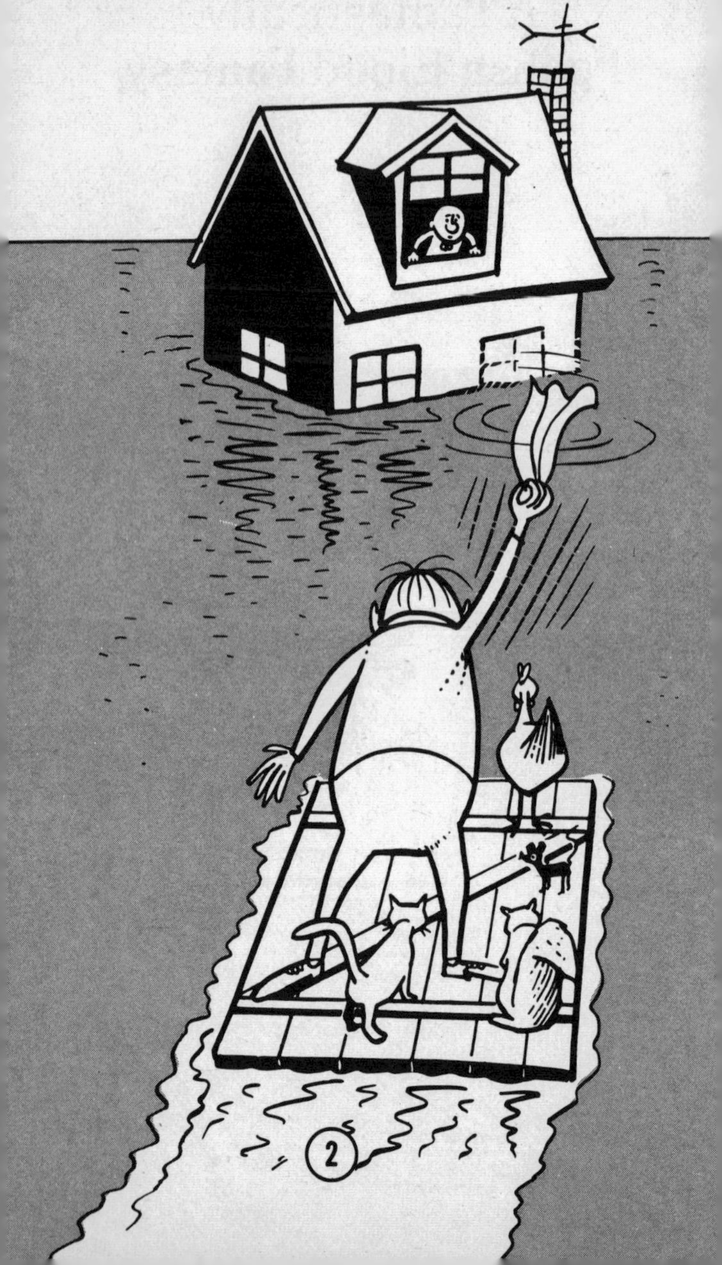
2

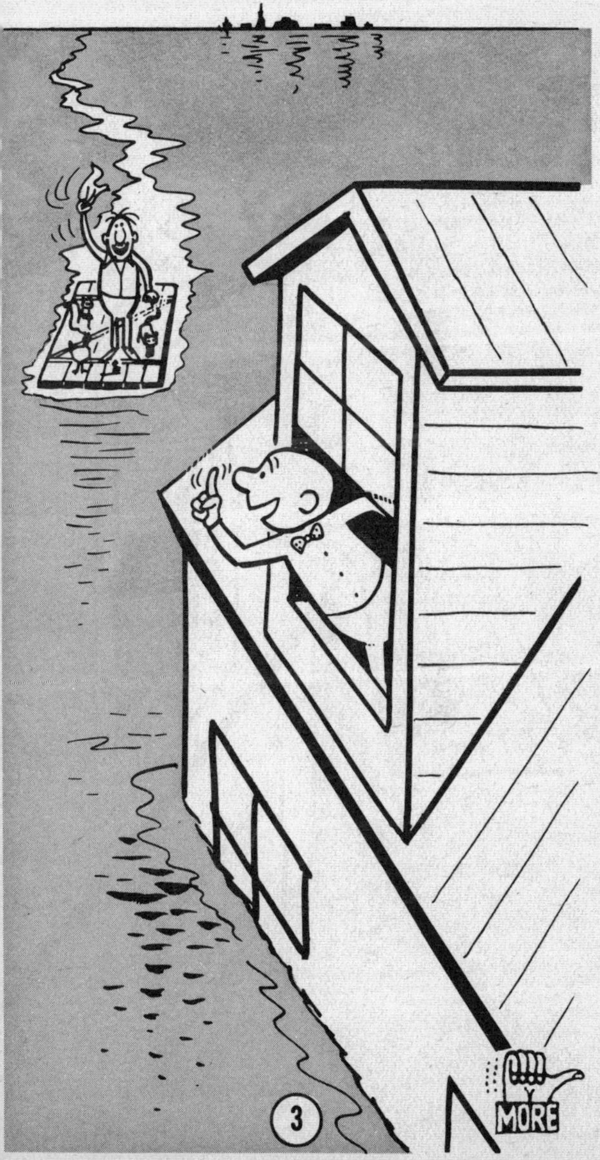
3
MORE

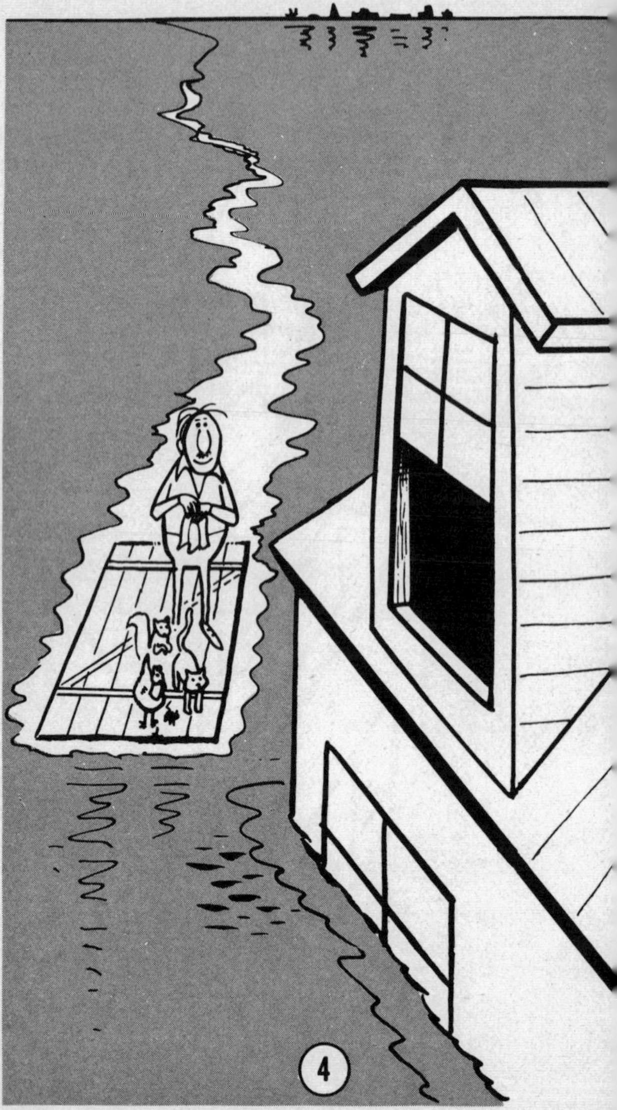
4

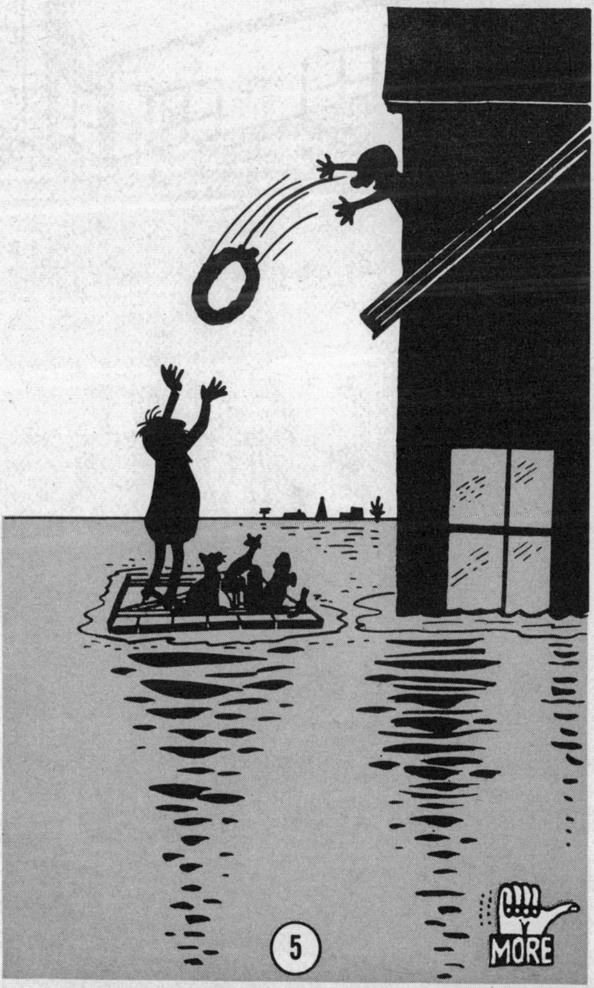
5
MORE

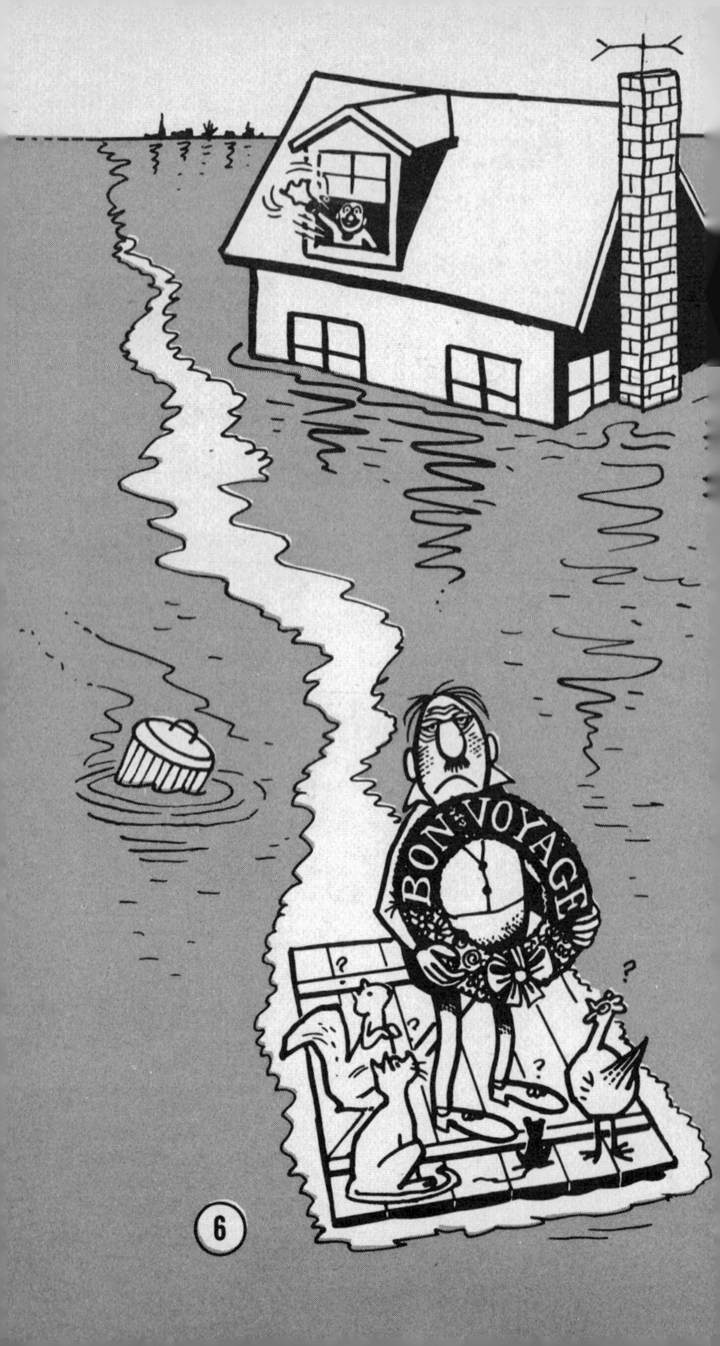
BON VOYAGE
6

An Extraordinary Aggregation of Flimsy Frailties

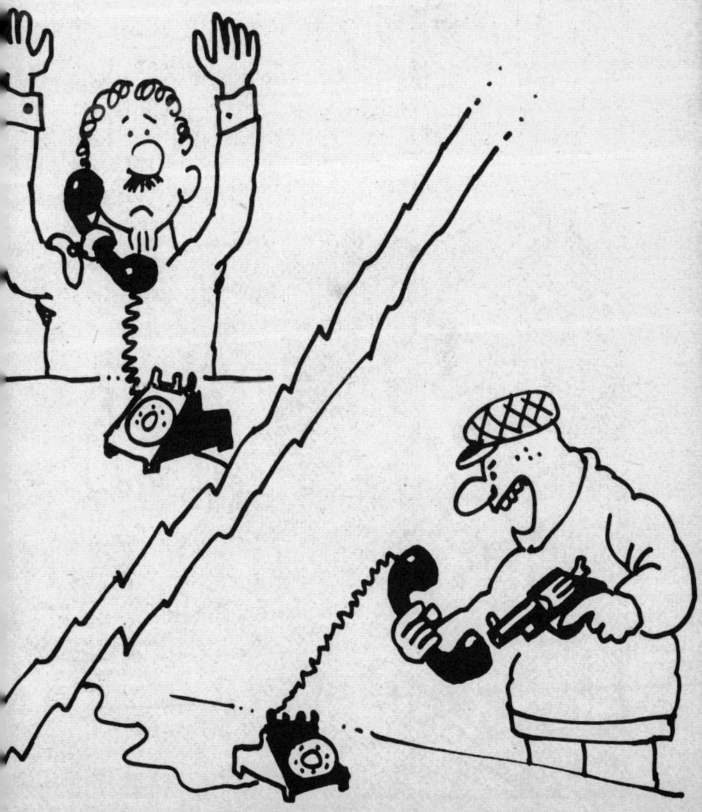

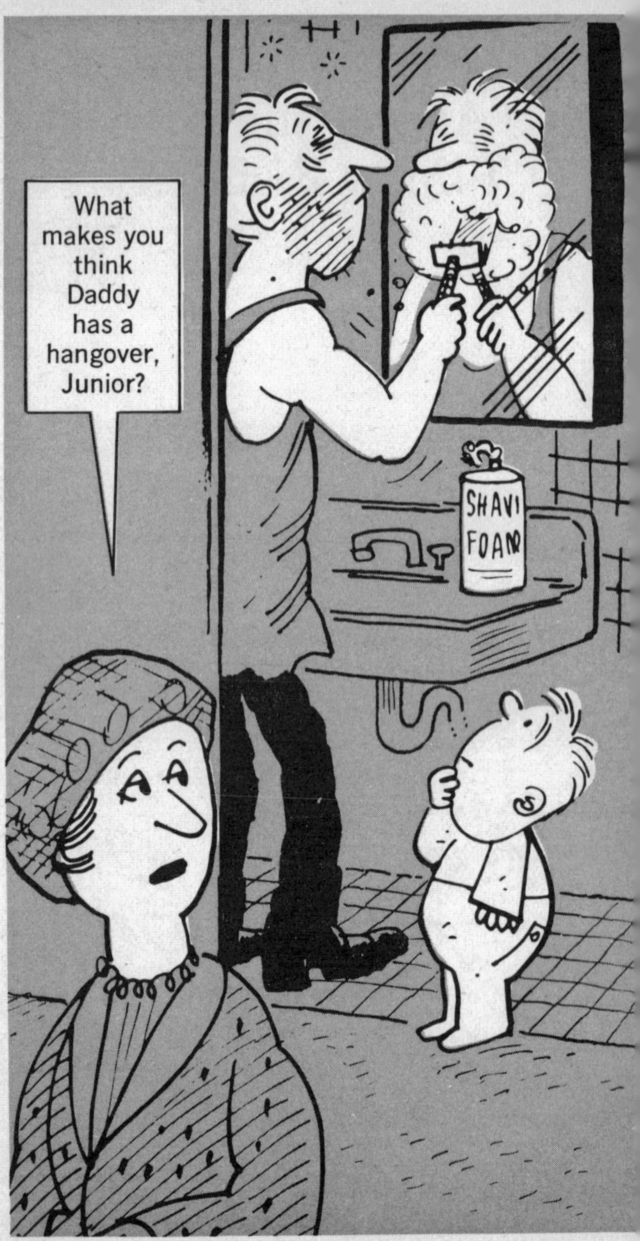
What makes you think Daddy has a hangover, Junior?
SHAVI FOAM

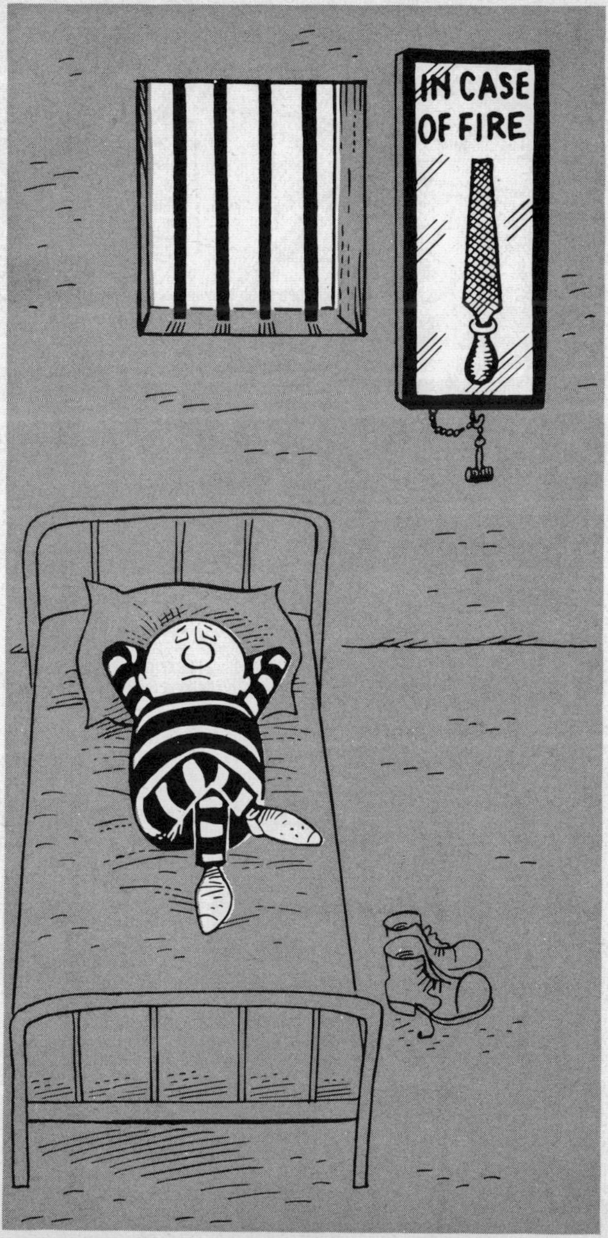
IN CASE
OF FIRE

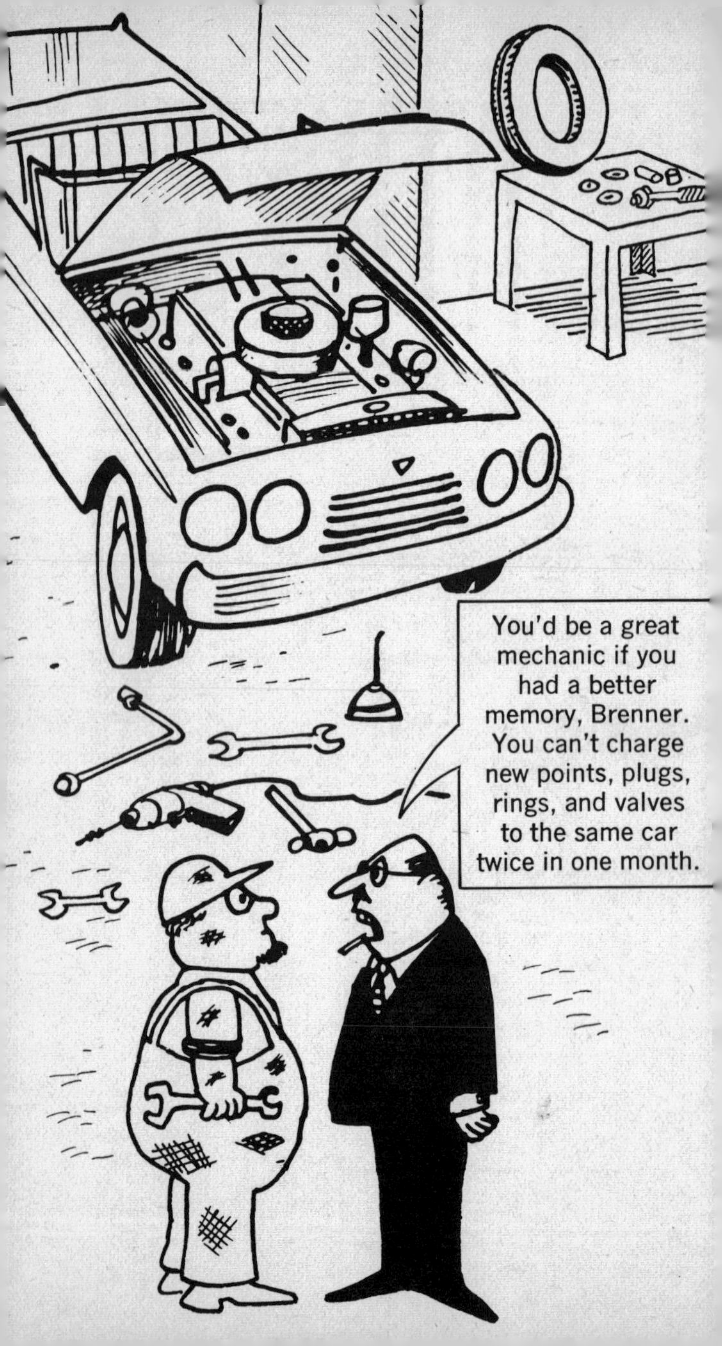
You'd be a great mechanic if you had a better memory, Brenner. You can't charge new points, plugs, rings, and valves to the same car twice in one month.

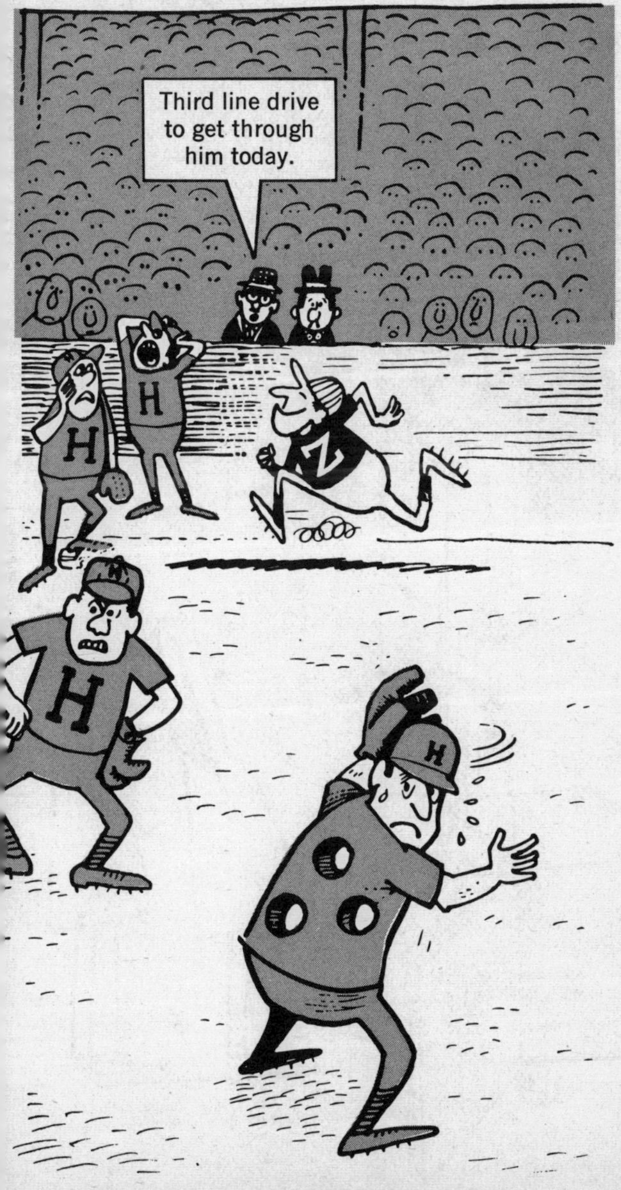
Third line drive to get through him today.

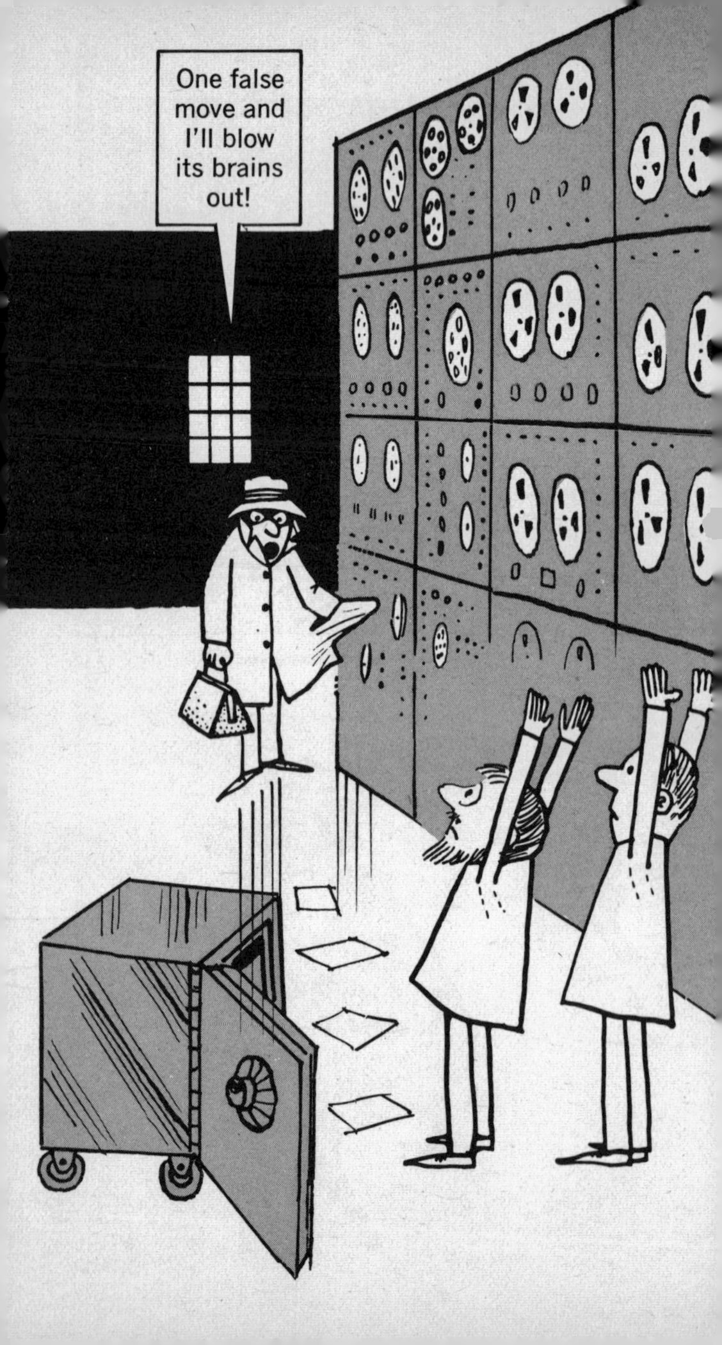
One false move and I'll blow its brains out!

A Handsomely Hackneyed Helicopter Happening

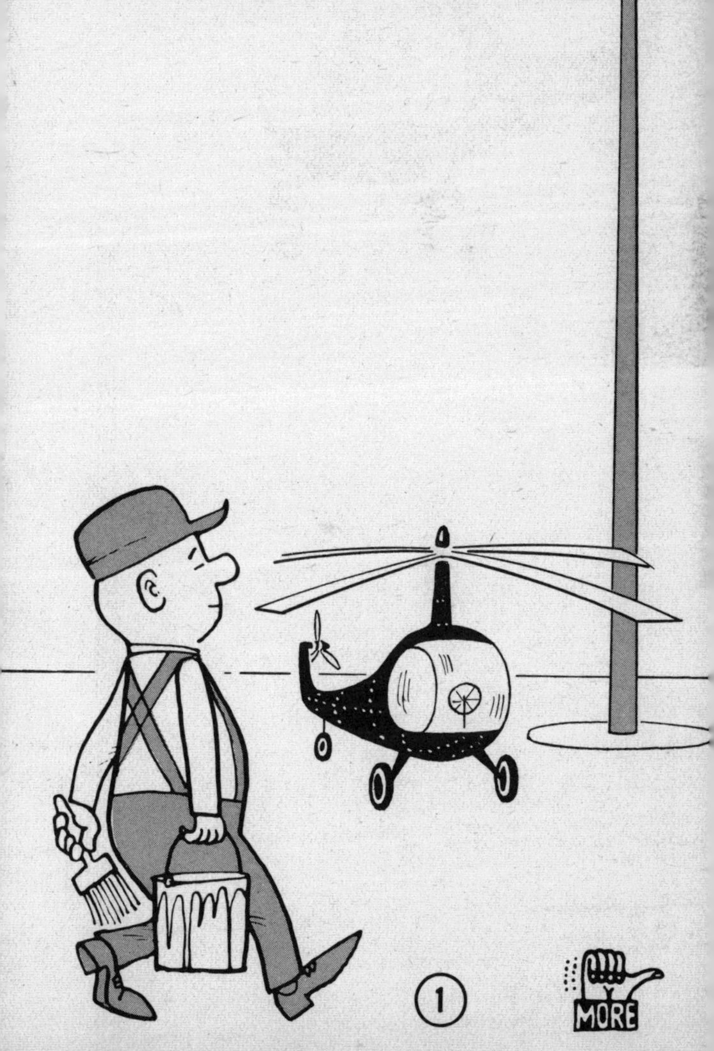
MORE

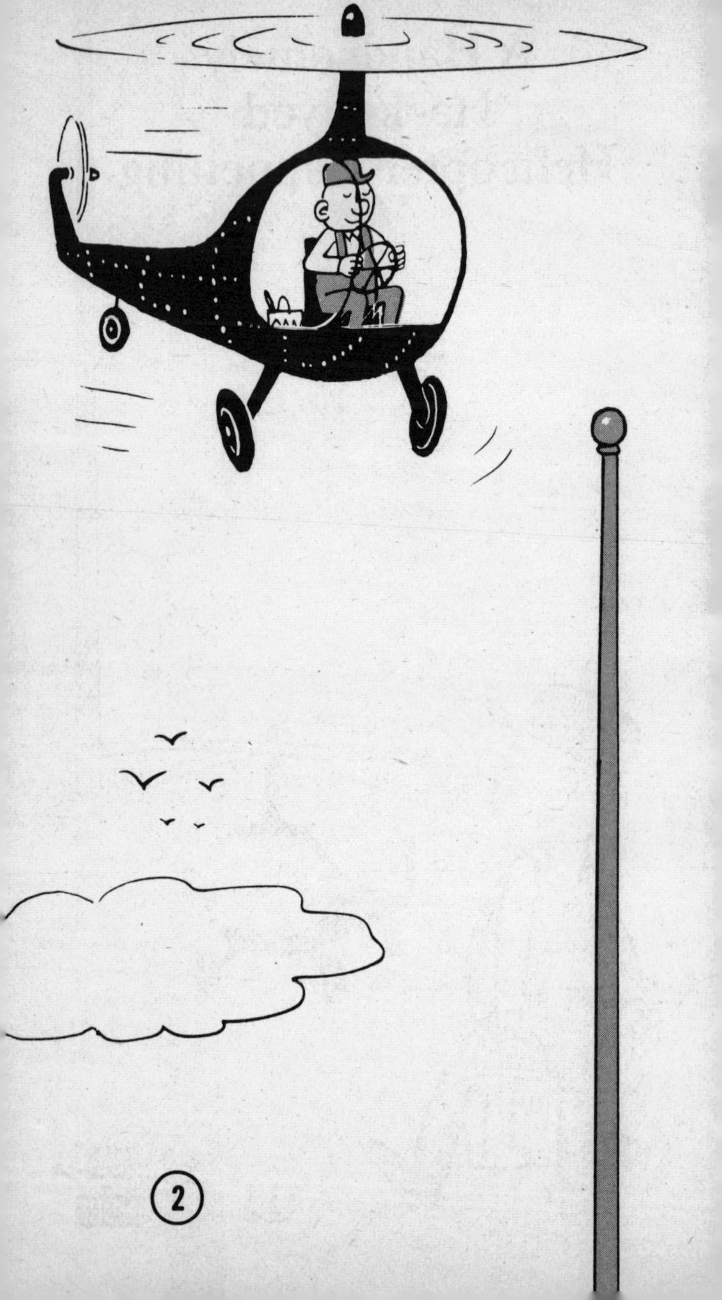
2

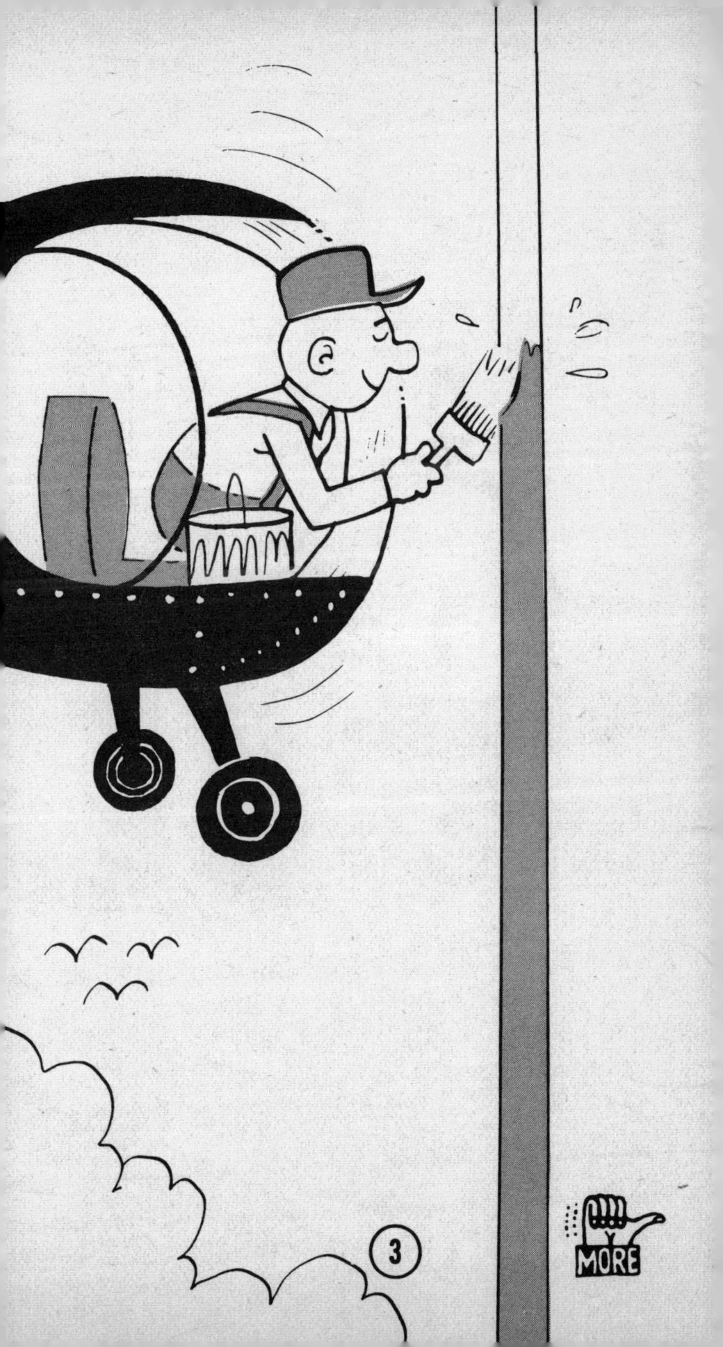
3
MORE

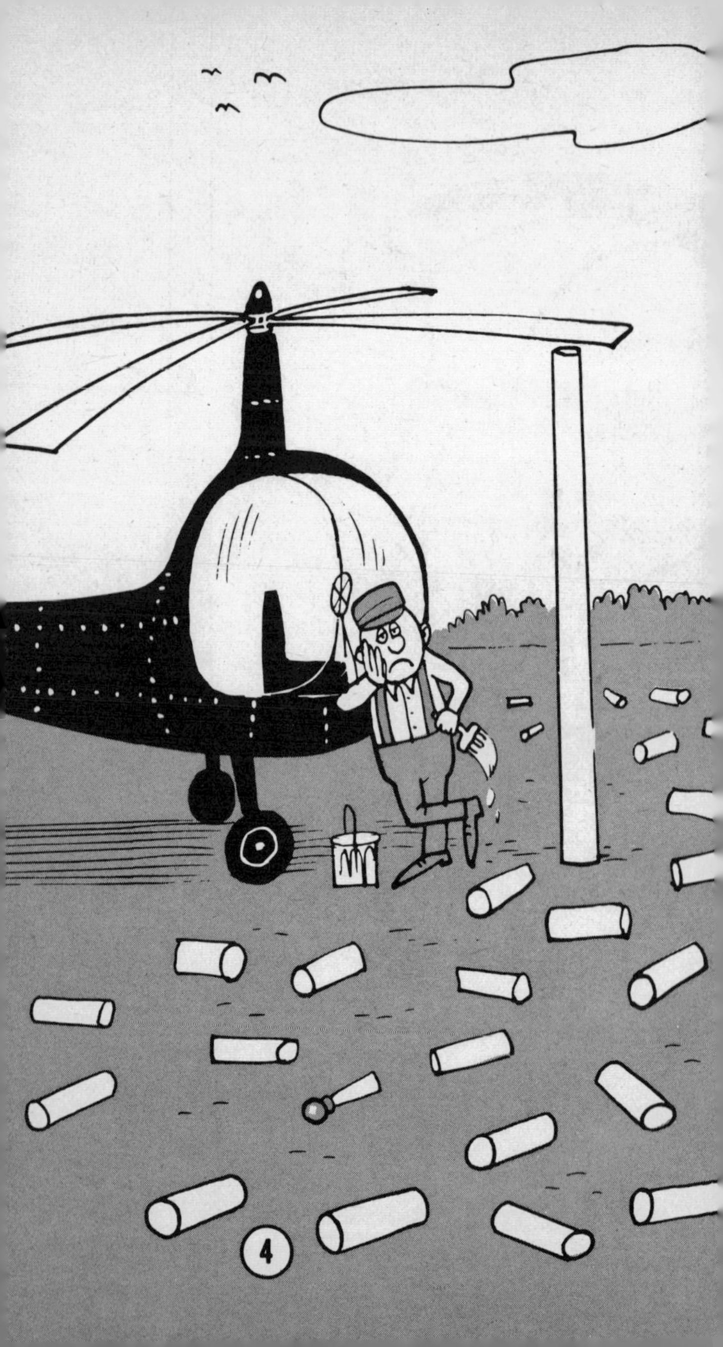
4

A Magnanimous Conglomeration of Mystifying Maladies

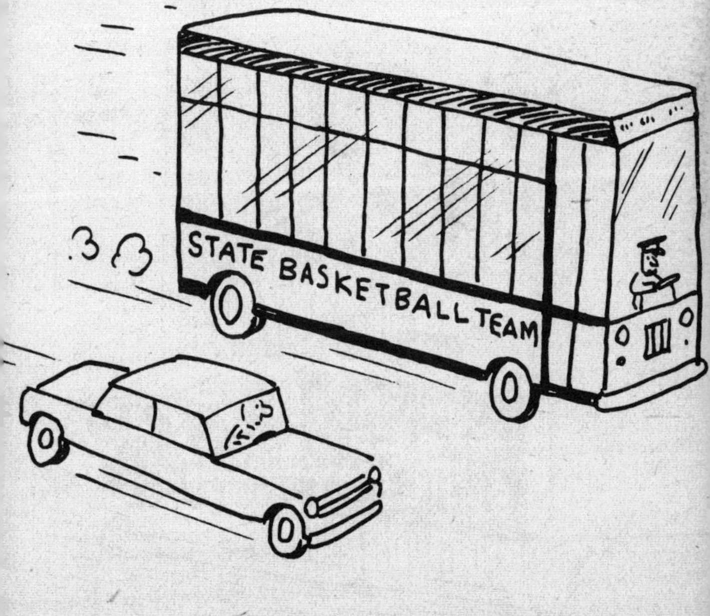
STATE BASKETBALL TEAM

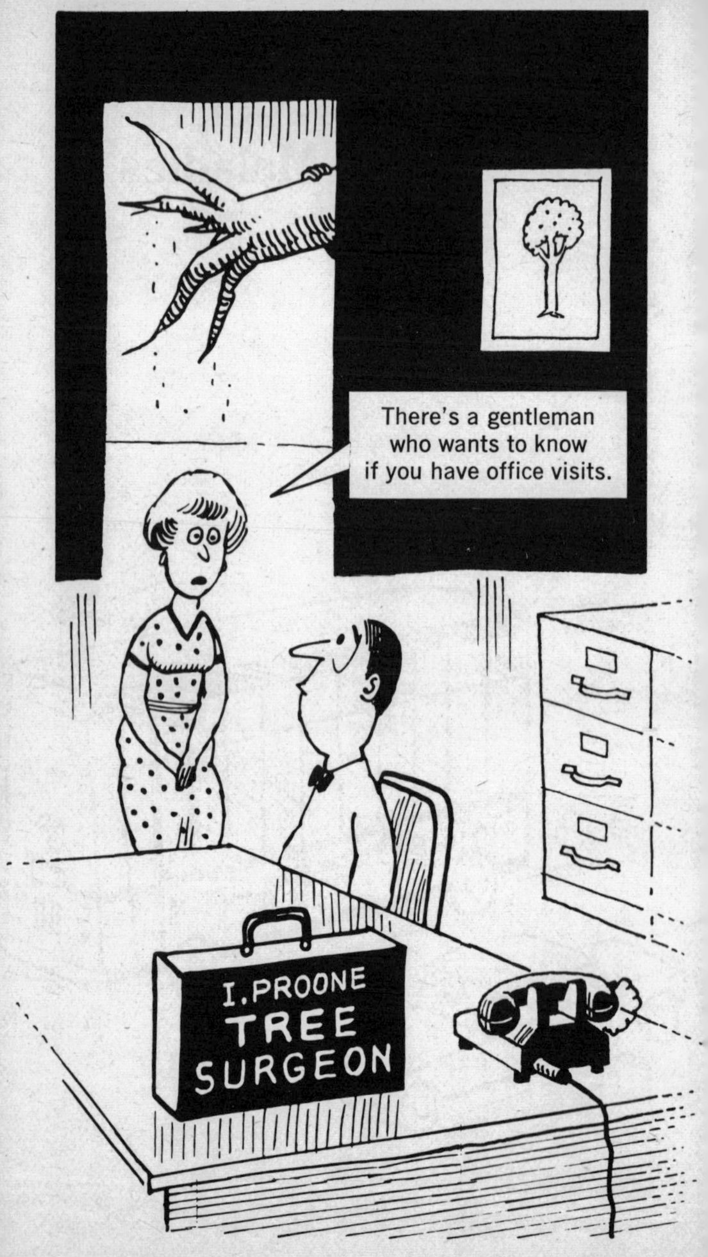
There's a gentleman who wants to know if you have office visits.
I. PROONE TREE SURGEON

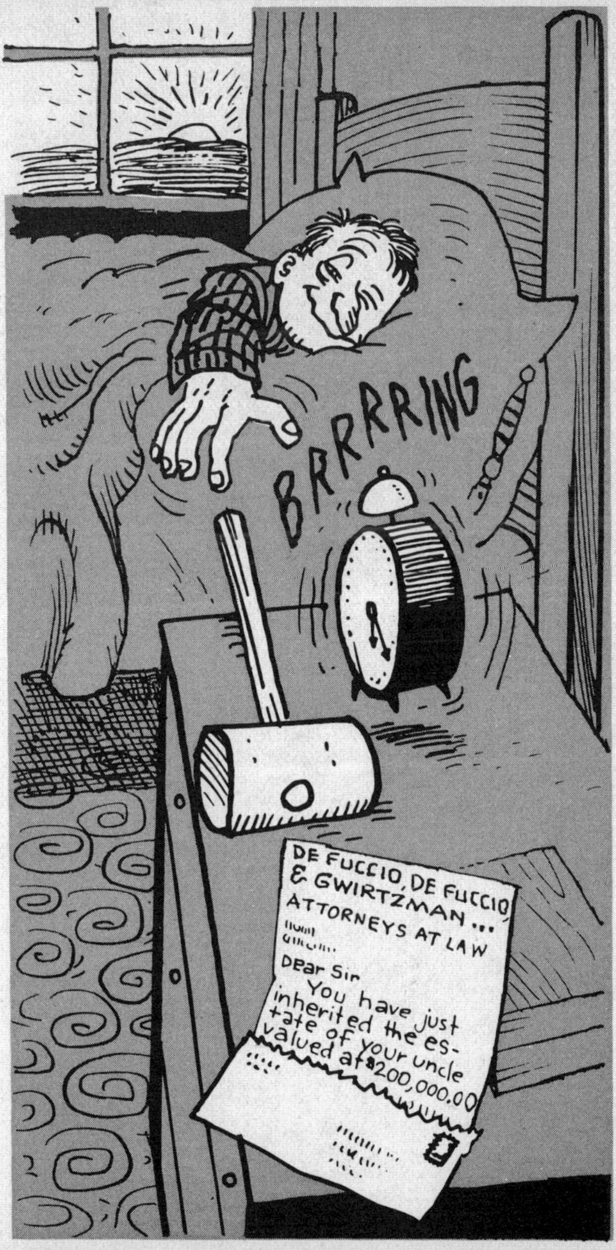
BRRRRRING
DE FUCCIO, DE FUCCIO
& GWIRTZMAN ...
ATTORNEYS AT LAW
Dear Sir
You have just inherited the estate of your uncle valued at $200,000.00

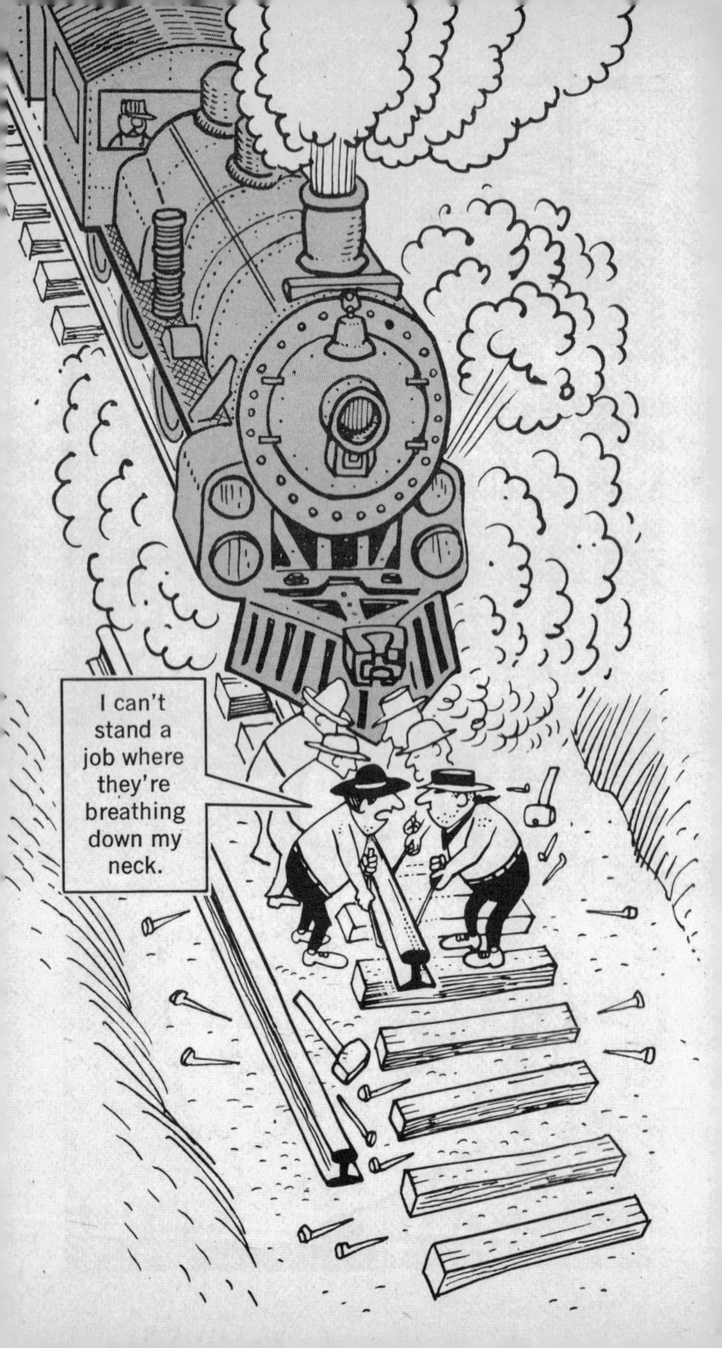
I can't stand a job where they're breathing down my neck.

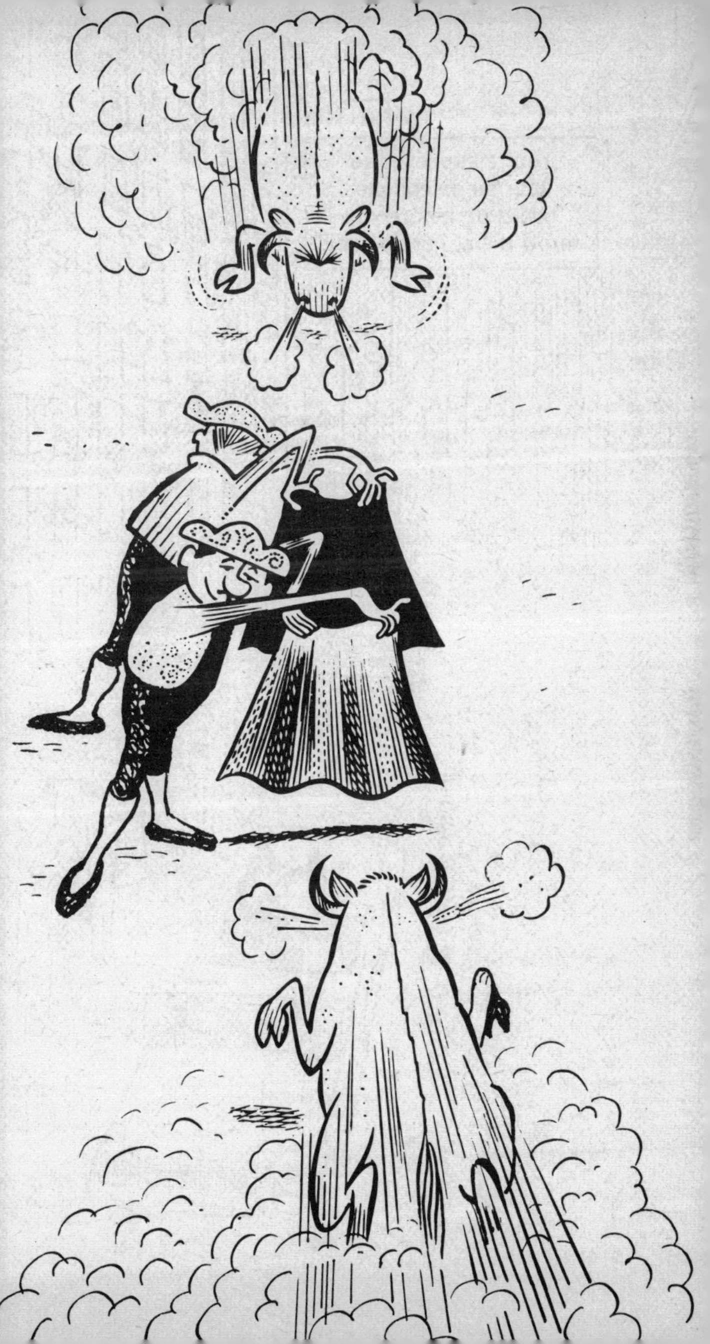

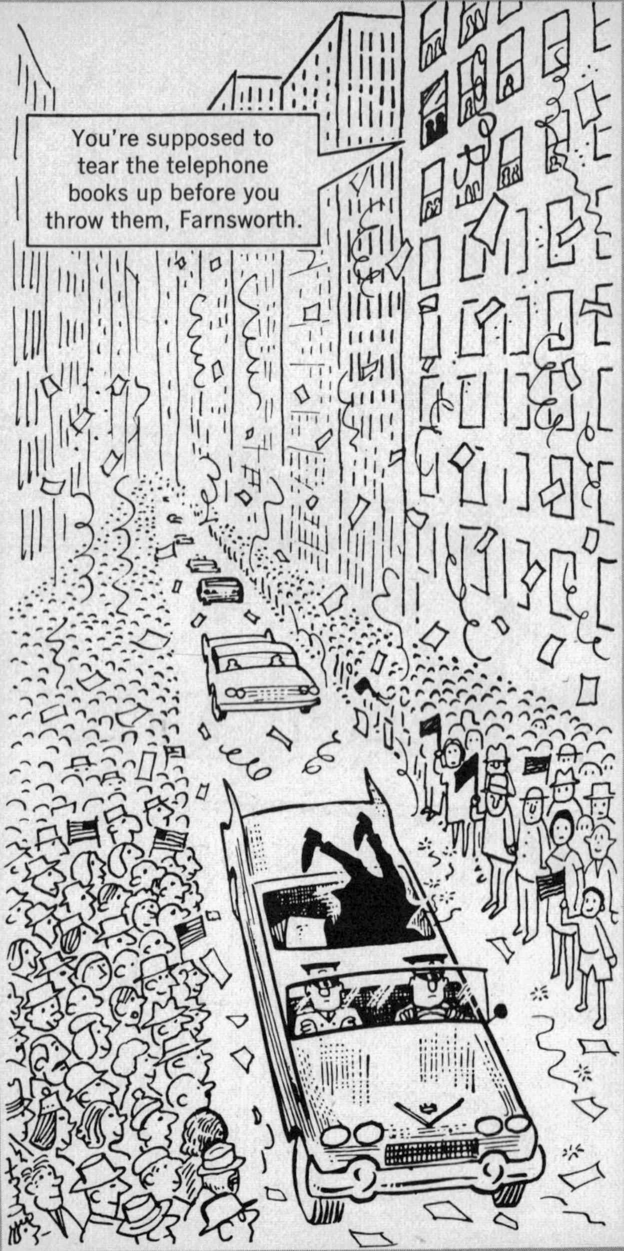
You're supposed to tear the telephone books up before you throw them, Farnsworth.

A Masterfully Morbid Medical Mission

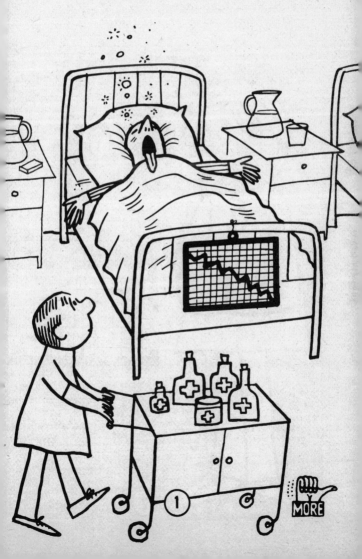

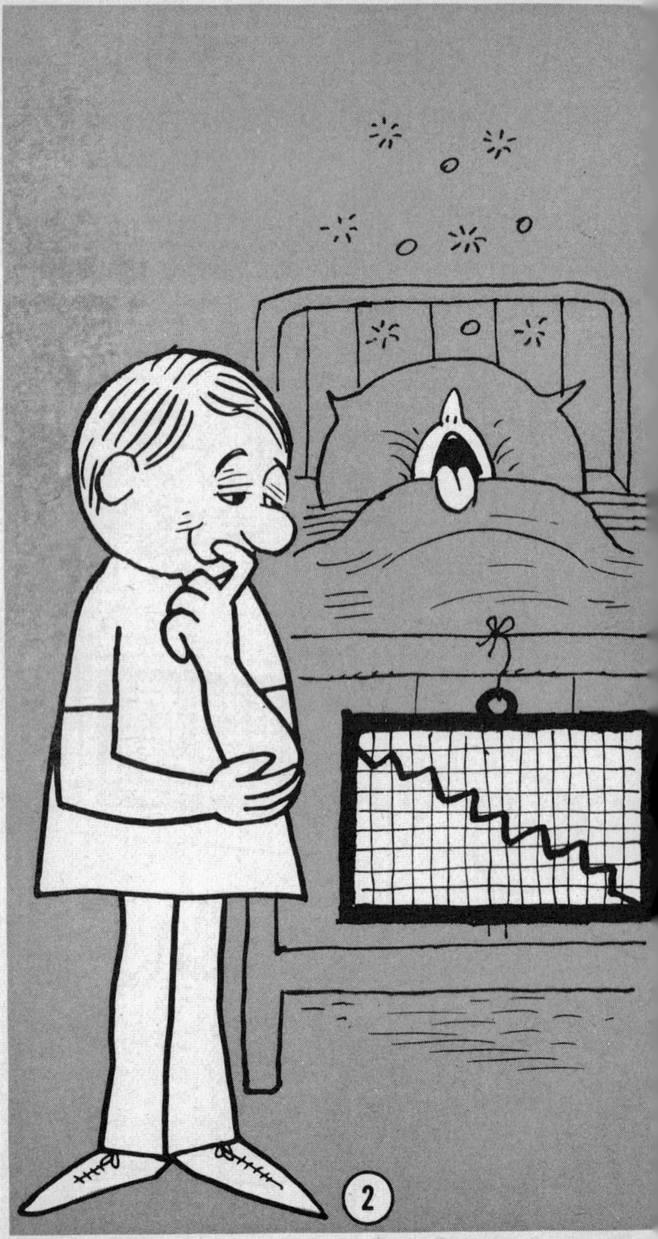
2

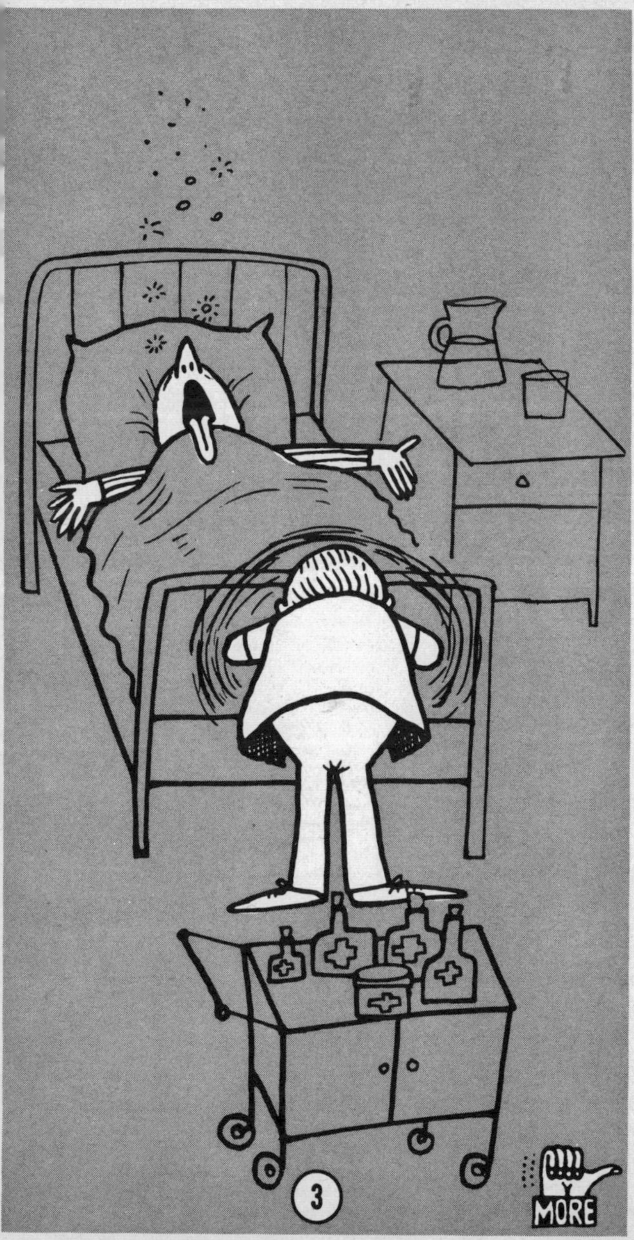
3
MORE

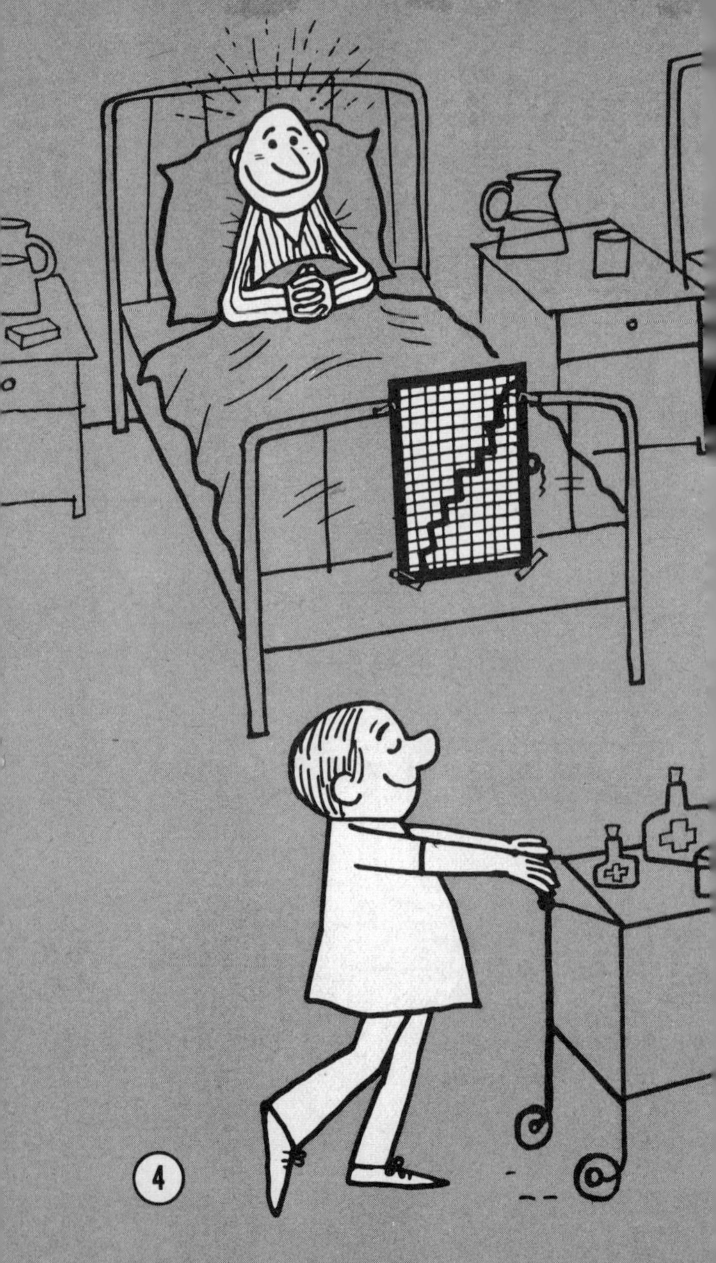
4

An Exhilarating Compilation of Perplexing Buffooneries

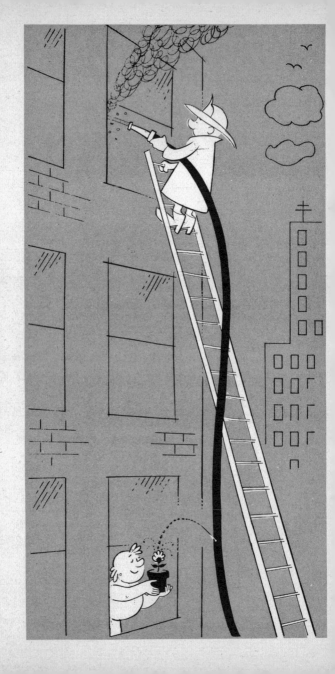

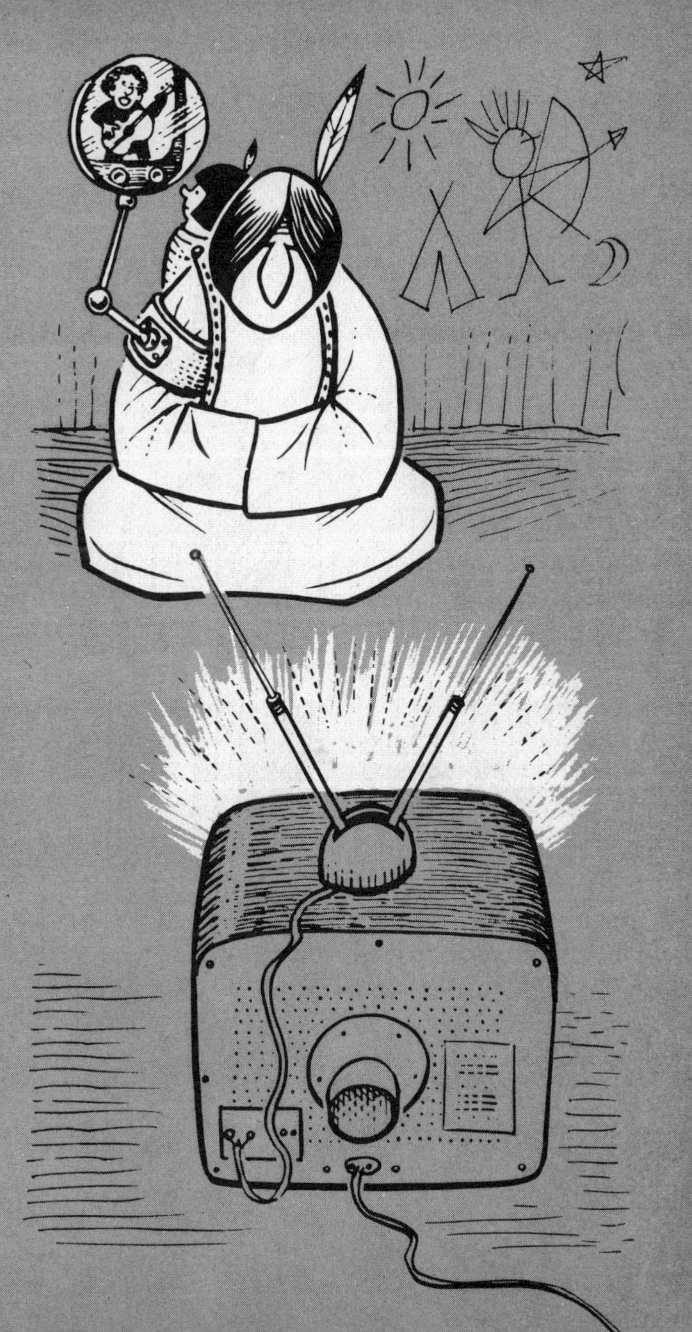

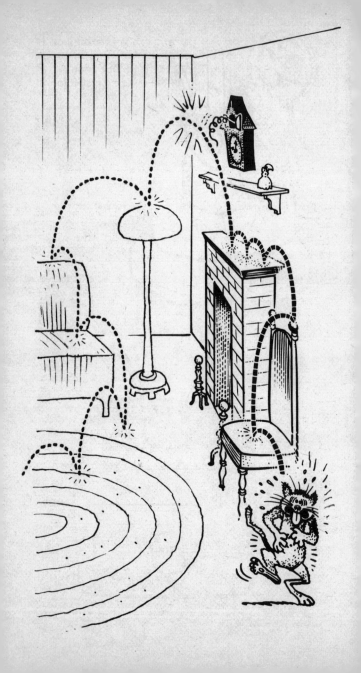

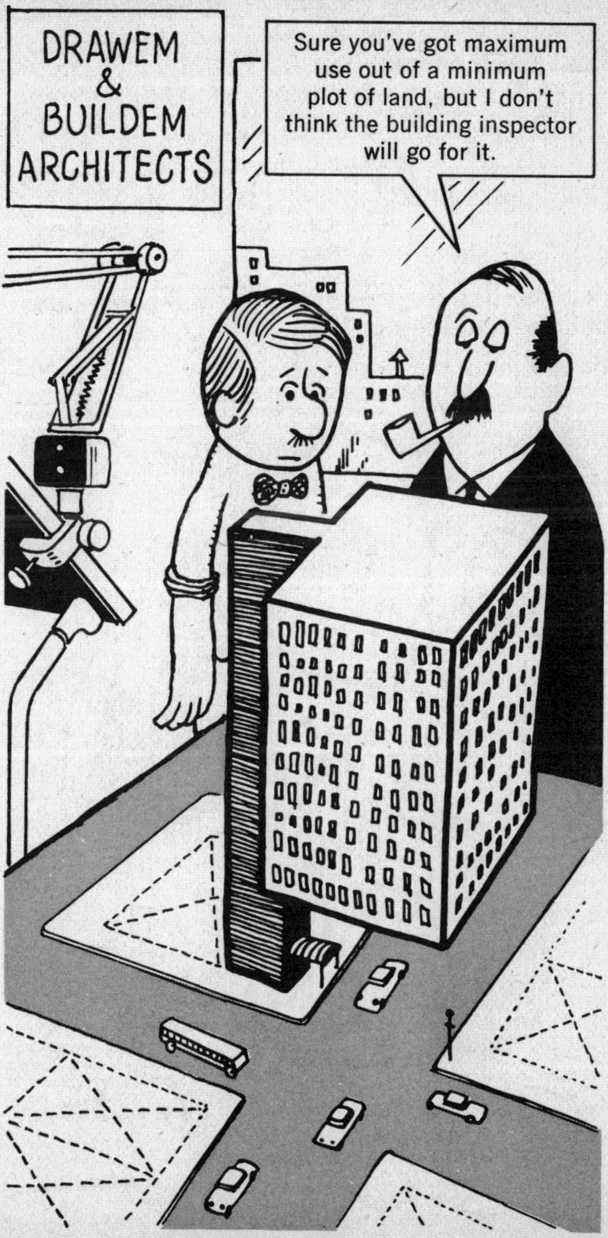
DRAWEM & BUILDEM ARCHITECTS
Sure you've got maximum use out of a minimum plot of land, but I don't think the building inspector will go for it.

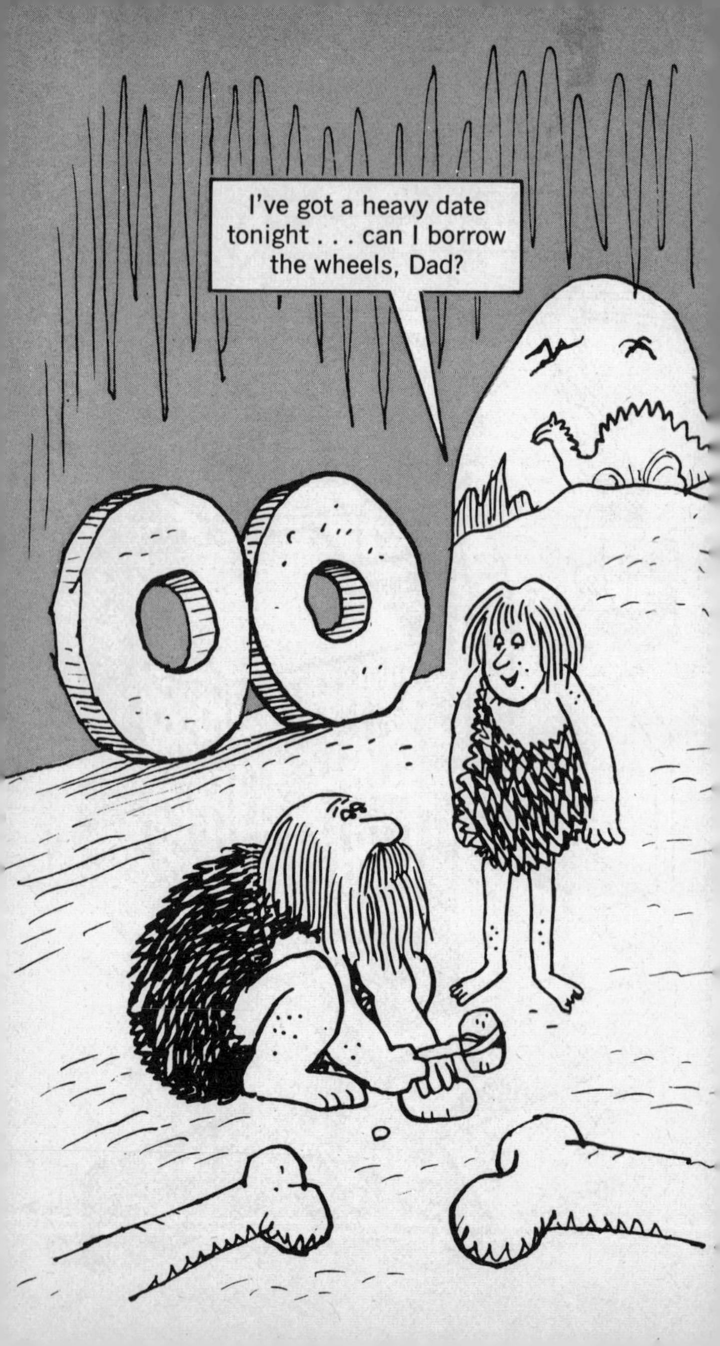
I've got a heavy date tonight . . . can I borrow the wheels, Dad?

An Appealingly Aimless Arrow Arrangement

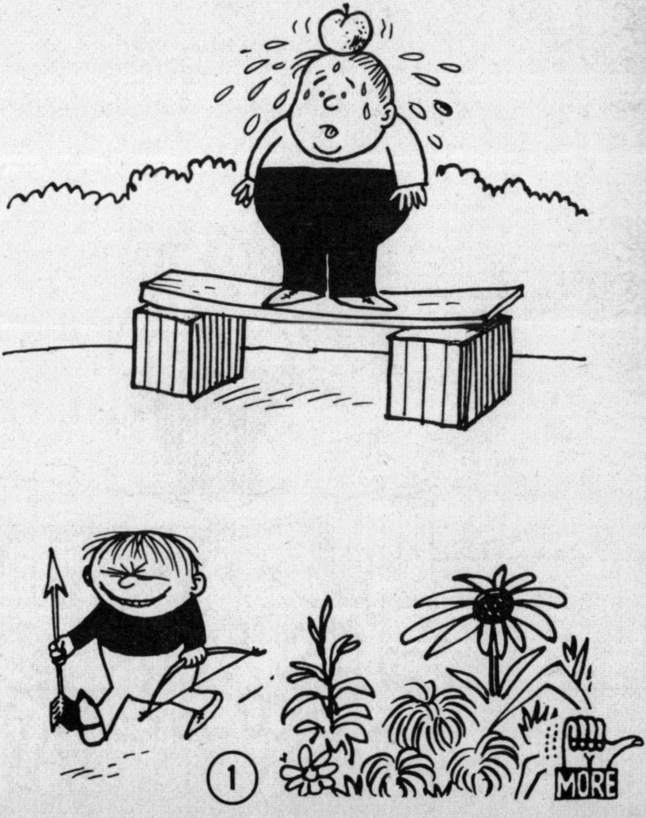
1
MORE

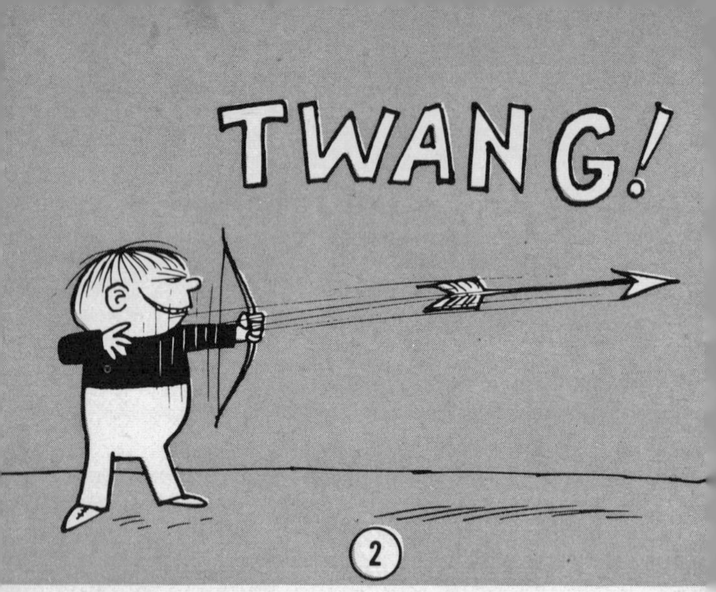
TWANG!
2

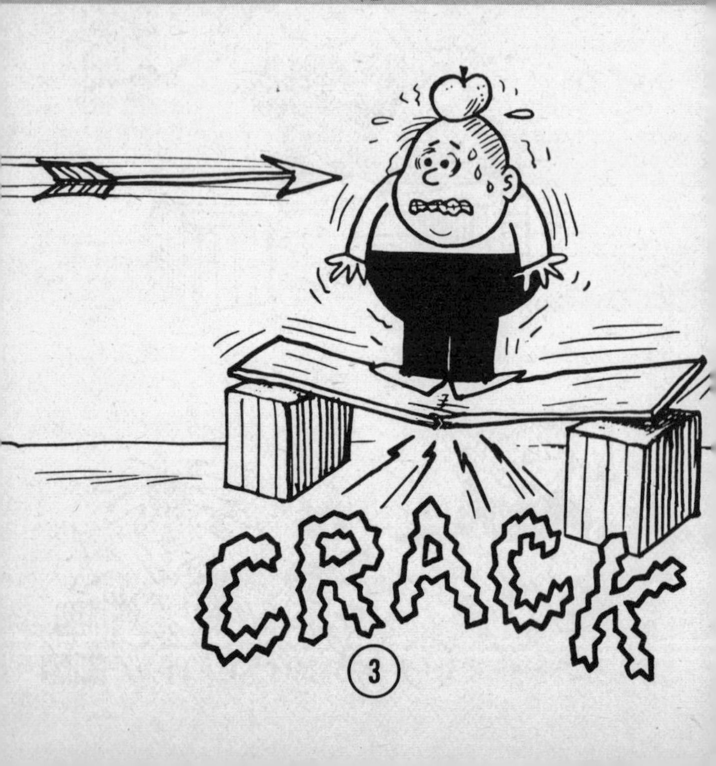
CRACK
3

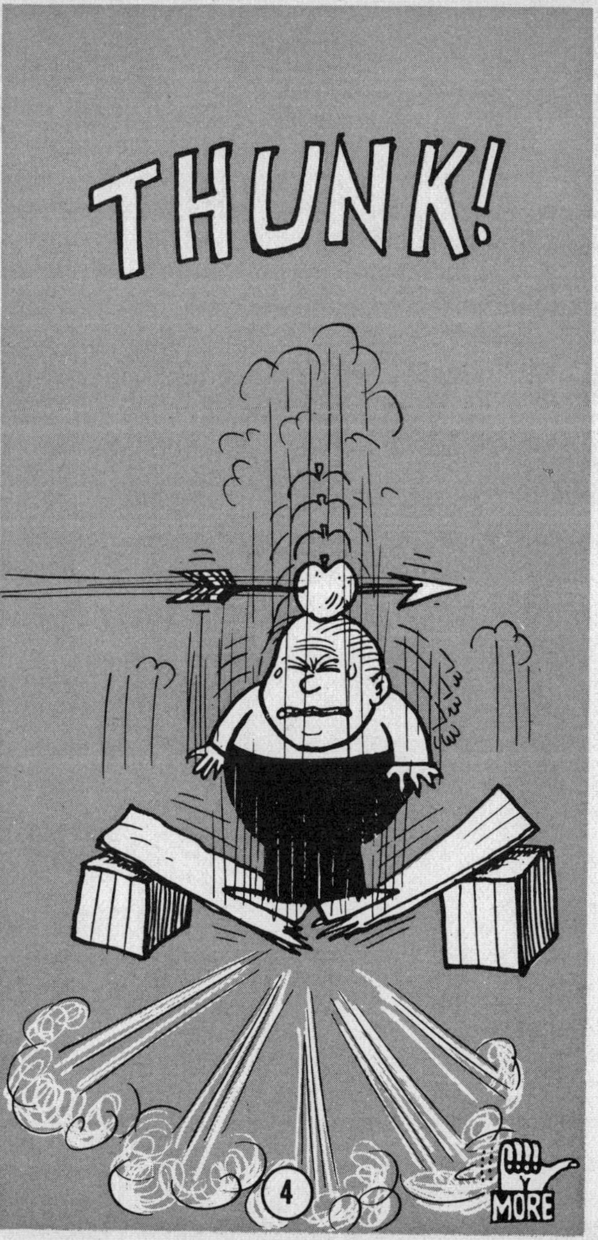
THUNK!
4
MORE

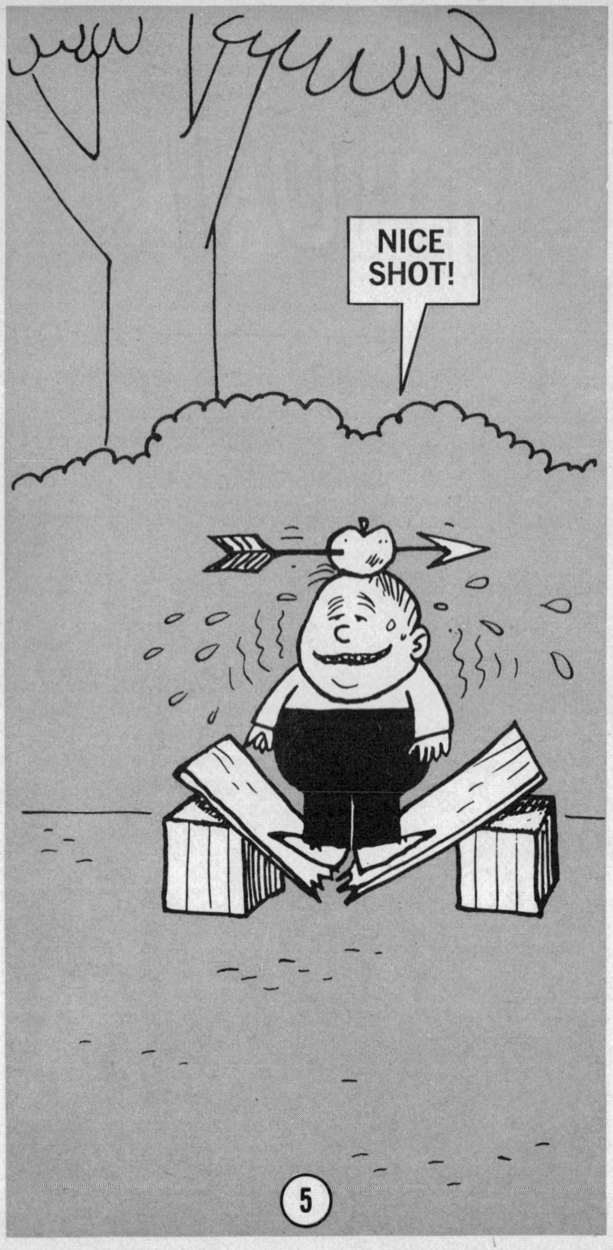
NICE
SHOT!
5

An Exemplary Cluster of Exhausted Inanities

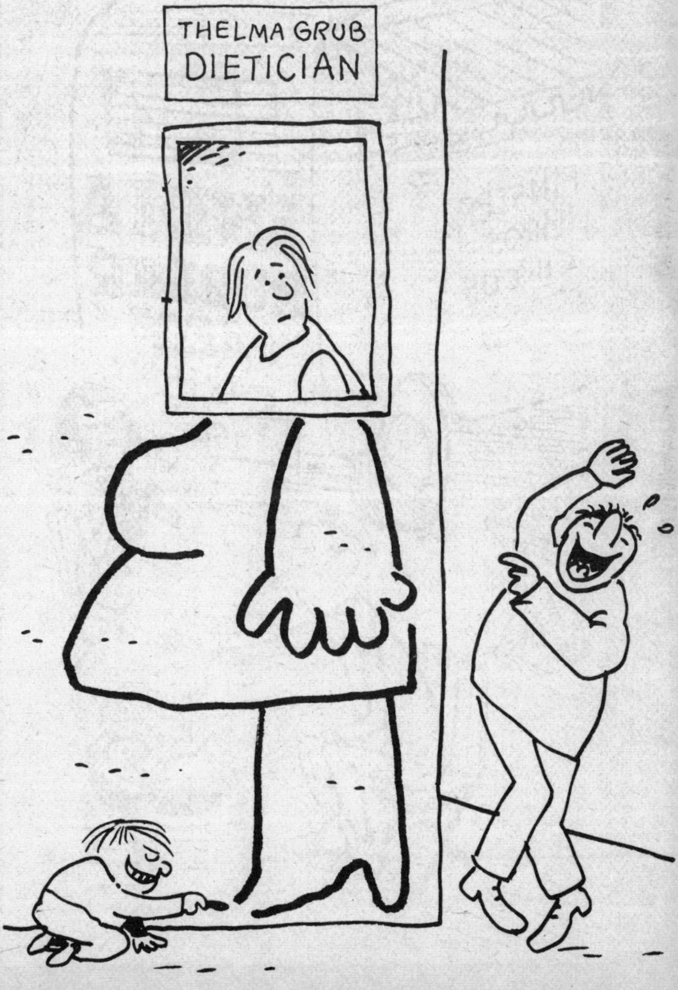
THELMA GRUB
DIETICIAN

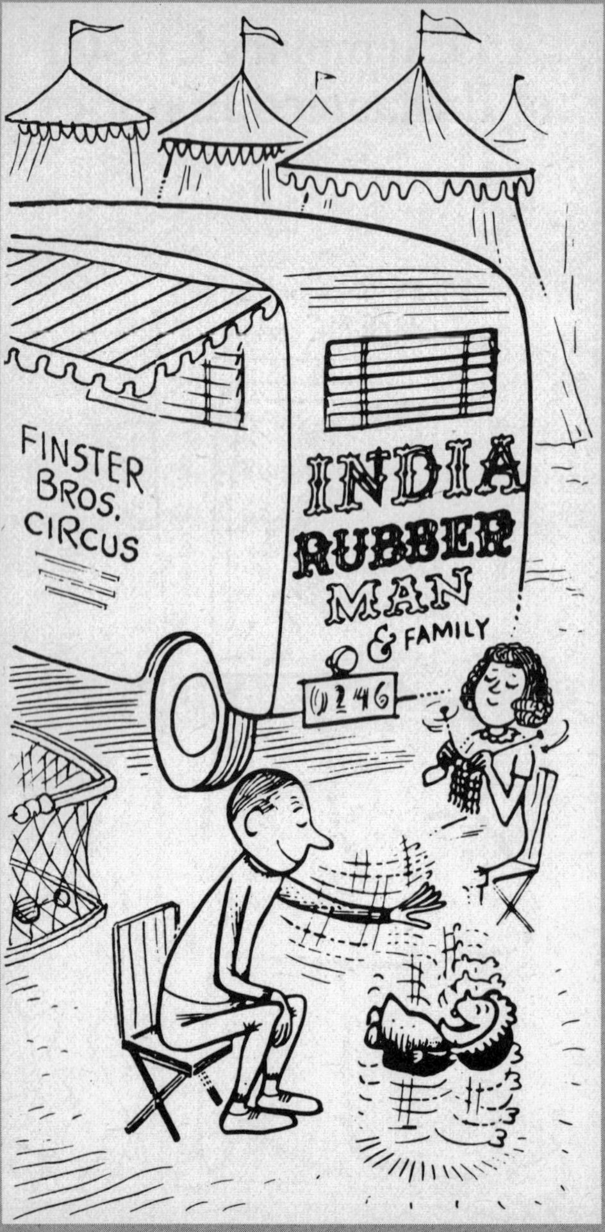
FINSTER BROS. CIRCUS
INDIA RUBBER MAN & FAMILY

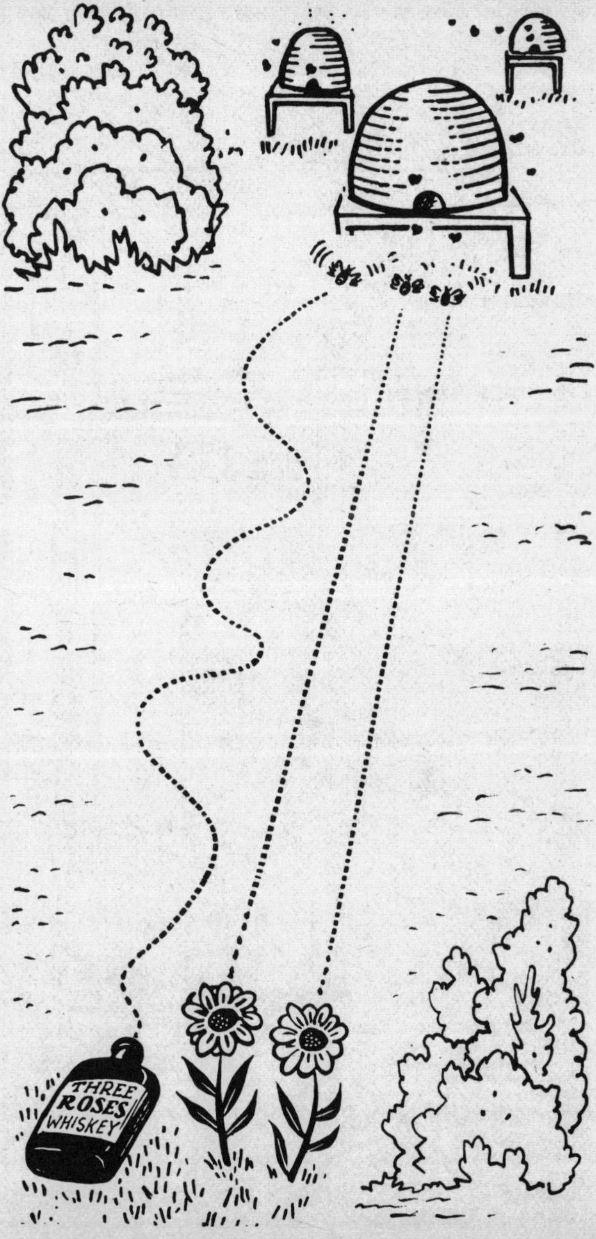
THREE
ROSES
WHISKEY

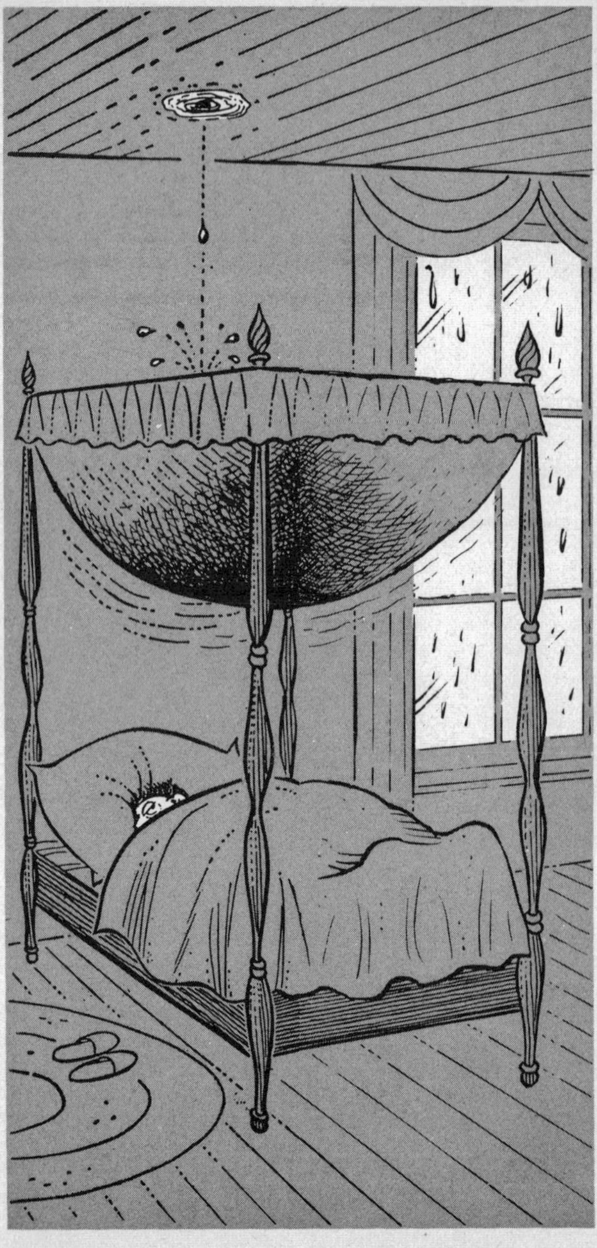

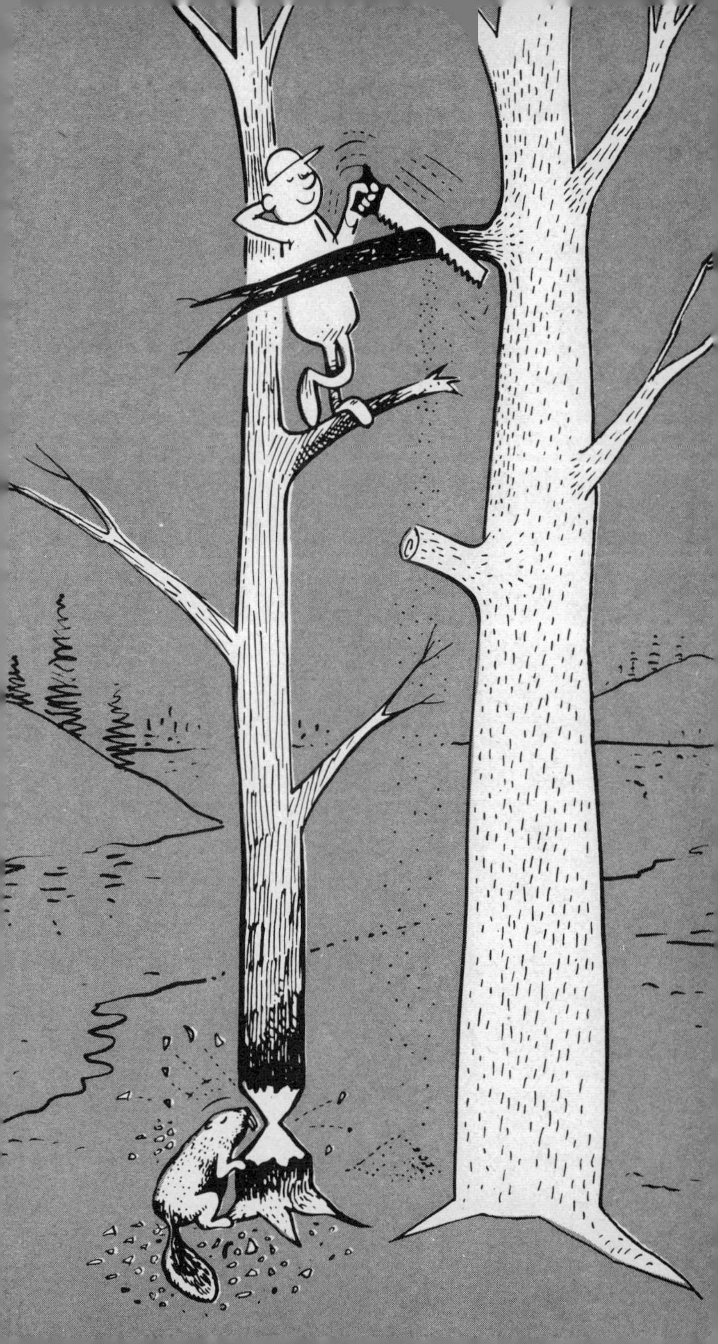

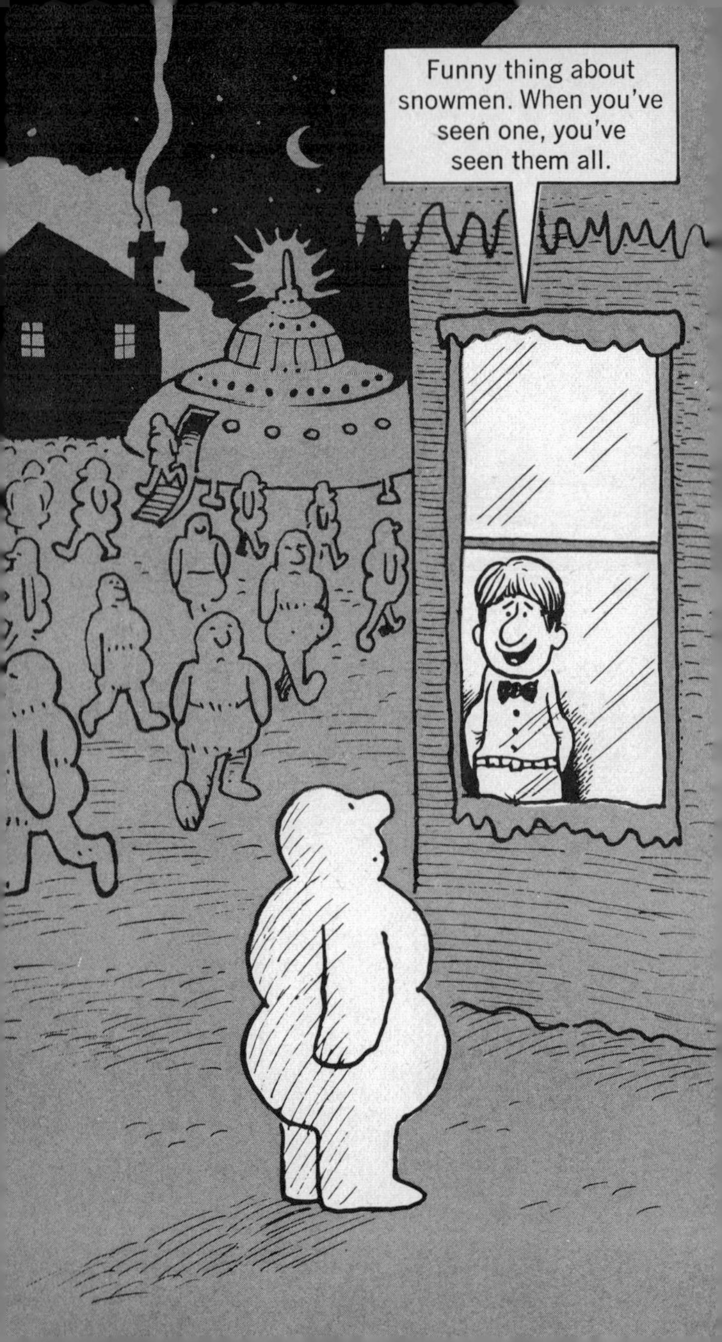
Funny thing about snowmen. When you've seen one, you've seen them all.

A Pleasurably Pitiful Prison Project

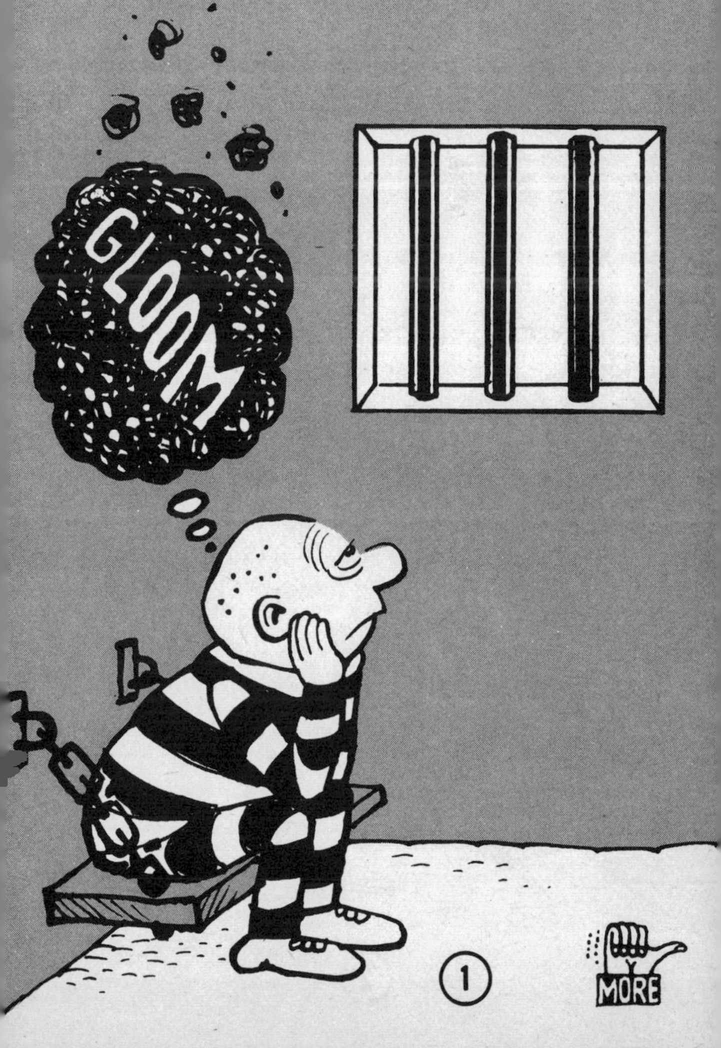
GLOOM

MORE

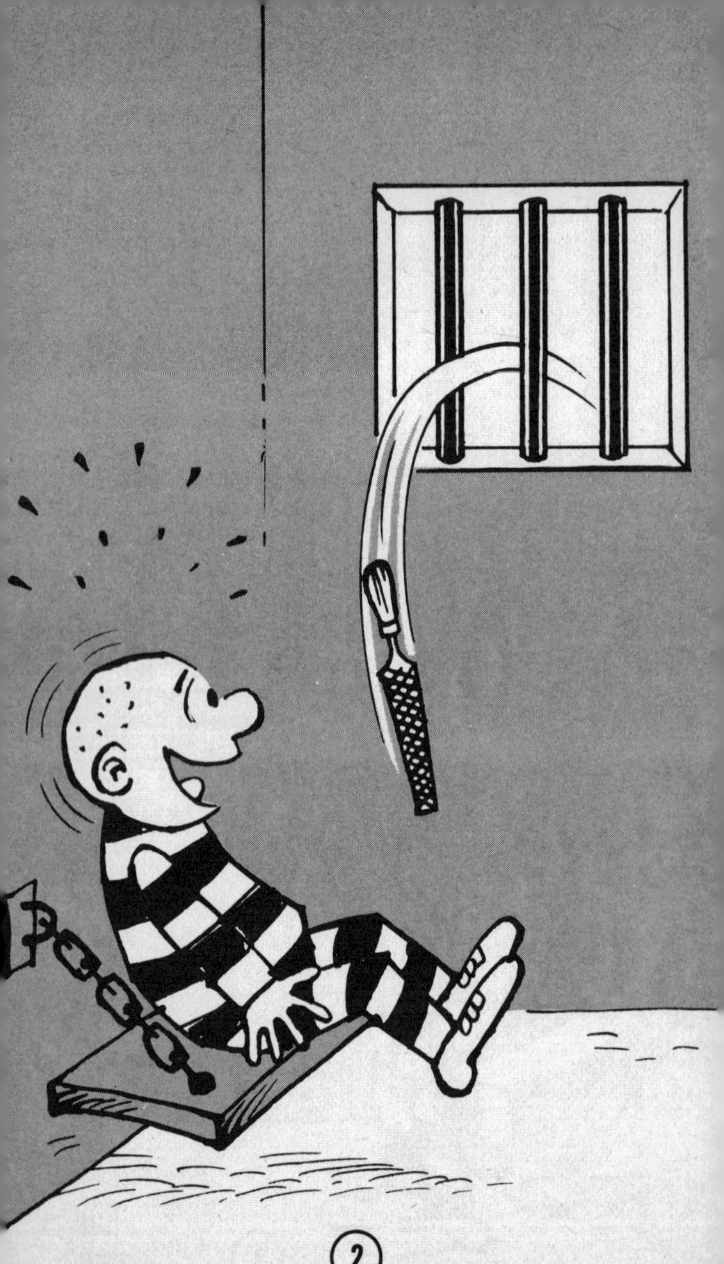

2

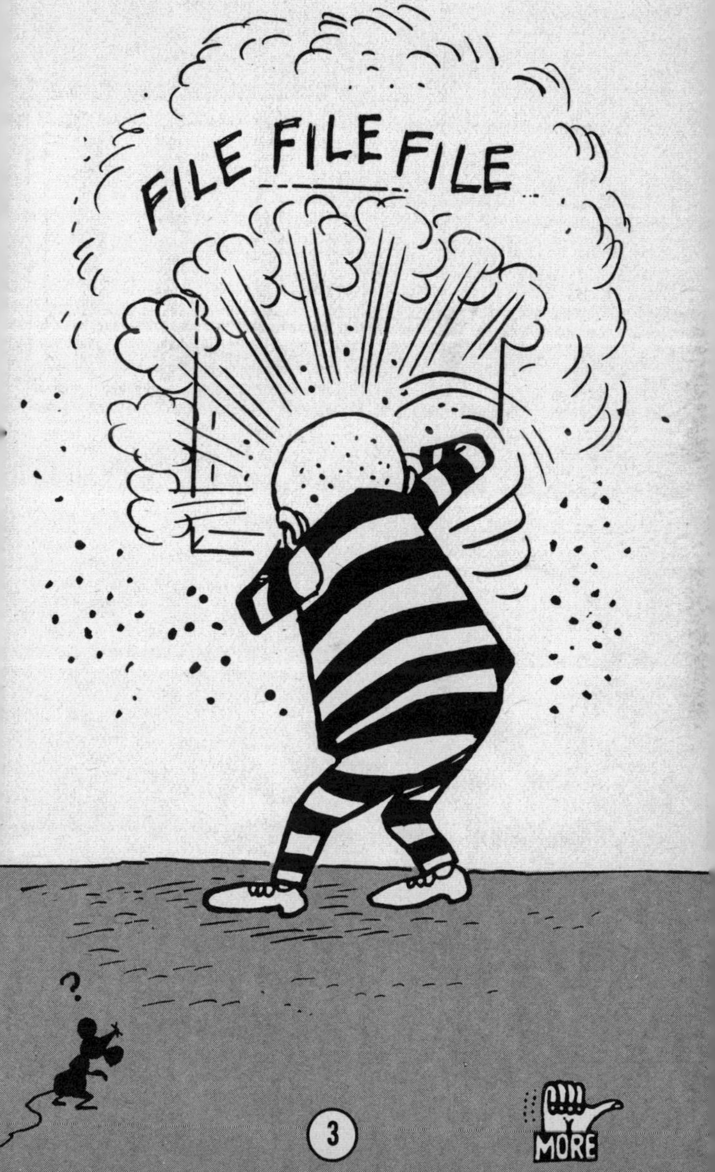
FILE FILE FILE
?
MORE

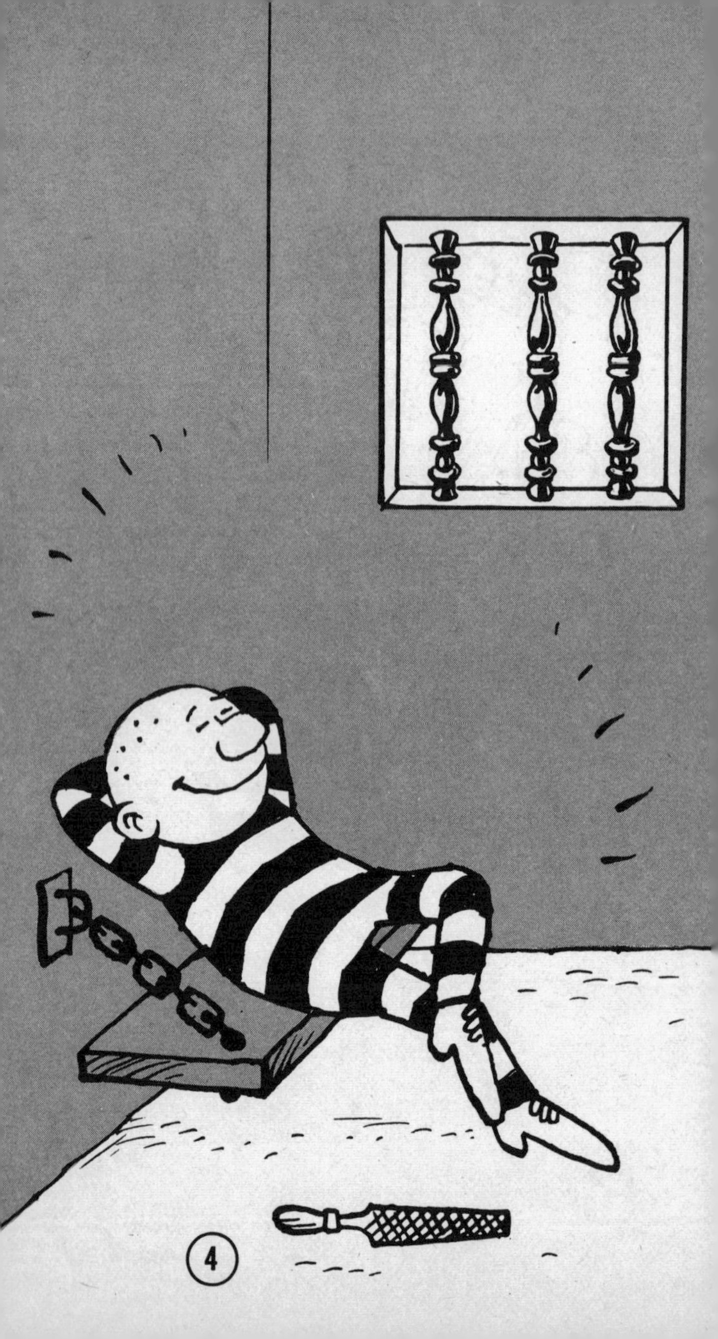
4

More Male Chauvinist Pigisms

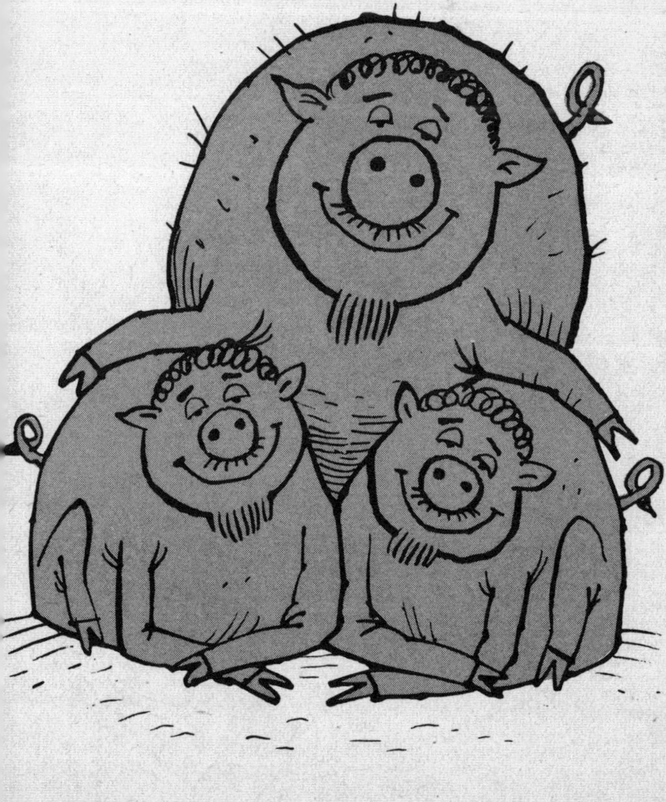

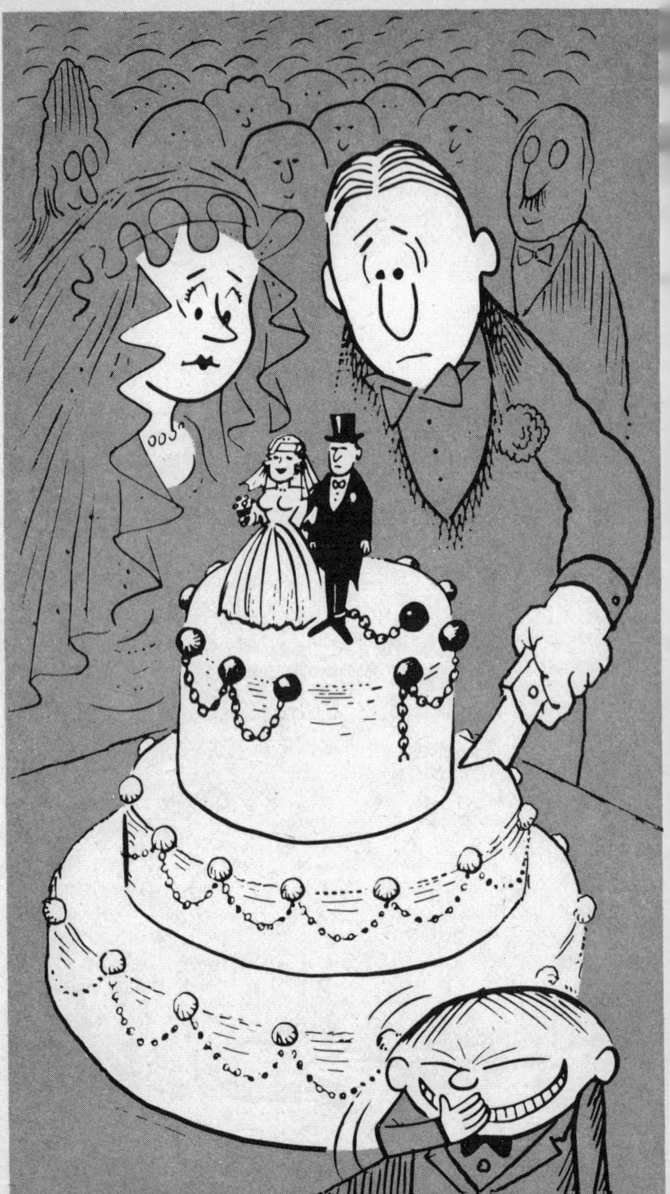

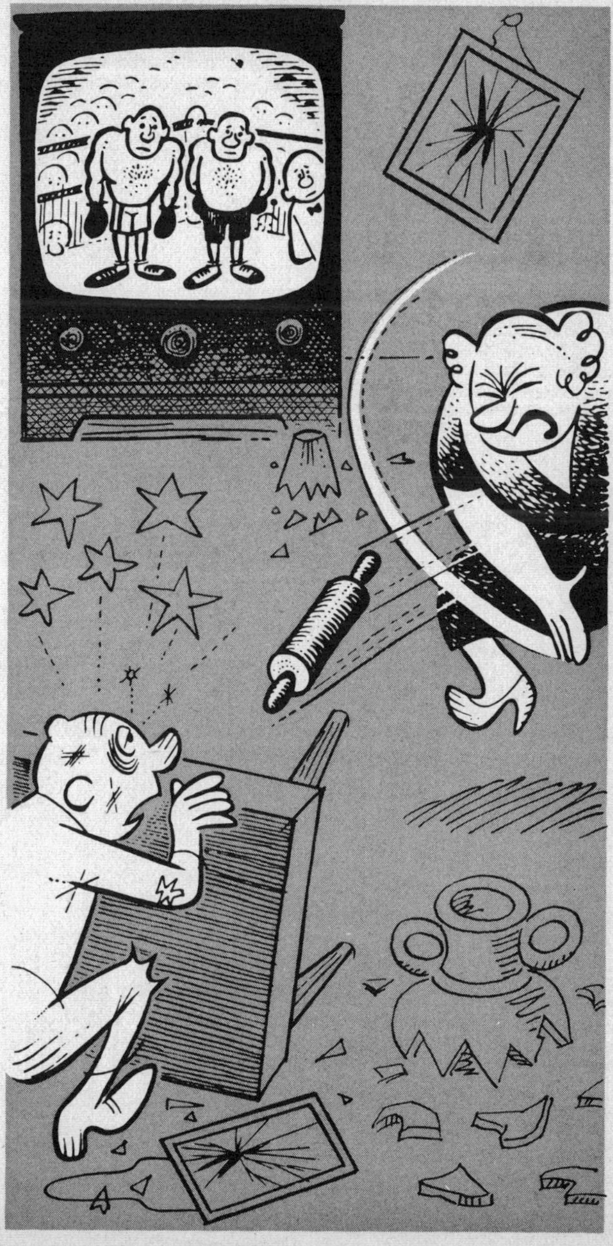

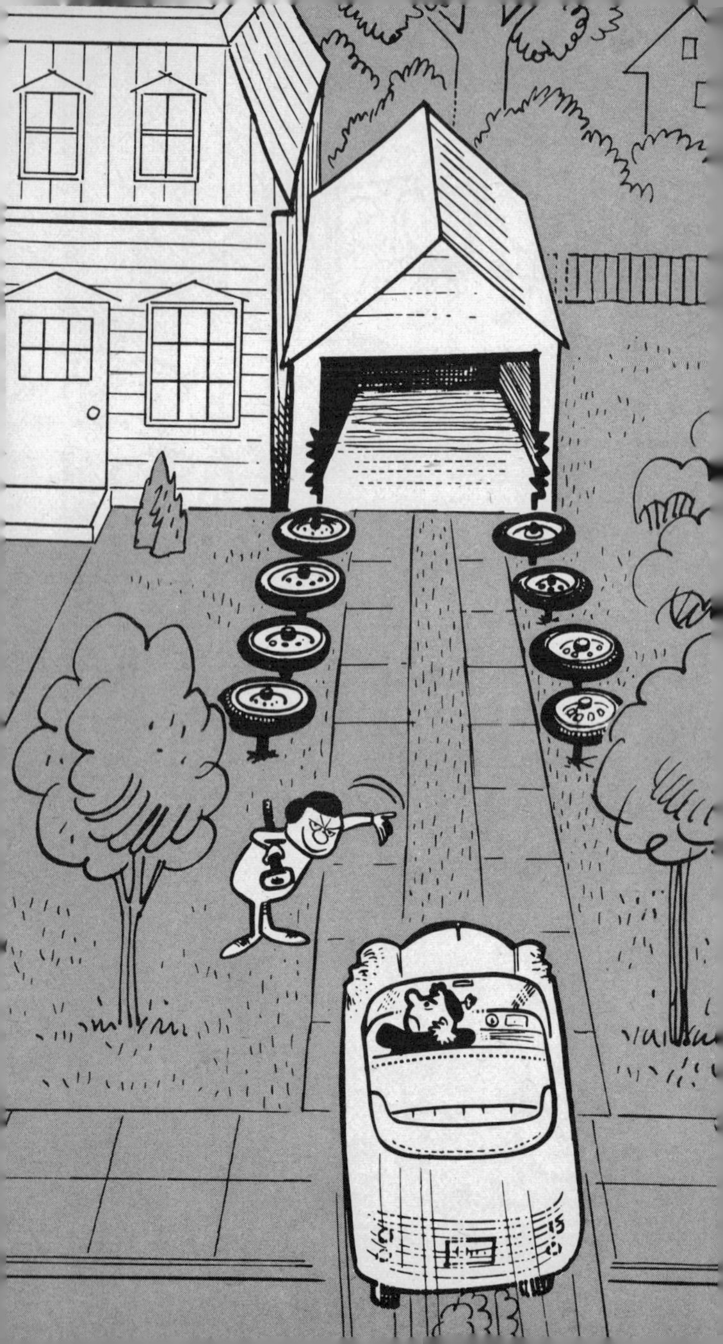

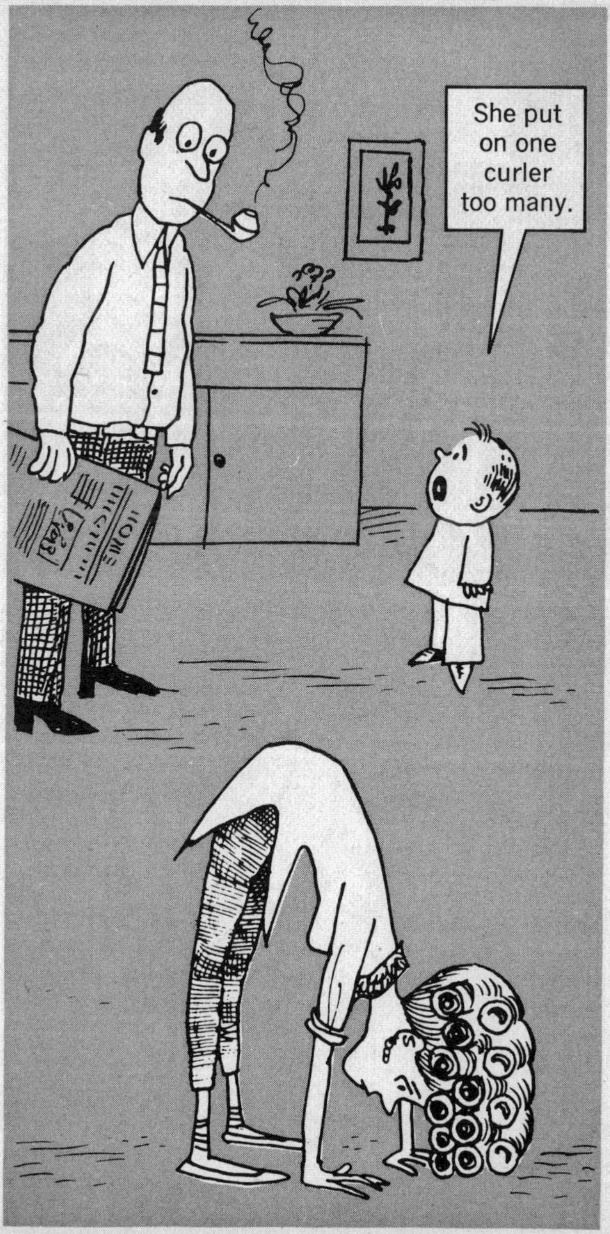
She put on one curler too many.

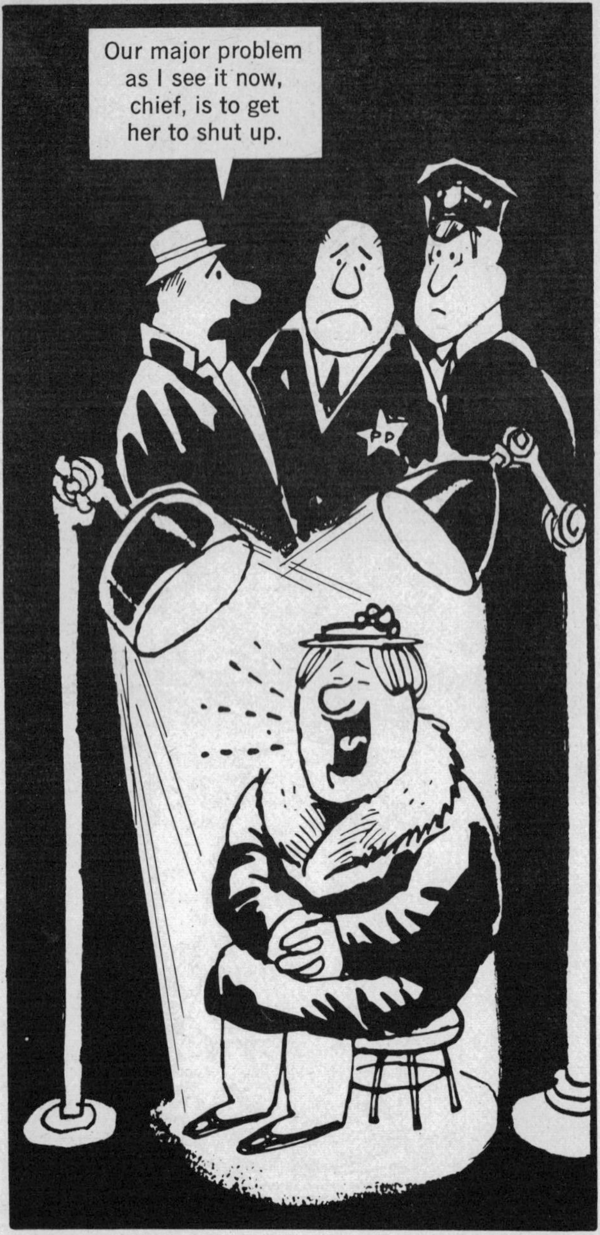
Our major problem as I see it now, chief, is to get her to shut up.

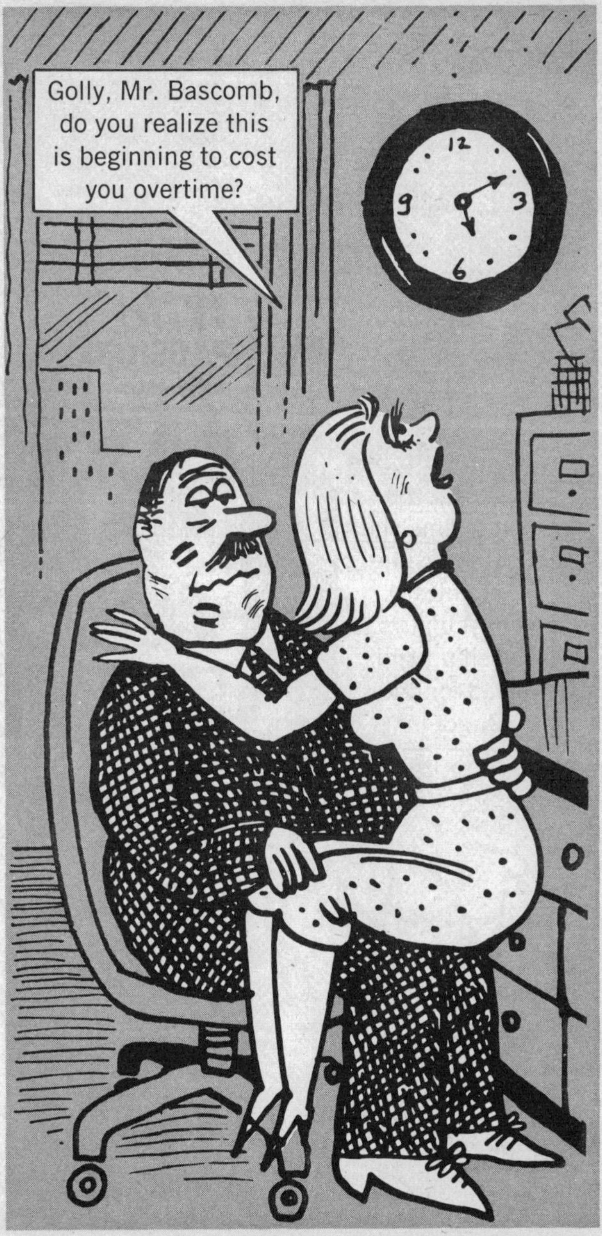
Golly, Mr. Bascomb, do you realize this is beginning to cost you overtime?

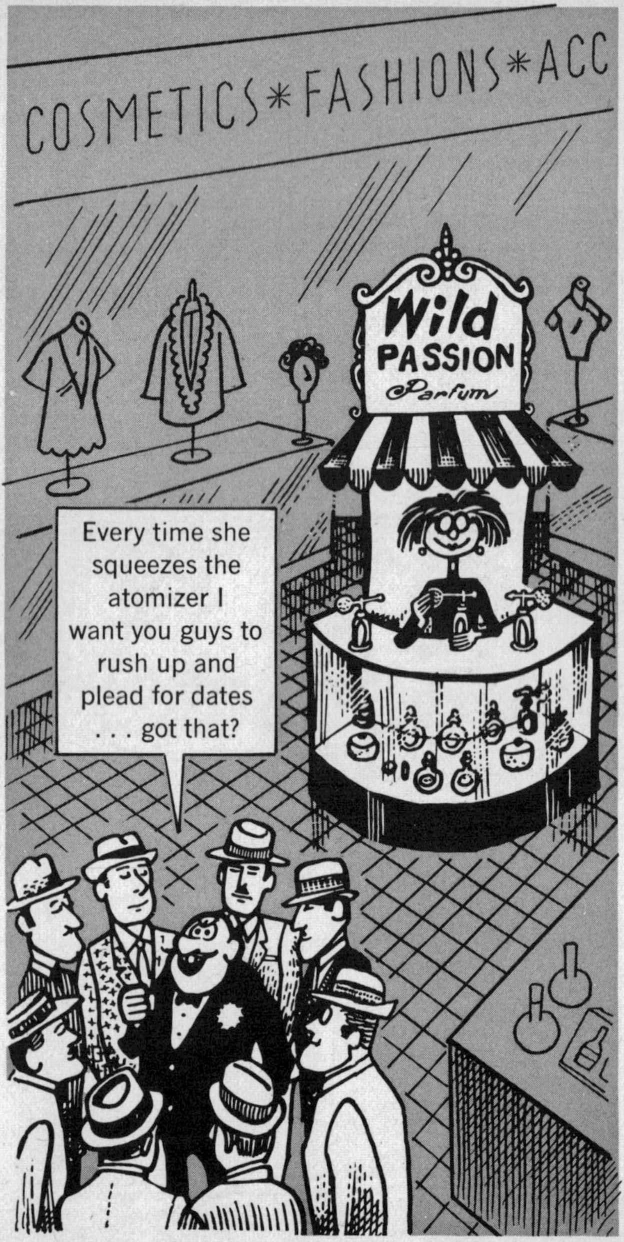
COSMETICS*FASHIONS*ACC
Wild PASSION Parfum
Every time she squeezes the atomizer I want you guys to rush up and plead for dates . . . got that?

A Constructively Crass Carpet Concoction

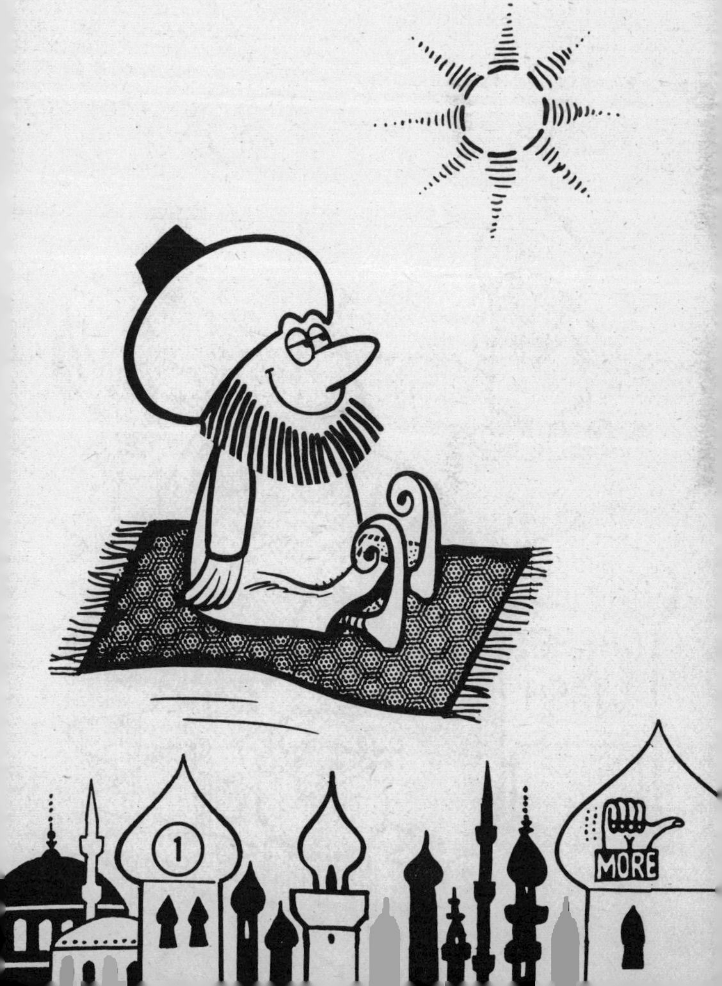
1
MORE

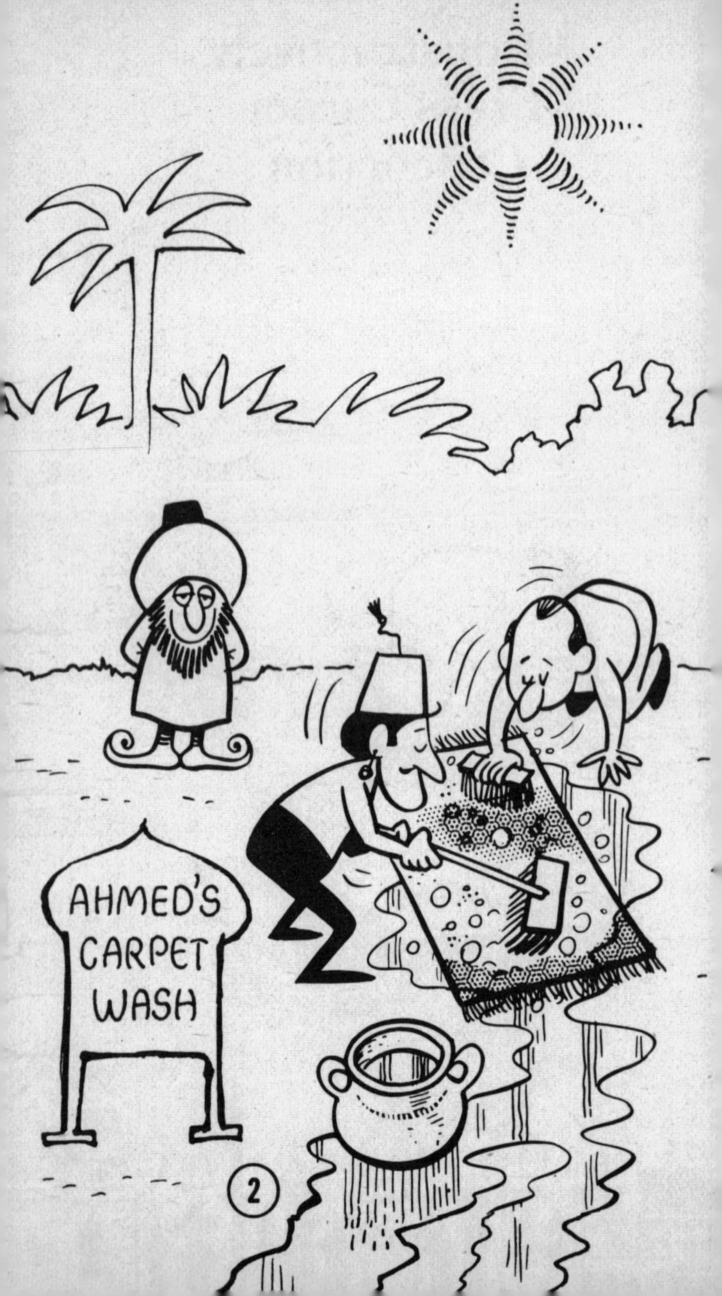
AHMED'S CARPET WASH
2

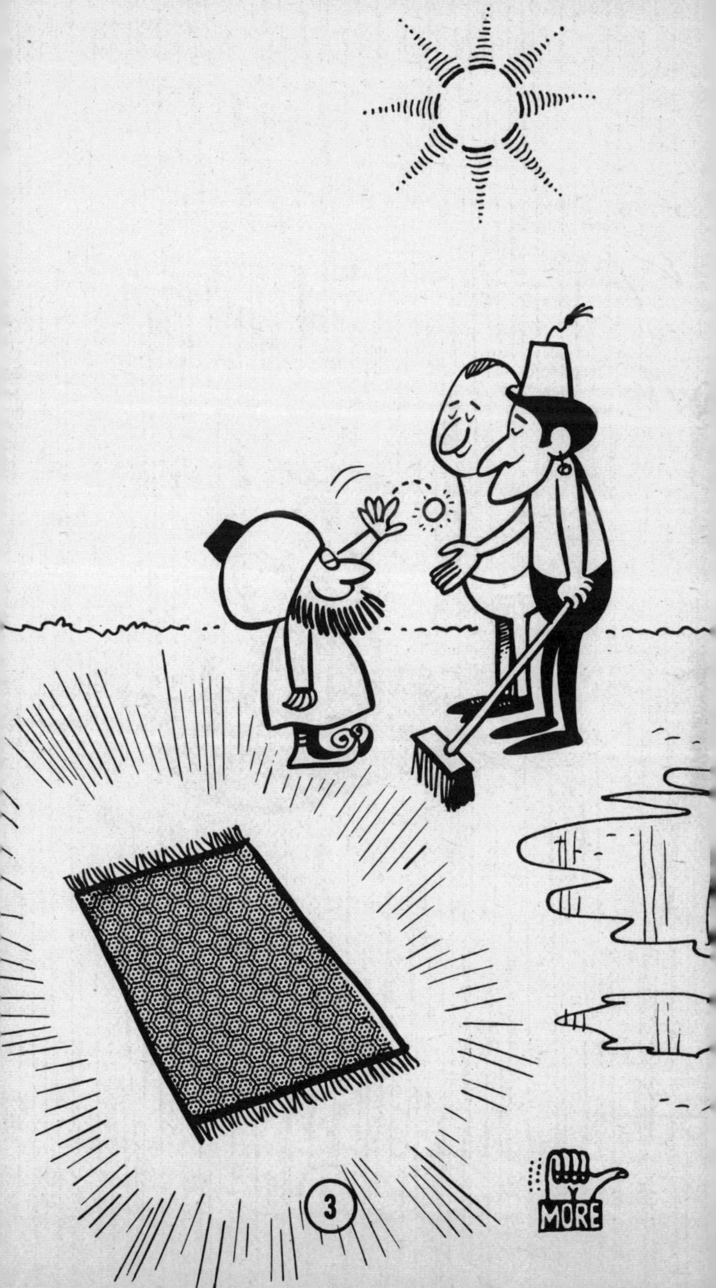
3
MORE

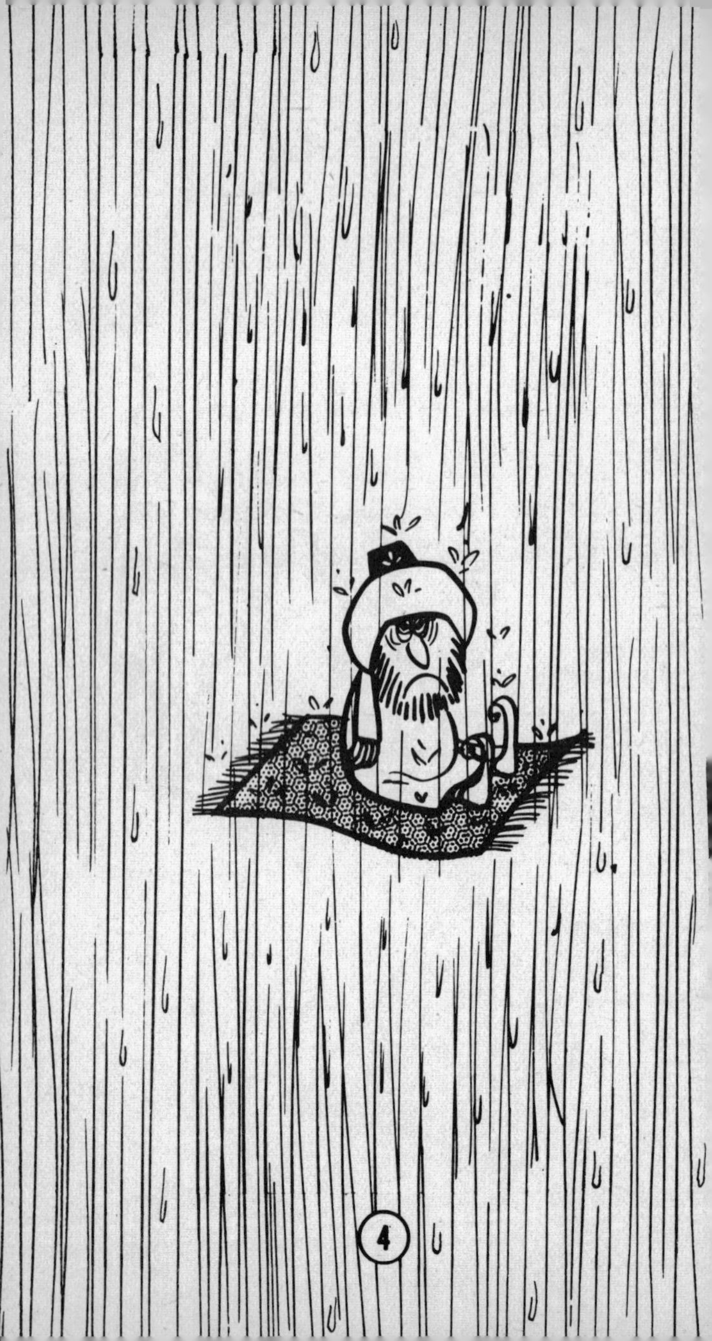
4

A Supreme Selection of Detrimental Detritus

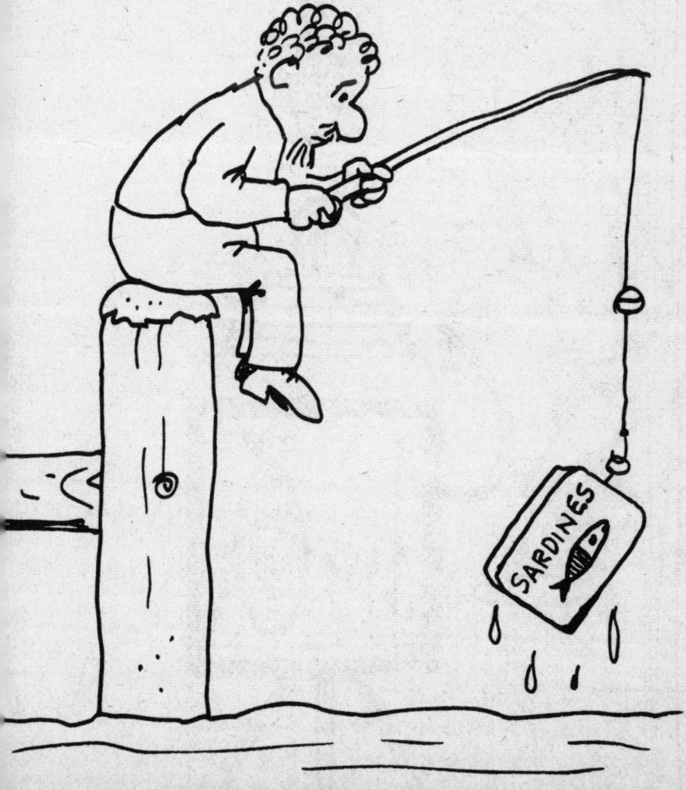
SARDINES

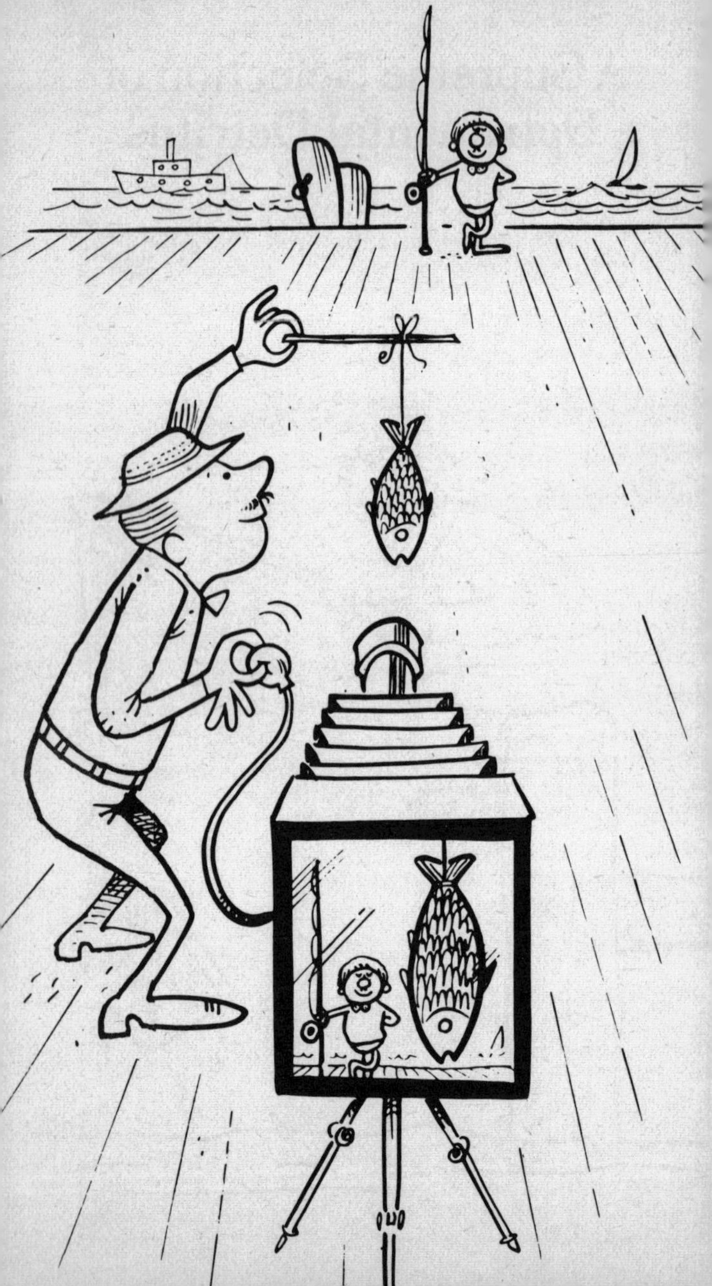

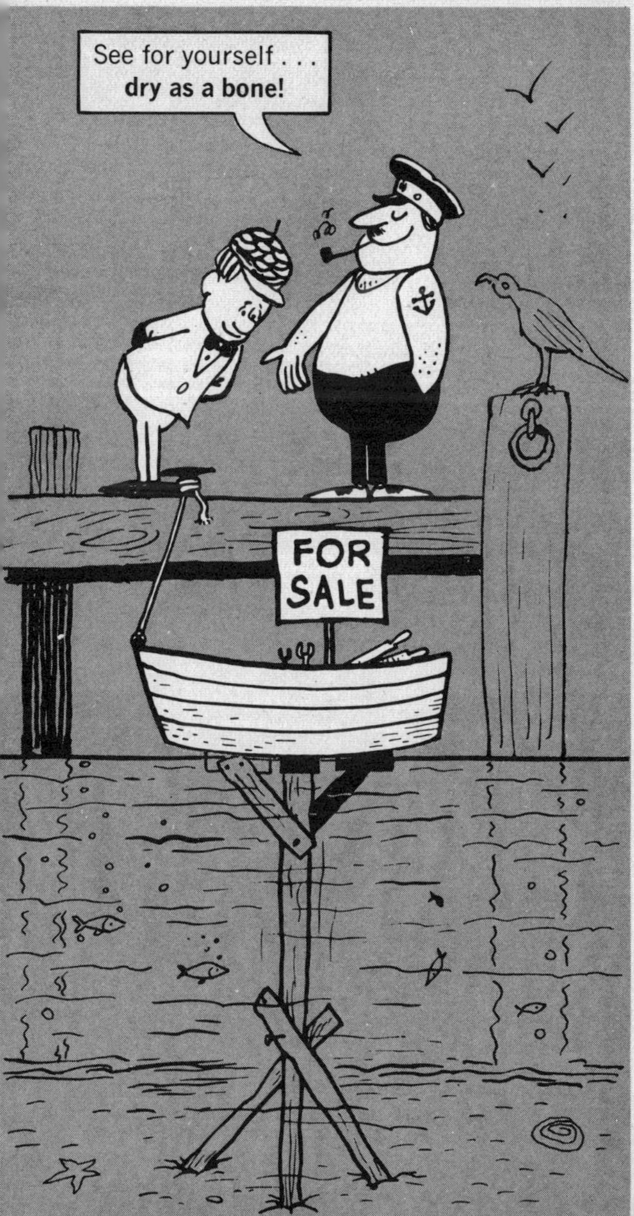
See for yourself . . . **dry as a bone!**
FOR SALE

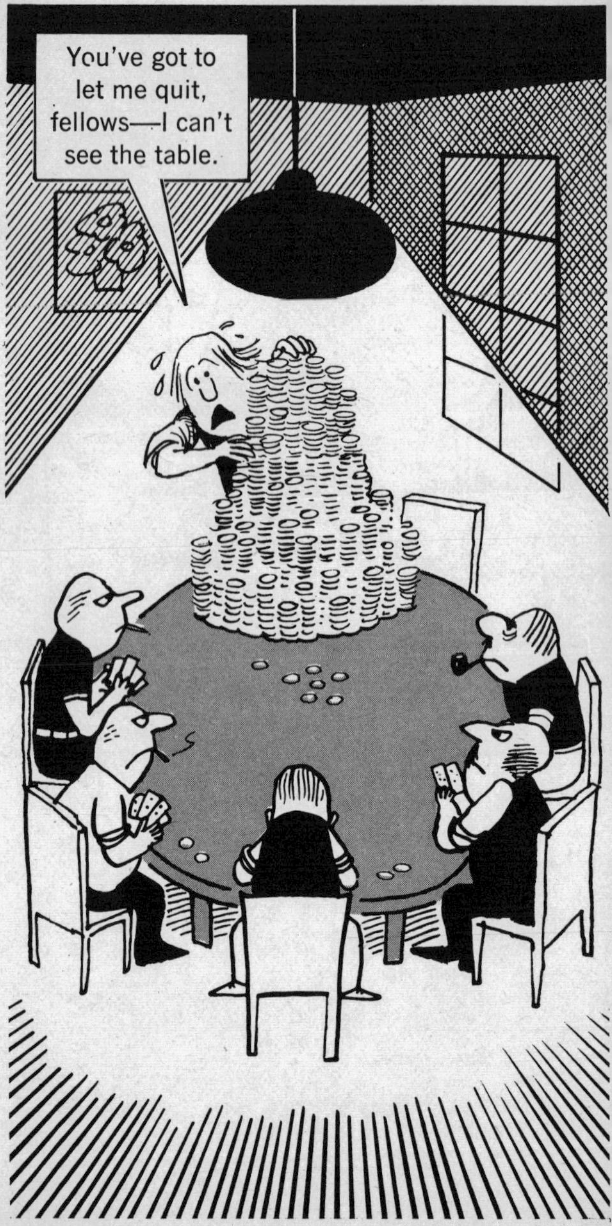
You've got to let me quit, fellows—I can't see the table.

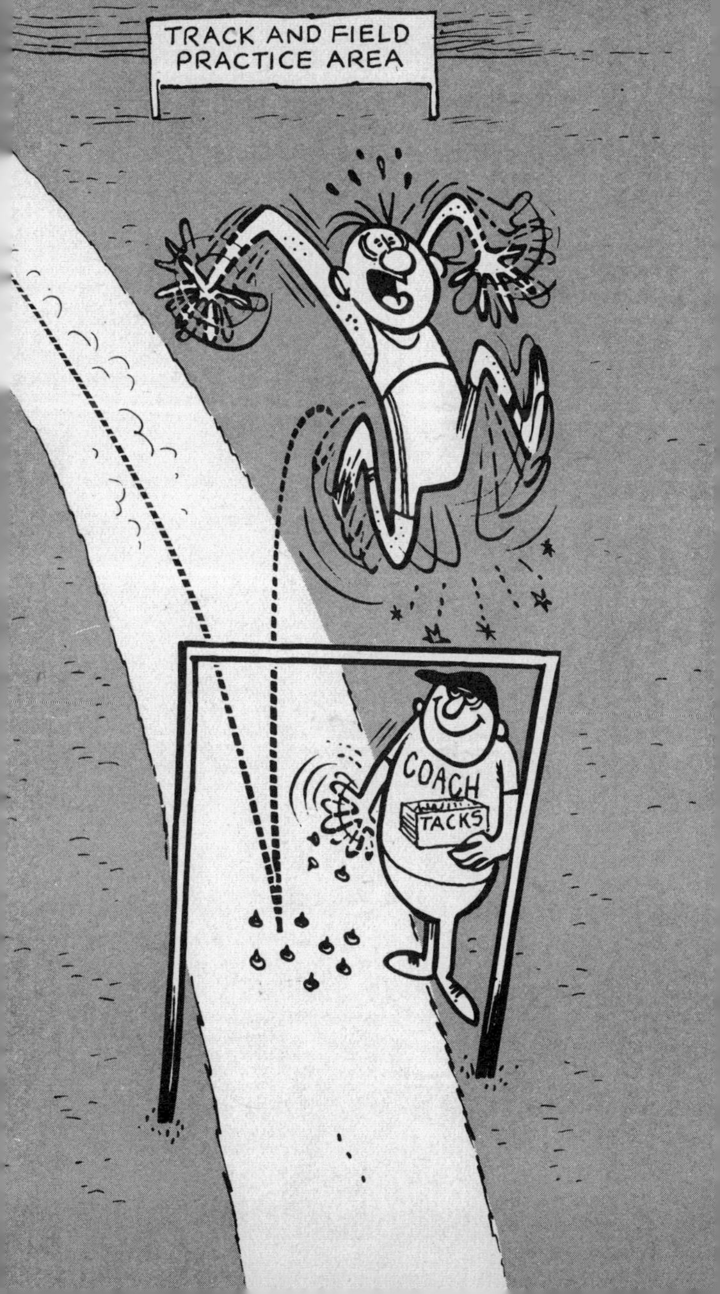
TRACK AND FIELD
PRACTICE AREA
COACH
TACKS

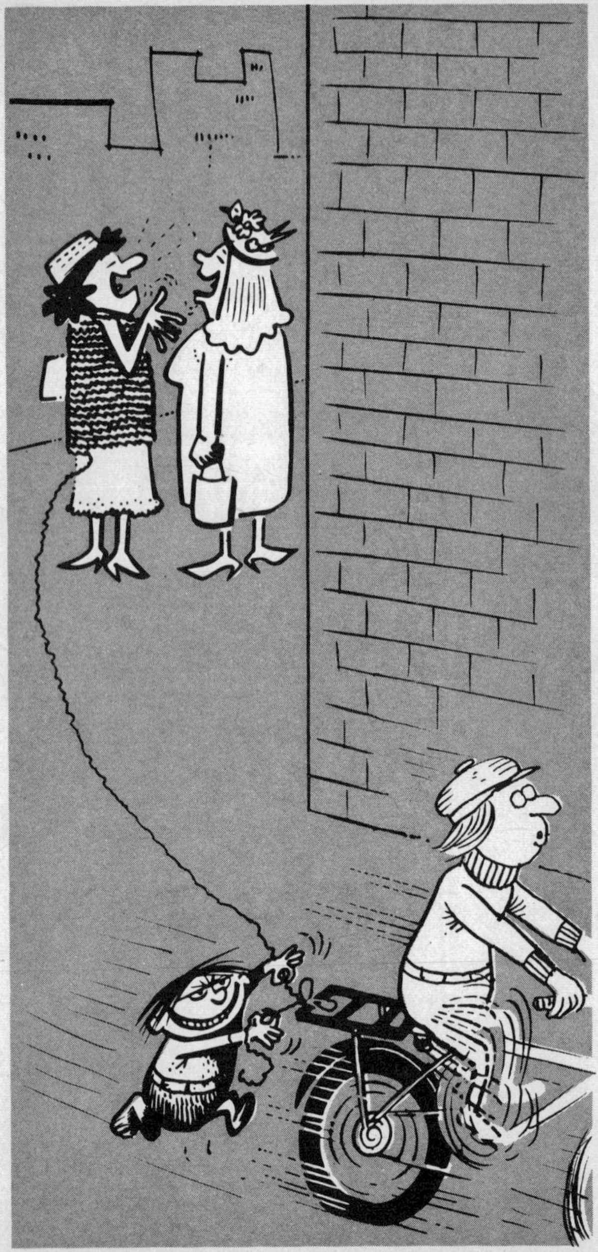

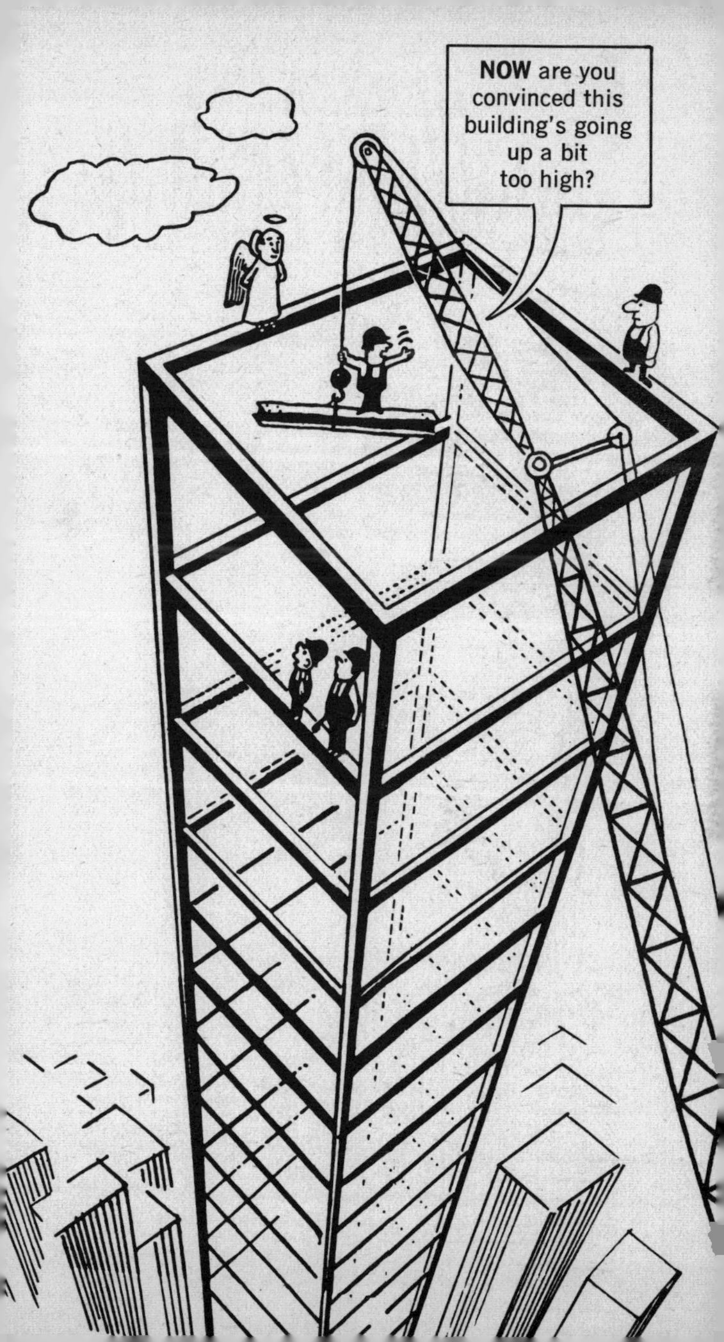
NOW are you convinced this building's going up a bit too high?

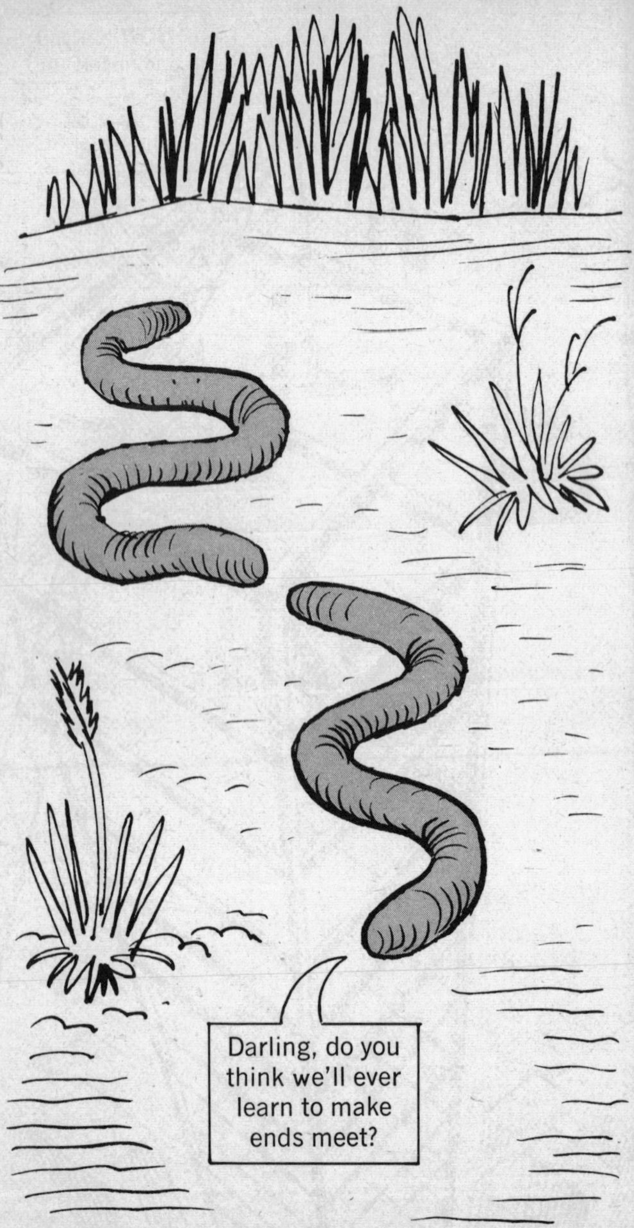
Darling, do you think we'll ever learn to make ends meet?

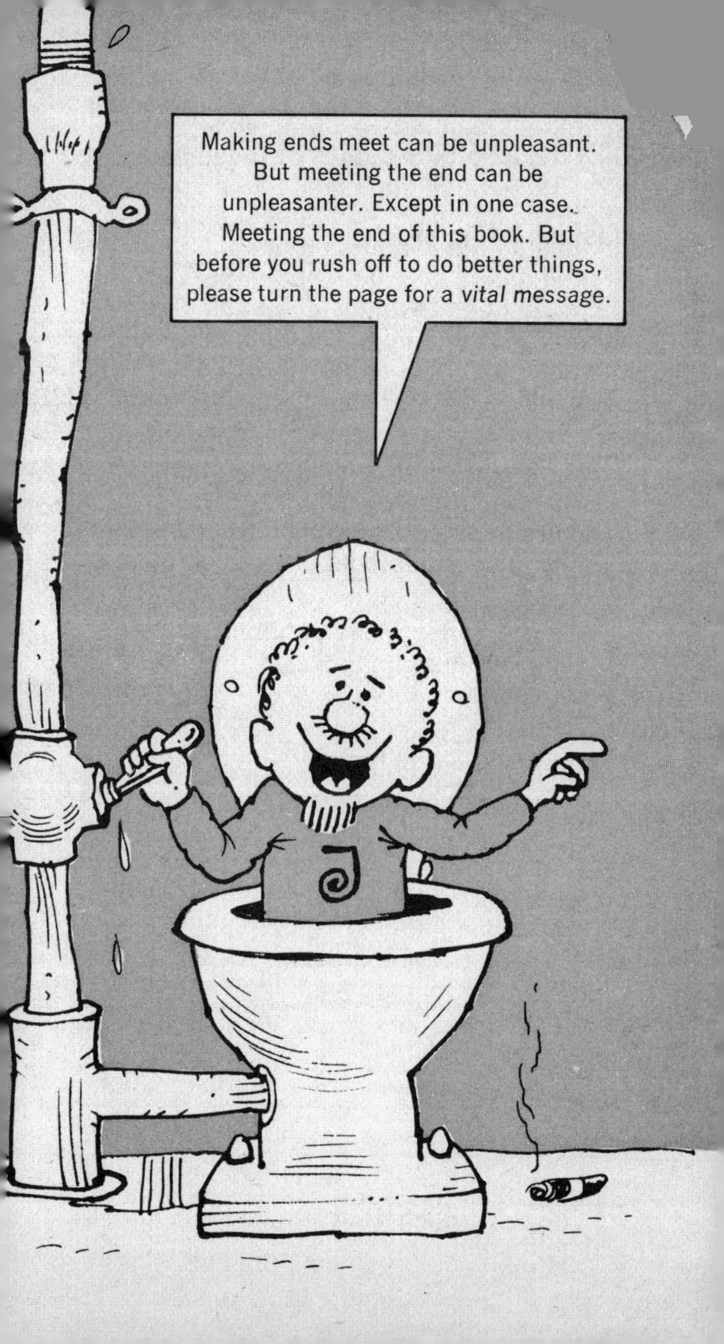
Making ends meet can be unpleasant. But meeting the end can be unpleasanter. Except in one case. Meeting the end of this book. But before you rush off to do better things, please turn the page for a *vital message*.
J

Hurry, hurry, while they last.

Only 12,256,678 copies of these treasured

classics left in stock.

☐ Al Jaffee Gags .... (#Y6856–$1.25)

☐ Al Jaffee Gags Again .... (#Y6652–$1.25)

☐ Al Jaffee Blows His Mind .... (#Y6759–$1.25)

☐ Mad's Al Jaffee Spews Out Snappy Answers
    to Stupid Questions .... (#T4987–75¢)

☐ Mad's Al Jaffee Spews Out MORE
    Snappy Answers to Stupid
    Questions .... (#Y6740–$1.25)

☐ The Mad Book of Magic
    by Al Jaffee .... (#Y6743–$1.25)

THE NEW AMERICAN LIBRARY, INC.,
P.O. Box 999, Bergenfield, New Jersey 07621

Please send me the SIGNET BOOKS I have checked above. I am
enclosing $_____(check or money order—no currency or
C.O.D.'s). Please include the list price plus 35¢ a copy to cover
handling and mailing costs. (Prices and numbers are subject to
change without notice.)

Name_____

Address_____

City_____State_____Zip Code_____
Allow at least 4 weeks for delivery